Ultimate KubeVirt for OpenShift Virtualization

Design, Deploy and Scale Hybrid Workloads in Kubernetes Using Kubevirt and Openshift to Unify Cloud-Native Infrastructure

Dhirendra Kumar

Ishan Khare

www.orangeava.com

First Published: October 2025

Published By: Orange Education Pvt Ltd, AVA®

Address: 9, Daryaganj, Delhi, 110002, India

275 New North Road Islington Suite 1314 London,
N1 7AA, United Kingdom

ISBN (PBK): 978-93-49888-10-4
ISBN (E-BOOK): 978-93-49888-62-3

Scan the QR code to explore our entire catalogue

www.orangeava.com

Dedicated To

My Beloved Parents:

Smt Tara Devi and Sri Baskit Sah.

And

My Wife, Geethashri Ananda as well as My Son, Naitik.

- Dhirendra Kumar

How We Learn and Evolve in Life

आचार्यत् पद्मादत्ते पादम् पादम् शषि्य स्वमेधायः
पादम् सब्रह्मचारभि्यःपादम् कालक्रमेण च

~

A student gets a quarter (knowledge) from his teacher, a quarter by his own intelligence.

A quarter from his fellow students, and a quarter in due course of time.

- Ishan Khare

About the Authors

Dhirendra Kumar is a seasoned DevOps engineer with deep expertise in cloud infrastructure and developer experience. He began his career at IBM in 2003, supporting Fortune 500 clients with virtualization and container orchestration using Kubernetes and OpenShift. Now based in Boston, he works at a leading fintech firm, where he scales infrastructure and builds automation solutions leveraging Kubernetes and AWS.

Dhirendra holds multiple industry certifications and is an active contributor to the open-source community. He is also passionate about IoT and cutting-edge technology innovations.

Ishan Khare is a distinguished engineer with a passion for technology and lifelong learning. He began his career as a full-stack developer, specializing in frontend (JavaScript and TypeScript) and backend (Python and Docker) at Wingify and ReBIT. He then focused on backend development with Golang at Goibibo/MakeMyTrip, deepening his expertise in building scalable systems.

Ishan's journey advanced into cloud-native engineering at Gojek Tech, where he worked extensively with Kubernetes, Istio, and Google Cloud in distributed systems and SRE. He further contributed to Kubernetes controllers at Porter.run, and became a founding engineer at Loft Labs. There, he played a critical role in building **vCluster** and **vCluster.pro**, leveraging Golang, Helm, and Kubernetes operators.

Recently, Ishan led development of a GPU cloud product at Cloudraft, integrating Golang, Kubernetes, and KubeVirt for a data center client. He now focuses on his own start-up, innovating at the intersection of GPU cloud, Kubernetes, and AI—including training custom models. Ishan also explores drone technology, from hardware assembly to software automation, reflecting his end-to-end engineering mindset.

About the Technical Reviewer

Sachin Lobo has 17 years of experience in designing and engineering applications and infrastructure solutions across enterprise environments. He has worked across various industries, including telecommunications and banking, contributing to large-scale distributed systems and infrastructure modernization projects. He has had the pleasure of mentoring both junior and senior engineers, fostering technical excellence, and knowledge sharing within development organizations. Over the years, he has worked with industry leaders such as Infosys, J.P. Morgan, and Reliance Jio, among others.

At the moment, Sachin works as a Staff Product Engineer at InfraCloud where he focuses on building and enhancing cloud-native solutions that enable organizations to adopt modern infrastructure practices. With deep expertise in technologies such as Python, Golang, Docker and Kubernetes, he specializes in creating scalable and reliable systems for enterprise clients.

He is particularly passionate about cloud-native tools and technologies, especially in the field of container orchestration and infrastructure automation. His work is driven by a commitment to simplifying infrastructure, and enabling platform teams to build robust, production-grade systems.

Sachin holds a Bachelor of Engineering in Information Technology, and is based in Mumbai, India. His comprehensive understanding of both traditional enterprise systems and modern cloud-native architectures uniquely positions him to bridge the gap between legacy infrastructure and contemporary virtualization solutions.

Acknowledgments

We would like to thank our family for their unwavering love and continuous support throughout the writing of this book. Their encouragement and belief in us served as the greatest motivators, and without them, this project would not have been possible. We are deeply grateful for their patience and understanding, as we dedicated countless hours to bringing this book to life!

Preface

In today's rapidly evolving cloud-native landscape, organizations are continuously seeking innovative ways to optimize infrastructure, and streamline operations. The convergence of traditional Virtual Machine (VM) workloads with agile, containerized applications presents a significant challenge, yet also a powerful opportunity. This book, ***Ultimate KubeVirt for OpenShift Virtualization*** is crafted to guide you through this transformative journey, bridging the gap between established virtualization paradigms and the dynamic world of Kubernetes.

The book serves as your comprehensive guide to leveraging KubeVirt within OpenShift, empowering you to manage VMs as first-class citizens within your Kubernetes clusters. We delve into the core architectural components of KubeVirt, providing you with a fundamental understanding of how it seamlessly integrates with OpenShift's robust ecosystem. Beyond theory, we adopt a practical approach, offering step-by-step instructions for setting up your environment, managing VM lifecycles, and configuring intricate networking and storage solutions tailored for virtualized workloads.

As you progress, you will explore the advanced topics crucial for modern IT environments, including implementing robust security measures, automating VM management with GitOps, and optimizing performance for demanding workloads. We also examine specialized use cases such as running GPU-accelerated VMs, and compare KubeVirt's capabilities with other virtualization strategies. Our goal is to equip you with the knowledge and practical skills necessary to confidently design, deploy, and operate a unified platform for both your VMs and containers, ensuring agility, scalability, and efficiency in your hybrid cloud strategy. This book is divided into 15 chapters, designed to systematically build your expertise:

Chapter 1: Introduction to KubeVirt for OpenShift Virtualization will introduce KubeVirt, its relevance, and the benefits of combining Kubernetes with VMs.

Chapter 2: Setting Up the Environment provides a detailed guide for installing and configuring OpenShift Virtualization.

Chapter 3: Understanding the KubeVirt Architecture offers a comprehensive overview of KubeVirt's core components, and how it uses Kubernetes CRDs.

Chapter 4: Managing Virtual Machines (VMs) covers defining, deploying, and lifecycle management of VMs as Kubernetes-native objects.

Chapter 5: Networking in OpenShift Virtualization delves into KubeVirt's networking architecture, including Multus and security considerations.

Chapter 6: Storage Integration explains persistent storage for VMs, focusing on DataVolumes and CDI.

Chapter 7: Security and Compliance explores the best practices for securing VMs, using RBAC, SELinux, and OpenShift policies.

Chapter 8: Automating Virtualization with GitOps introduces GitOps principles for managing VM configurations and CI/CD pipelines.

Chapter 9: Monitoring and Performance Optimization focuses on setting up monitoring and optimizing VM performance, using Prometheus and Grafana.

Chapter 10: Programming KubeVirt Functionality guides developers on extending and automating KubeVirt using the Go client library.

Chapter 11: KubeVirt vs. vCluster compares these two methods for running virtual machines within Kubernetes environments.

Chapter 12: Cloning, Golden VM Images, and the CDI Project covers advanced VM lifecycle management, including cloning and golden images with CDI.

Chapter 13: KubeVirt in Hybrid and Multi-Cloud Environments explores using KubeVirt to manage VMs across diverse cloud and on-premises infrastructures.

Chapter 14: Advanced Topics in KubeVirt delves into advanced use cases such as running GPU-accelerated workloads within VMs.

Chapter 15: Best Practices and Future Trends concludes the book by discussing the best practices and emerging trends in virtualization and cloud-native technologies.

Get a Free eBook

We hope you are enjoying your recently purchased book! Your feedback is incredibly valuable to us, and to all other readers looking for great books.

If you found this book helpful or enjoyable, we would truly appreciate it, if you could take a moment to leave a short review with a 5 star rating on Amazon. It helps us grow, and lets other readers discover our books.

As a thank you, we would love to send you a free digital copy of this book, and a **30%** discount code on your next cart value on our official websites:

www.orangeava.com

www.orangeava.in (For Indian Subcontinent)

☑ **Here's how:**

Leave a review for the book on Amazon.

Take a screenshot of your review, and send an email to **info@orangeava.com** (it can be just the confirmation screen).

Once, we receive your screenshot, we will send you the digital file, within 24 hours.

Thank you so much for your support – it means a lot to us!

Downloading the code bundles and colored images

Please follow the links or scan the QR codes to download the ***Code Bundles and Images*** of the book:

https://github.com/ava-orange-education/Ultimate-KubeVirt-for-OpenShift-Virtualization

The code bundles and images of the book are also hosted on ***https://rebrand.ly/29c0d3***

In case there's an update to the code, it will be updated on the existing GitHub repository.

Errata

We take immense pride in our work at **Orange Education Pvt Ltd,** and follow best practices to ensure the accuracy of our content to provide an indulging reading experience to our subscribers. Our readers are our mirrors, and we use their inputs to reflect and improve upon human errors, if any, that may have occurred during the publishing processes involved. To let us maintain the quality and help us reach out to any readers who might be having difficulties due to any unforeseen errors, please write to us at :

errata@orangeava.com

Your support, suggestions, and feedback are highly appreciated.

DID YOU KNOW

Did you know that Orange Education Pvt Ltd offers eBook versions of every book published, with PDF and ePub files available? You can upgrade to the eBook version at **www.orangeava.com** and as a print book customer, you are entitled to a discount on the eBook copy. Get in touch with us at: **info@orangeava.com** for more details.

At **www.orangeava.com**, you can also read a collection of free technical articles, sign up for a range of free newsletters, and receive exclusive discounts and offers on Print Books and eBooks.

PIRACY

If you come across any illegal copies of our works in any form on the internet, we would be grateful if you would provide us with the location address or website name. Please contact us at **info@orangeava.com** with a link to the material.

ARE YOU INTERESTED IN AUTHORING WITH US?

If there is a topic that you have expertise in, and you are interested in either writing or contributing to a book, please write to us at **business@orangeava.com**. We are on a journey to help developers and tech professionals to gain insights on the present technological advancements and innovations happening across the globe and build a community that believes Knowledge is best acquired by sharing and learning with others. Please reach out to us to learn what our audience demands and how you can be part of this educational reform. We also welcome ideas from tech experts and help them build learning and development content for their domains.

REVIEWS

Please leave a review. Once you have read and used this book, why not leave a review on the site that you purchased it from? Potential readers can then see and use your unbiased opinion to make purchase decisions. We at Orange Education would love to know what you think about our products, and our authors can learn from your feedback. Thank you!

For more information about Orange Education, please visit **www.orangeava.com**.

Table of Contents

CHAPTER 1
Introduction to KubeVirt for OpenShift Virtualization

Introduction

This chapter will talk about Virtualization which has transformed IT infrastructure from single-application servers to efficient, resource-optimized systems. With the rise of cloud-native technologies, organizations are increasingly adopting containers for their agility and scalability. However, many enterprises still rely on Virtual Machines (VMs) for legacy applications and compliance needs.

KubeVirt addresses this challenge by extending Kubernetes to manage VM workloads alongside containerized applications. It enables businesses to unify their infrastructure, improve resource utilization, and modernize legacy systems, without disrupting operations. OpenShift Virtualization, powered by KubeVirt, further enhances this capability by providing enterprise-grade tools for VM lifecycle management, security, and hybrid cloud deployments. Together, these technologies bridge the gap between traditional virtualization and modern cloud-native environments, supporting a gradual transition toward fully containerized ecosystems.

Structure

In this chapter, we will cover the following topics:

- Evolution of virtualization and cloud-native applications
- KubeVirt and its relevance
- Benefits of combining Kubernetes and Virtual Machines
- Overview of OpenShift Virtualization
- Key use cases for KubeVirt in hybrid workloads
- Comparison with traditional virtualization platforms

Evolution of Virtualization and Cloud-Native Applications

Virtualization has come a long way, from the early days of partitioning servers to the full-fledged cloud computing revolution, allowing businesses to get the most of their resources, do with less, and make the move to virtual infrastructures much more easily. But as organizations adopt cloud-native architectures, traditional machines (VMs) are left running alongside containerized applications, requiring creative solutions, for which KubeVirt provides a way.

The Evolution of Virtualization

It all started a long time back, when Virtualization was introduced to use the hardware efficiently. The legacy of establishing a data center was to run a single application on a single physical server which resulted in poor resource utilization and additional costs. By utilizing hypervisors, multiple **Virtual Machines (VMs)** can now operate on one server, providing **greater resource efficiency and flexibility.**

- **Mainframe Era (1960s–1970s):** IBM introduced virtualization in mainframes, allowing multiple users to run isolated workloads.
- **Server Virtualization (1990s–2000s):** VMware popularized x86 server virtualization, enabling multiple OS instances on a single server.
- **Data Center Consolidation:** Organizations adopted hypervisors such as VMware ESXi, Microsoft Hyper-V, KVM, and IBM LPAR to reduce hardware footprints, and increase agility.

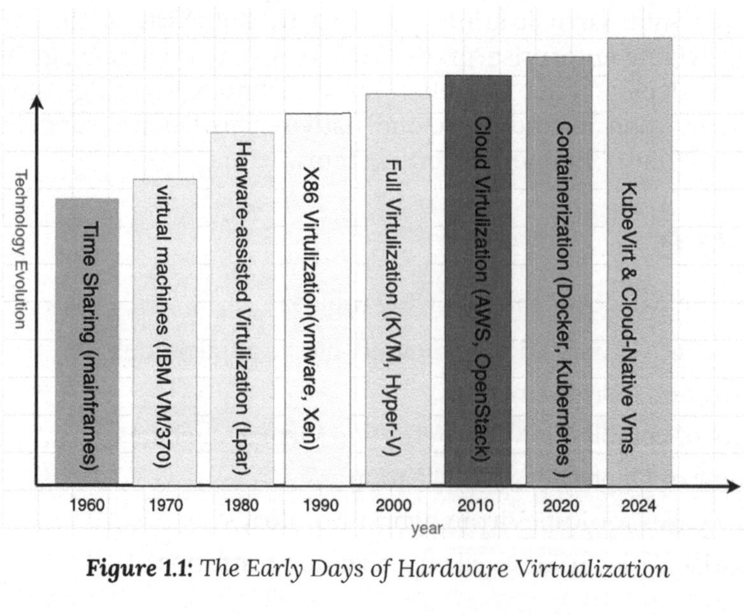

Figure 1.1: *The Early Days of Hardware Virtualization*

The Rise of Cloud Computing

As virtualization matured, cloud computing emerged, shifting the focus from on-premises infrastructure to on-demand services. Infrastructure-as-a-Service (IaaS) platforms such as AWS EC2, Azure, IBM, HPE, and GCP leveraged virtualization to provide scalable computing resources.

- **Public Cloud (2006-Present):** AWS pioneered cloud services, allowing enterprises to rent virtualized infrastructure, instead of maintaining physical servers.
- **Private and Hybrid Clouds:** OpenStack, VMware vSphere, and Azure Stack enabled enterprises to create private cloud environments, while integrating with public cloud services.
- **Limitations:** Despite its benefits, VM-based cloud computing faced challenges in speed, resource efficiency, and orchestration complexity.

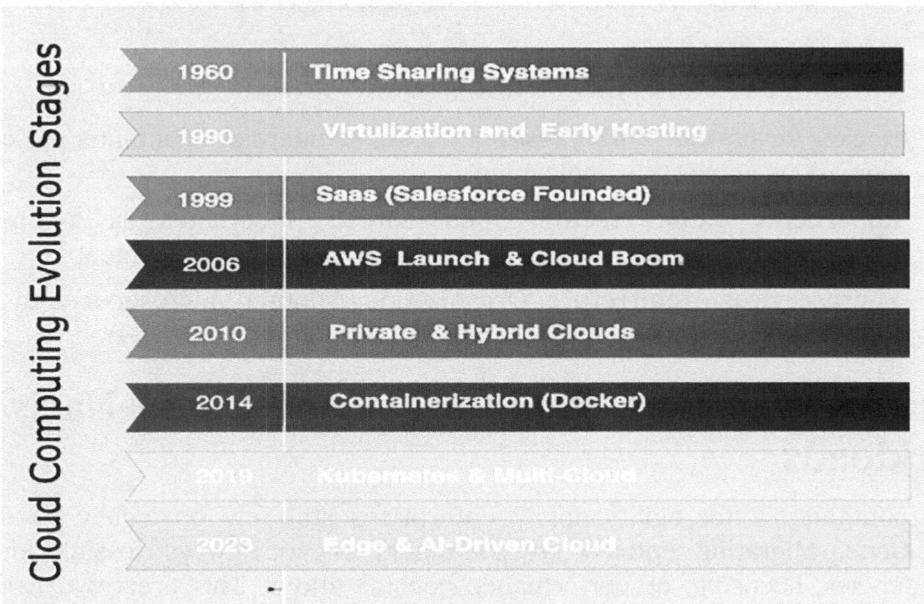

Figure 1.2: *The Rise of Cloud Computing*

The Shift to Cloud-Native Applications

The Emergence of Containers: Containers introduced a new paradigm for deploying and managing applications. Unlike VMs, which virtualize hardware, containers virtualize the operating system, making them lightweight and faster to deploy.

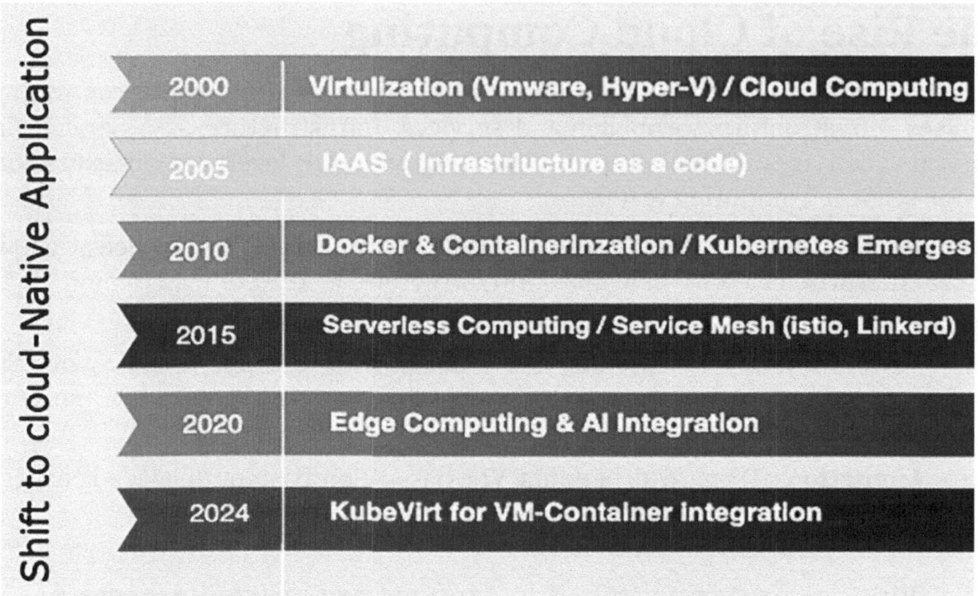

Figure 1.3: *The Emergence of Containers*

- **Docker Revolution (2013-Present):** Docker standardized container packaging, simplifying application deployment.
- **Kubernetes (2014-Present):** Open-sourced Kubernetes as a powerful orchestration tool, enabling large-scale containerized deployments.
- **Microservices Architecture:** Organizations adopted microservices to break monolithic applications into independently deployable services.

Challenges in Managing Legacy and Cloud-Native Workloads

While containers offer agility, many enterprises still rely on legacy VM-based applications. Migrating entirely to containers is not always feasible due to dependencies, licensing, or performance considerations. This creates a need for hybrid environments that support both VMs and containers seamlessly.

- **Coexistence of VMs and Containers:** Enterprises need solutions that integrate VMs within Kubernetes environments.
- **Resource Efficiency and Orchestration:** Managing VMs alongside containers requires consistent networking, storage, and compute management.
- **Security and Compliance:** Legacy applications often require specific security and compliance policies that must be maintained in a containerized infrastructure.

Introduction to KubeVirt: Bridging the Gap

KubeVirt is an open-source project that allows users to run **virtual machines inside Kubernetes.** It enables enterprises to run VM-based workloads within Kubernetes clusters, leveraging Kubernetes-native capabilities for networking, storage, and automation.

- **Seamless Integration:** KubeVirt allows VMs to run as Kubernetes objects, simplifying management.
- **Unified Orchestration:** IT teams can use Kubernetes tools such as kubectl and Helm to manage both VMs and containers.
- **Hybrid Cloud Ready:** KubeVirt supports multi-cloud and on-premises deployments, aligning with hybrid cloud strategies.

Benefits of KubeVirt in Cloud-Native Environments

KubeVirt provides several advantages for organizations looking to modernize their infrastructure, without abandoning legacy applications.

- **Flexibility:** Run VMs alongside containers, without separate orchestration platforms.
- **Efficiency:** Utilize Kubernetes' resource scheduling to optimize VMs and container workloads.
- **Cost Savings:** Reduce reliance on traditional hypervisors, while leveraging Kubernetes' automation.
- **Future-Proofing:** Enable gradual migration from VMs to containers, without disrupting operations.

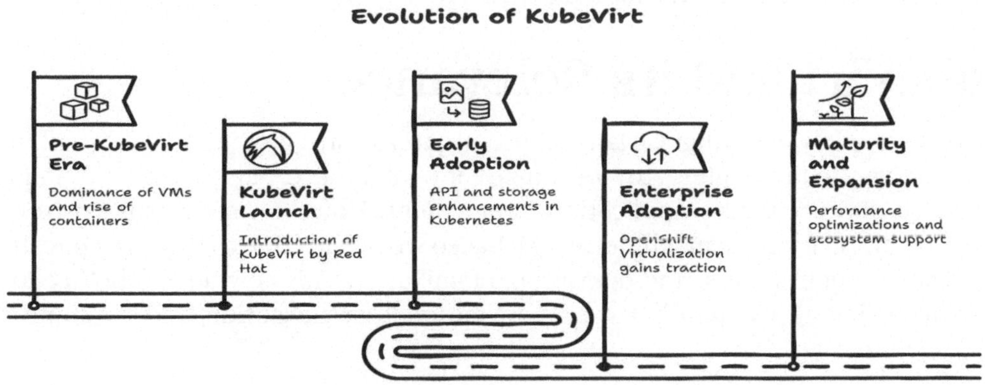

Figure 1.4: *Key Evolutionary Stages for KubeVirt*

Adaptation

Figure 1.5 shows the adaptation:

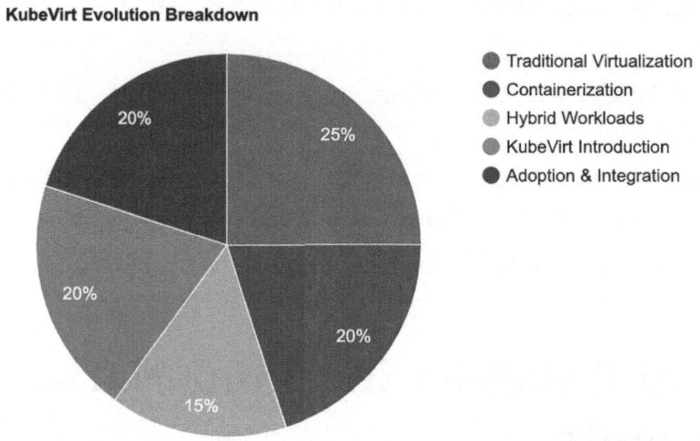

Figure 1.5: *KubeVirt Adaptation*

1. **Traditional Virtualization:** Hypervisors and VM-based workloads before Kubernetes.
2. **Containerization:** Rise of Docker, Kubernetes, and microservices.
3. **Hybrid Workloads:** Initial efforts to run VMs alongside containers in Kubernetes.
4. **KubeVirt Introduction:** Development of KubeVirt to run VMs within Kubernetes.
5. **Adoption and Integration:** Growing enterprise adoption, integration with OpenShift, and multi-cloud environments.

KubeVirt and its Relevance

In today's rapidly evolving IT landscape, organizations are increasingly adopting cloud-native technologies to optimize infrastructure management, improve scalability, and accelerate application deployment. However, many enterprises still rely on traditional virtual machine or VM-based workloads due to legacy applications, compliance requirements, and operational familiarity. This is where KubeVirt comes into play, bridging the gap between conventional virtualization and containerized environments.

KubeVirt extends Kubernetes, the leading container orchestration platform, to run and manage virtual machines alongside containers seamlessly. It provides a unified platform where organizations can integrate their existing VM workloads into modern Kubernetes-based environments, enabling hybrid cloud adoption, and easing the transition to cloud-native computing.

The Evolution of Virtualization and the Rise of Containers

Traditional Virtualization

Virtualization technology has been a cornerstone of IT infrastructure for decades, allowing multiple virtual machines to run on a single physical server. Popular hypervisors such as VMware ESXi, Microsoft Hyper-V, and KVM (Kernel-based Virtual Machine) have enabled efficient resource utilization, improved scalability, and isolated workloads.

However, as cloud-native computing gained momentum, organizations began shifting toward containerized architectures. Containers offer:

- Lightweight runtime environments compared to VMs.
- Faster startup times due to the absence of full operating system overhead.
- Better scalability and orchestration using Kubernetes.

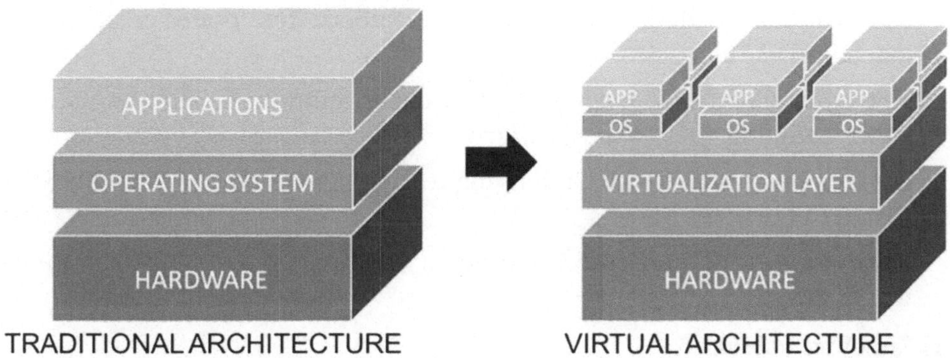

Figure 1.6: *Architecture of Traditional System vs. Virtual System*

Challenges in Managing Legacy VM-Based Workloads

Despite the benefits of containerization, many enterprises still rely on traditional VMs for:

- Running stateful applications, and legacy software.

- Compliance and security requirements in regulated industries.
- Workloads that require full OS support not available in containers.

These challenges necessitate a solution that allows organizations to run both containers and VMs on a single platform, while leveraging the power of Kubernetes. This is where KubeVirt becomes highly relevant.

What is KubeVirt?

KubeVirt is an open-source virtualization solution designed to run virtual machines within Kubernetes clusters. Developed by the Kubernetes community, and backed by Red Hat, KubeVirt enables organizations to modernize their infrastructure by integrating VMs into their Kubernetes environments, without requiring a separate hypervisor or dedicated virtualization platform.

Key Components of KubeVirt

KubeVirt extends Kubernetes by introducing the following core components:

- **Virtual Machine (VM) Custom Resource:** Defines and manages virtual machines as native Kubernetes objects.
- **virt-launcher:** A pod that hosts the virtual machine, ensuring seamless VM execution within Kubernetes.
- **virt-handler:** A daemon running on Kubernetes nodes responsible for managing VM lifecycles.
- **virt-controller:** Manages high-level orchestration tasks, such as VM creation and scheduling.
- **libvirt and QEMU/KVM:** Underlying technologies that provide VM execution within Kubernetes pods.
- **KubeVirt API:** Extends the Kubernetes API to support virtualization-related workloads.

Why is KubeVirt Relevant?

- **Unifying VM and Container Workloads:** KubeVirt eliminates the need for separate infrastructure stacks by running both VMs and containers on Kubernetes, allowing organizations to streamline their DevOps and CI/CD pipelines, without migrating legacy applications immediately.
- **Enabling Hybrid Cloud and Multi-Cloud Strategies:** KubeVirt supports hybrid cloud deployments, allowing enterprises to run VM workloads on-premises, in public clouds, or across multiple cloud providers, while benefiting from Kubernetes' orchestration capabilities.
- **Modernizing Legacy Applications:** Many enterprises operate legacy applications that cannot be easily containerized. KubeVirt provides a path for

incremental modernization, allowing organizations to refactor applications at their own pace, while maintaining Kubernetes-native management.

- **Simplified Management and Automation:** With KubeVirt, IT teams can use Kubernetes-native tools (for example, kubectl, Helm, and GitOps) to manage virtual machines, bringing consistency to Infrastructure as Code (IaC) practices.
- **Cost Efficiency and Resource Optimization:** KubeVirt helps optimize hardware utilization by allowing VMs and containers to share compute resources, reducing the need for separate virtualization infrastructure.

Benefits of Combining Kubernetes and Virtual Machines

The integration of KubeVirt into Kubernetes environments offers many advantages:

- **Unified Management:** Organizations can manage both containerized and VM-based workloads, using a single Kubernetes control plane, simplifying administration, and reducing the need for multiple platforms.
- **Improved Resource Efficiency:** By running VMs and containers within the same cluster, organizations can optimize resource allocation, reduce hardware waste, and achieve better density and cost-effectiveness.
- **Hybrid Cloud Compatibility:** KubeVirt enables organizations to seamlessly extend their infrastructure across on-premises data centers and cloud environments, facilitating hybrid cloud adoption and migration strategies.
- **Enhanced Automation and CI/CD Integration:** Traditional VMs can be included in modern DevOps workflows, enabling automated deployments, scaling, and integration with Kubernetes-native tools such as Helm, GitOps, and CI/CD pipelines.
- **Security and Isolation:** KubeVirt allows organizations to leverage Kubernetes security policies, while maintaining VM-level isolation, ensuring secure multi-tenancy and workload separation.
- **Simplified Modernization of Legacy Applications:** Legacy applications that cannot be easily containerized can still be managed within Kubernetes clusters, allowing gradual modernization, without disrupting business operations.

Overview of OpenShift Virtualization

OpenShift Virtualization, an enterprise-grade solution powered by KubeVirt, is designed to integrate traditional virtual machine workloads into modern Kubernetes-based container environments. As organizations embrace cloud-native architectures, they face the challenge of managing legacy VMs, while leveraging the flexibility and scalability of containers. OpenShift Virtualization bridges this gap by enabling users to run and manage VMs within an OpenShift cluster, ensuring a unified infrastructure for both containerized and non-containerized applications.

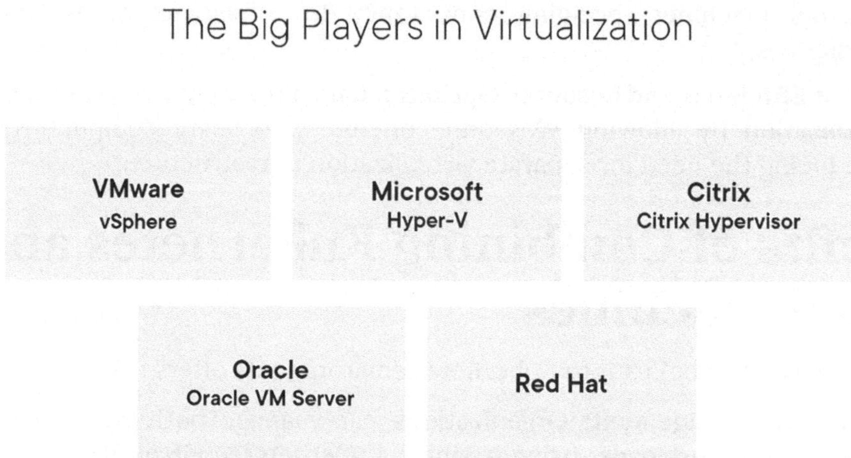

Figure 1.7: *Companies Who Support Virtualization Hardware*

Evolution of Virtualization and Containerization

Virtualization has long been a cornerstone of data center efficiency, enabling multiple workloads to run on shared hardware through hypervisors. This approach revolutionized IT infrastructure by optimizing resource utilization, improving disaster recovery, and simplifying application management. However, the rise of Kubernetes and containerization introduced a new paradigm that emphasizes microservices, rapid scaling, and automation.

While containers provide lightweight and portable execution environments, many enterprises still rely on VMs for critical applications that require specific dependencies or regulatory compliance. OpenShift Virtualization addresses this need by allowing organizations to modernize their infrastructure, without abandoning their existing investments in VM-based workloads.

Key Components of OpenShift Virtualization

OpenShift Virtualization extends Kubernetes by integrating the following core components:

- **KubeVirt:** The core technology that enables VM management within Kubernetes.

- **Virtual Machine Operator (VMO):** Automates the lifecycle management of VMs within OpenShift.
- **CDI (Containerized Data Importer):** Facilitates data import and storage management for VM images.
- **Networking and Storage Integration:** Ensures seamless connectivity and persistent storage support for VMs.
- **OpenShift Web Console and CLI:** Provides an intuitive interface for VM creation, monitoring, and management.

By leveraging these components, OpenShift Virtualization allows enterprises to run VMs alongside containers, using the same Kubernetes-based orchestration, security, and CI/CD pipelines.

Benefits of OpenShift Virtualization

The integration of virtualization within OpenShift offers several advantages:

- **Unified Management:** Centralized control for both VM and containerized workloads.
- **Enhanced Scalability:** Dynamic resource allocation, based on workload demands.
- **Security and Compliance:** OpenShift's robust security features extend to VMs.
- **Hybrid Cloud Readiness:** Seamless migration and interoperability across on-premise and cloud environments.
- **Developer Efficiency:** Enables DevOps teams to develop, test, and deploy applications, without infrastructure silos.

Hybrid Cloud Adoption and Future Trends

As enterprises increasingly adopt hybrid cloud strategies, OpenShift Virtualization plays a crucial role in enabling workload portability and multi-cloud deployments. Organizations can gradually transition from VM-based infrastructure to containerized applications, ensuring business continuity, while embracing modern cloud-native architectures.

By understanding the fundamentals of OpenShift Virtualization, cloud architects, DevOps professionals, and IT leaders can harness its capabilities to drive innovation and operational efficiency. The following chapters will delve deeper into technical implementations, best practices, and real-world use cases for OpenShift Virtualization in enterprise environments.

Key Use Cases for KubeVirt in Hybrid Workloads

As enterprises navigate the transition to cloud-native architectures, many organizations find themselves managing both containerized applications and legacy virtual machines. KubeVirt, an extension of Kubernetes, offers a unified platform that enables the seamless operation of VMs alongside containers. This lesson will explore the primary use cases where KubeVirt excels in hybrid workloads, enabling organizations to achieve operational efficiency, scalability, and modernization, without disrupting the existing infrastructure.

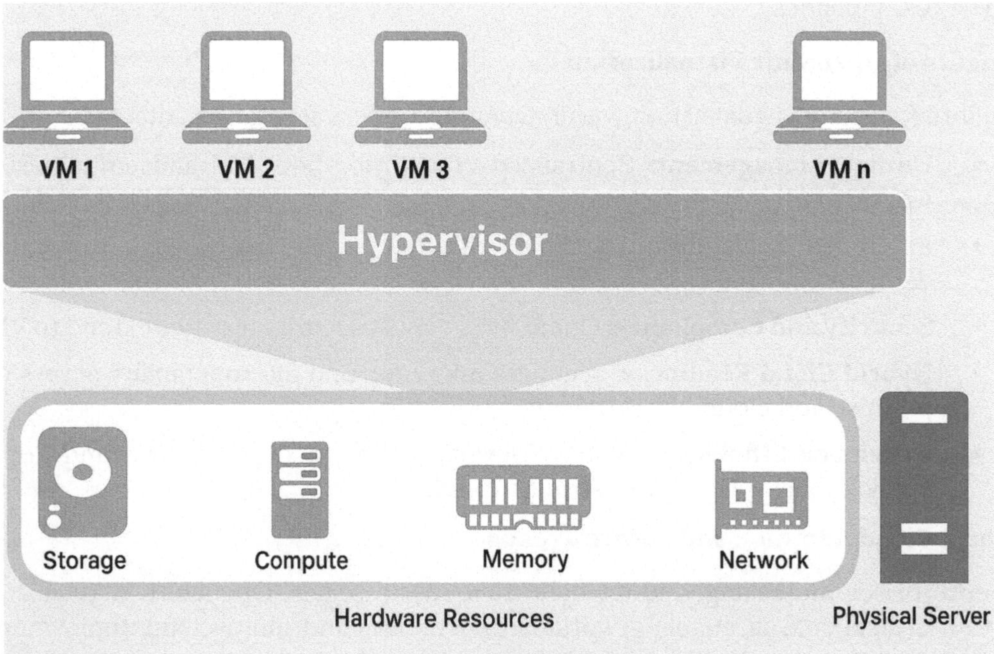

Figure 1.8: *Architecture of High-Level VM Management Using KubeVirt*

Bridging Legacy Applications with Cloud-Native Environments

Many enterprises still rely on traditional VM-based applications that are not yet ready for containerization. KubeVirt allows organizations to run these legacy applications within a Kubernetes environment, enabling gradual modernization. By hosting VMs in Kubernetes clusters, enterprises can leverage Kubernetes' scheduling, networking, and security capabilities, while maintaining their existing workloads.

Benefits:

- Seamless integration of VMs and containers.
- Improving resource utilization with Kubernetes orchestration.
- Reducing operational overhead by managing both workload types on a single platform.

Hybrid Cloud Deployments

Organizations adopting hybrid cloud strategies require flexibility in deploying and managing workloads across on-premises and public cloud environments. KubeVirt facilitates hybrid cloud scenarios by allowing workloads to run in both environments, without requiring fundamental changes to the applications.

Use Case Examples:

- Running a primary database on-premises, while leveraging cloud-based microservices.
- Migrating workloads incrementally from private data centers to the cloud.
- Ensuring business continuity by enabling workload failover between on-prem and cloud infrastructure.

Dev/Test Environments for Legacy Applications

Developers often need to test and validate legacy applications in controlled environments before full-scale deployment. KubeVirt provides a consistent, containerized environment where developers can spin up VM-based workloads, alongside Kubernetes-native services.

Key Advantages:

- Rapid provisioning of VM-based test environments.
- Enhanced CI/CD pipelines integrating legacy applications with containerized workloads.
- Cost reduction by consolidating resources, instead of maintaining separate virtualization platforms.

Multi-Tenancy and Secure Workload Isolation

Enterprises with stringent security and compliance requirements need isolation between workloads. KubeVirt allows organizations to enforce strong security boundaries between VM-based and containerized workloads, ensuring compliance with regulatory standards.

Security Enhancements:

- Network policies to segregate VM traffic within Kubernetes.
- RBAC (Role-Based Access Control) for secure multi-tenant environments.
- Integration with services meshes like Istio for enhanced security and observability.

Disaster Recovery and High Availability

Mission-critical applications require robust disaster recovery and high availability strategies. KubeVirt, integrated with Kubernetes' resilience features, enables organizations to implement automated failover, snapshot-based recovery, and high availability for VM workloads.

Implementation Examples:

- **Automated backup and recovery** using Kubernetes-native storage solutions.
- **Live migration of VMs** across nodes to prevent downtime.
- **Geographically distributed** deployments for disaster resilience.

Major Comparison with Traditional Virtualization Platforms

Virtualization has been a cornerstone of modern IT infrastructure, enabling organizations to maximize resource utilization, enhance scalability, and improve workload management. Traditionally, hypervisor-based virtualization platforms such as VMware vSphere, Microsoft Hyper-V, and KVM have dominated enterprise environments. However, with the rise of cloud-native workloads and containerized applications, new approaches such as KubeVirt have emerged, offering an innovative fusion of virtual machine and container-based orchestration within Kubernetes.

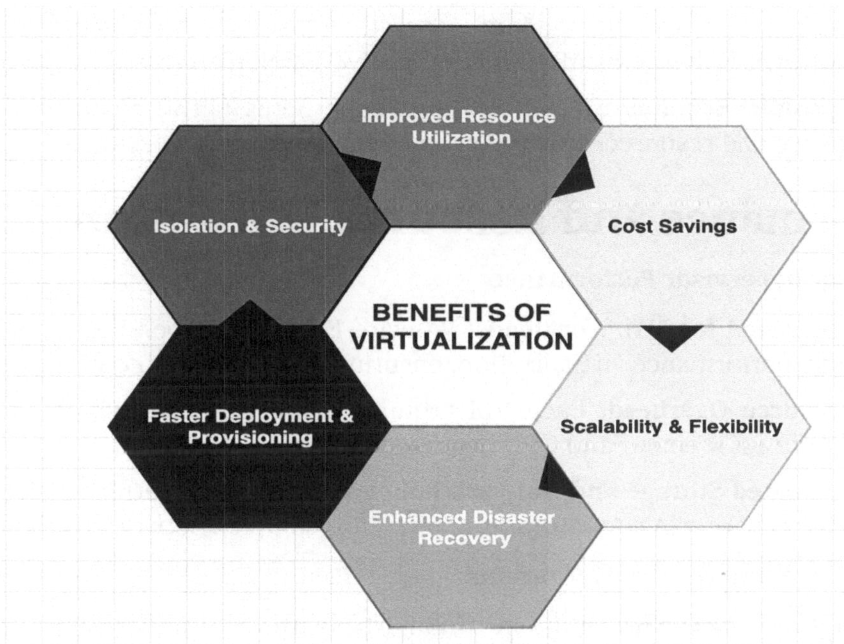

Figure 1.9: *Benefits of Virtualization in Real Application*

This topic will provide a detailed comparison between traditional virtualization platforms and KubeVirt, highlighting their architectural differences, management paradigms, performance trade-offs, and real-world applicability.

Architecture and Deployment Model

Traditional Virtualization Platforms: Traditional virtualization platforms rely on hypervisors (Type-1 or Type-2) that abstract physical hardware to create and manage virtual machines. Some key architectural characteristics include:

- **Hypervisor-based Isolation:** Each VM runs with a guest OS, and its own virtualized hardware, isolated from other VMs.
- **Dedicated Management Layer:** Platforms such as VMware vSphere employ a dedicated management layer (vCenter) for provisioning and monitoring VMs.
- **Fixed Resource Allocation:** CPU, memory, and disk resources are statically allocated to VMs, leading to potential underutilization.

KubeVirt's Cloud-Native Approach: KubeVirt, an extension to Kubernetes, integrates virtualization capabilities directly within container orchestration, offering:

- **Container-Oriented VM Management:** Virtual Machines are defined as Kubernetes Custom Resources (CRs), and are managed alongside containers.

- **Unified Platform:** Instead of separate hypervisor management, KubeVirt leverages Kubernetes APIs and declarative YAML manifests.
- **Dynamic Scheduling and Scaling:** Kubernetes-native features like auto-scaling and resource-efficient scheduling benefit VM workloads.

Performance and Resource Utilization

Traditional Hypervisor Performance

- **Optimized for VM Workloads:** VMware ESXi and Hyper-V are designed for high-performance virtualization, ensuring near-native execution speeds.
- **Resource Overhead:** Each VM requires a full OS stack which can lead to significant memory and CPU overhead.
- **Dedicated Storage and Network Policies:** Traditional platforms often rely on SAN/NAS or vSAN for storage, and require complex network configurations.

KubeVirt Performance Considerations

- **Lighter Footprint:** VMs in KubeVirt share the underlying Kubernetes infrastructure, reducing overhead compared to traditional VMs.
- **Seamless Integration with Kubernetes Networking and Storage:** Enables the use of Container Network Interface (CNI) plugins and CSI-based storage backends.
- **Potential Latency Concerns:** As Kubernetes was not originally designed for VMs, there may be additional scheduling delays compared to dedicated hypervisor solutions.

Management and Automation

Traditional Platforms' Management Tools

- **GUI-Driven Management:** vSphere, Hyper-V, and XenCenter provide graphical interfaces for VM administration.
- **Limited CI/CD Integration:** Automation tools such as Ansible and Terraform are often required for operational efficiency.
- **Complex Licensing:** Enterprise deployments often incur additional licensing costs for management features.

KubeVirt's Kubernetes-Based Management

- **API-Driven Control:** Full integration with Kubernetes API enables automation, using Kubernetes-native tools such as Helm and Operators.
- **GitOps and CI/CD Compatibility:** Easily integrates into DevOps workflows with tools like ArgoCD and Flux.

- **Open-Source and Cost-Efficient:** Reduces proprietary licensing costs, and encourages innovation in VM orchestration.

Security and Isolation

Traditional Hypervisors' Security Posture

- **Hardware-Enforced Isolation:** Leveraging Intel VT-x and AMD-V for secure VM execution.
- **Dedicated Security Controls:** Enterprise-grade security features like VM encryption and secure boot.
- **Attack Surface:** Hypervisors, while robust, introduce a single point of failure, if compromised.

KubeVirt's Security Features

- **Pod Security Policies:** VM workloads benefit from Kubernetes-native security policies.
- **Namespace-Based Multi-Tenancy:** Enhanced isolation compared to traditional VM segmentation.
- **SELinux and Seccomp Integration:** Additional security layers inherited from Kubernetes environments.

Use Cases and Suitability

Feature	Traditional Virtualization	KubeVirt
Best For	Enterprise IT, Datacenter VMs	Cloud-native VMs, hybrid workloads
Scalability	Horizontal scaling via clusters	Kubernetes auto-scaling
Management Complexity	Requires separate hypervisor management	Unified Kubernetes-based control
Cost Efficiency	Licensing and infrastructure costs	Open-source, lower cost
Performance Overhead	Higher due to full OS per VM	Lower with Kubernetes integration

Figure 1.10: *Major Differences between Traditional Virtualization and KubeVirt*

Conclusion

KubeVirt and OpenShift Virtualization have emerged as powerful solutions that bridge this gap, enabling enterprises to run traditional virtual machines alongside modern containerized workloads within a unified Kubernetes ecosystem.

Throughout this book, we will explore the evolution of virtualization, the rise of cloud-native architectures, and the strategic role that KubeVirt plays in hybrid cloud adoption. We will examine the technical underpinnings of KubeVirt, its seamless integration into OpenShift, and its ability to enhance workload portability, automation, and operational efficiency.

By leveraging KubeVirt, enterprises can modernize their IT infrastructure incrementally, ensuring that legacy applications continue to operate, while embracing the agility of Kubernetes. OpenShift Virtualization further extends these capabilities by providing an enterprise-grade, developer-friendly platform that simplifies VM lifecycle management, security, and hybrid cloud deployment.

Looking ahead, the convergence of virtualization and cloud-native technologies will continue to evolve, driven by innovations in automation, security, and scalability. As Kubernetes cements itself as the de-facto orchestration layer for modern workloads, solutions like KubeVirt will play an increasingly significant role in shaping the future of IT infrastructure.

CHAPTER 2
Setting Up the Environment

Introduction

Deploying **KubeVirt** within an **OpenShift** environment requires careful preparation to ensure a stable, performant, and scalable virtualization infrastructure. Kubernetes is designed for containerized workloads, KubeVirt extends its capabilities to support Virtual Machines (VMs), enabling enterprises to modernize infrastructure, without abandoning legacy applications. However, integrating virtualization into a Kubernetes-native environment comes with **specific prerequisites**, including platform compatibility, hardware configurations, networking setups, and security considerations.

This chapter will provide a **structured approach to preparing the environment** for KubeVirt deployment, ensuring that all critical dependencies are met before deploying and managing virtualized workloads. We will cover the essential aspects such as **hardware and software requirements, OpenShift configurations, networking best practices, security hardening, and installation verification.**

Structure

In this chapter, we will cover the following topics:

- Prerequisites for KubeVirt Deployment
- Installing OpenShift Virtualization Operator
- Configuring Cluster Resources for Virtualization
- Networking Setup and Integration
- Verifying and Troubleshooting the Installation
- Tools for Environment Preparation

Prerequisites for KubeVirt Deployment

KubeVirt is a powerful virtualization extension for Kubernetes that enables the orchestration of virtual machines, alongside container workloads. Deploying KubeVirt within an OpenShift environment requires careful planning and adherence to specific prerequisites to ensure a stable and efficient setup. This section will cover the technical and infrastructural requirements necessary for a successful KubeVirt deployment, including platform compatibility, hardware specifications, networking considerations, and software dependencies.

Platform Compatibility

KubeVirt is designed to run on Kubernetes-based platforms, with OpenShift being one of the most robust choices due to its enterprise-grade features. Before deploying KubeVirt, one needs to ensure the following:

- **Kubernetes Version:** KubeVirt requires Kubernetes version **1.21** or later, with CRI-O or containerd as the container runtime.
- **OpenShift Version:** OpenShift 4.8 or newer is recommended, as it provides integrated Operator Lifecycle Management (OLM) for KubeVirt installation, and seamless networking support.
- **Kernel Version:** The host operating system should have a kernel version 4.18 or later to support KVM (Kernel-based Virtual Machine) capabilities.
- **Underlying Infrastructure:** Whether deploying on bare metal or a cloud provider, ensure that the underlying infrastructure supports nested virtualization, if needed.

OpenShift clusters hosted on AWS, need to ensure that the EC2 instances running worker nodes are of type **`m5.xlarge`** or higher, as these support hardware virtualization extensions necessary for KubeVirt. Using *Figure 2.1*, we are trying to understand the difference between KVM and QEMU.

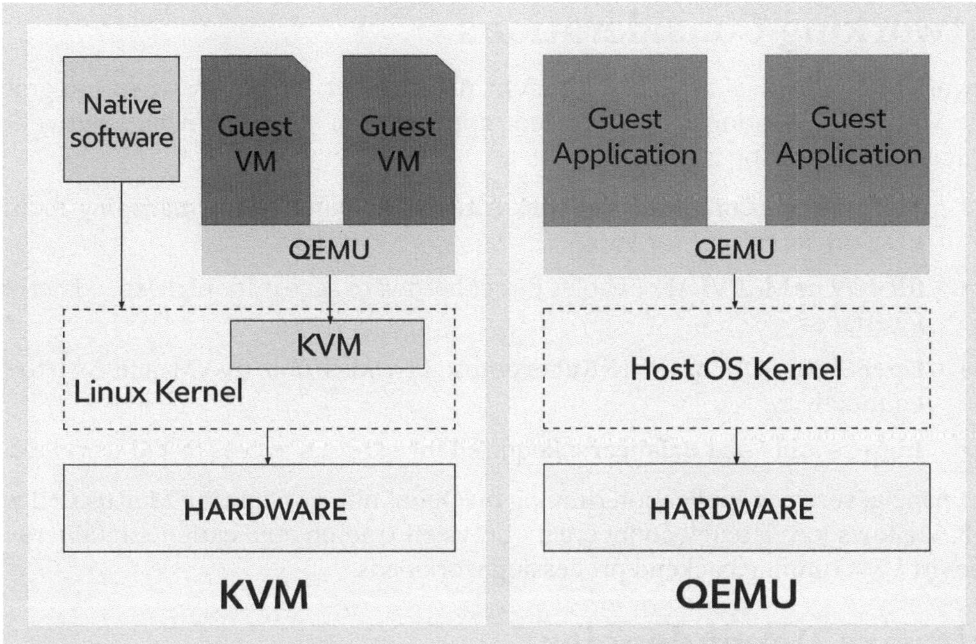

Figure 2.1: *KVM and QEMU Architecture*

Hardware Requirements

The hardware hosting KubeVirt must meet the minimum specifications to run VMs efficiently. The key hardware considerations include:

- **CPU:** Nodes must support hardware virtualization extensions (Intel VT-x or AMD-V).

```
ubuntu $ lscpu  | grep Virtualization
Virtualization type:            full
ubuntu $ 
```

Figure 2.2: *Hardware Support for Virtualization*

- **Memory:** A minimum of **16GB RAM** per node is recommended for running multiple virtual machines alongside containerized workloads.
- **Storage:** Persistent storage with support for block and file storage is required. OpenShift Data Foundation (ODF), or NFS-backed PVCs are common choices.
- **Networking:** Need to ensure a network interface capable of supporting SR-IOV (Single Root I/O Virtualization) if high-performance networking is needed.

Networking Considerations

Networking is a critical aspect of KubeVirt deployment, especially when integrating VMs with the existing containerized applications. The following networking configurations must be in place:

- **Multus CNI (Container Network Interface):** Required for managing multiple network interfaces for VMs.
- **SR-IOV or MACVLAN:** Enables direct hardware access for high-speed network interfaces.
- **OpenShift SDN or OVN-Kubernetes:** Provides pod-to-VM and VM-to-VM connectivity.
- **Ingress and Load Balancers:** Required for external access to VM workloads.

In a financial services application running on OpenShift, configuring **Multus CNI with SR-IOV** allows low-latency connectivity between trading application containers and KubeVirt VMs running backend processing workloads.

Software Dependencies

Several software dependencies must be installed and configured, before deploying KubeVirt:

- **KubeVirt Operator:** Manages the lifecycle of KubeVirt components within OpenShift.
- **KVM and QEMU:** The worker nodes must have `qemu-kvm` installed for virtualization.
- **Libvirt:** Provides VM management and networking capabilities.
- **CDI (Containerized Data Importer):** Enables VM disk image import and cloning.
- **Persistent Storage Classes:** Ensure that storage classes such as `rook-ceph-block` or `local-storage` are available.

For a hybrid cloud scenario where VMs need to be migrated between OpenShift clusters, **CDI-backed PVCs with Ceph RBD** enable persistent volume snapshots and replication.

Security and Access Control

Security policies must be in place to ensure compliance and isolation of VMs:

- **SELinux and AppArmor:** Should be configured in `permissive` mode, if troubleshooting issues arise.

- **RBAC (Role-Based Access Control):** Set up appropriate permissions for developers and administrators managing KubeVirt.
- **Network Policies:** Restrict VM traffic, using OpenShift's NetworkPolicy objects.
- **Pod Security Standards (PSS):** Ensure compliance with OpenShift's security profiles.

In a healthcare deployment where patient data is processed within KubeVirt VMs, configuring **RBAC with strict least privilege**, and enabling **TLS encryption for VM-to-VM communication** ensures regulatory compliance (HIPAA, GDPR).

Installation Readiness Check

Before deploying KubeVirt, one needs to verify system readiness, using the following commands:

***Figure 2.3:** Hardware Support for Virtualization*

```
# Need to validate that KubeVirt Operator can be installed
https://docs.redhat.com/en/documentation/openshift_container_
platform/4.8/html/cli_tools/openshift-cli-oc
oc get packagemanifest -n openshift-marketplace | grep kubevirt
# Verify CDI installation
oc get cdi -n kubevirt
```

OpenShift deployment, running **preflight checks using OpenShift's OperatorHub** need to ensure that all dependencies, including CDI and Multus CNI, are correctly configured, before deploying KubeVirt.

Installing OpenShift Virtualization Operator

OpenShift Virtualization is a critical component that enables users to run and manage virtual machines alongside containerized workloads within OpenShift clusters. This feature is powered by KubeVirt, an open-source project designed to extend Kubernetes with virtualization capabilities. To leverage this functionality, administrators must install the OpenShift Virtualization Operator which orchestrates the deployment and management of virtualized workloads.

Prerequisites

Before proceeding with the installation, one needs to ensure that the following requirements are met:

- **OpenShift Cluster:** A running OpenShift Container Platform (OCP) cluster, version 4.6 or later.
- **Cluster Administrator Access**: The user performing the installation should have cluster administrator privileges.
- **Sufficient Resources:** Adequate CPU, memory, and storage to support virtual machine workloads.
- **Operator Lifecycle Manager (OLM):** OLM should be enabled to manage the installation, and upgrades of operators.

Step 1: Accessing the OpenShift Web Console

a. Need to log into the **OpenShift web console**, using an account with cluster administrator privileges.

b. Need to navigate to the **Administrator** perspective to access cluster-wide settings and configurations.

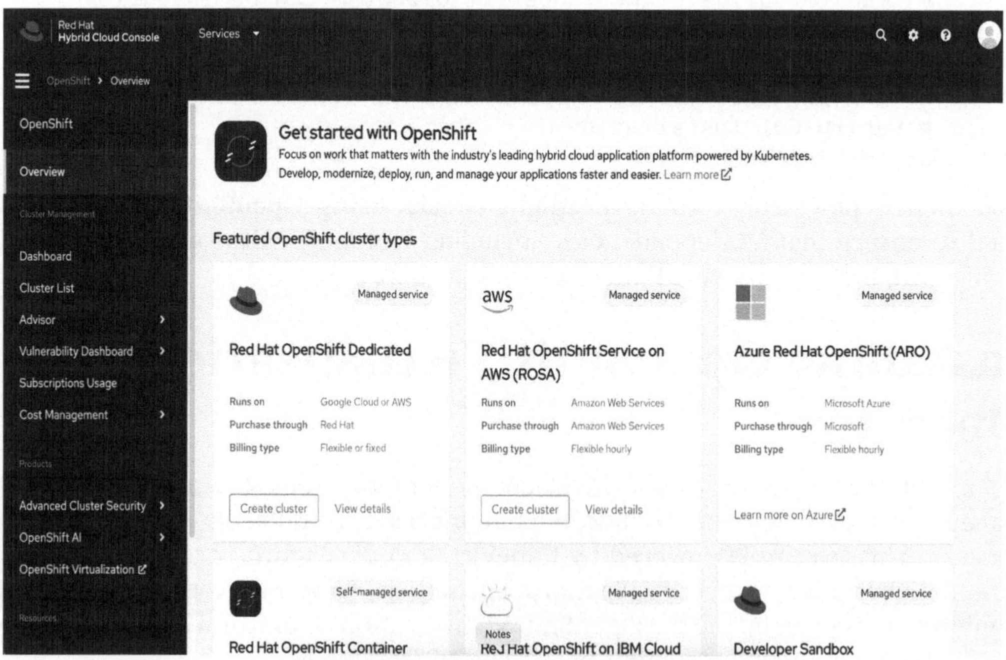

Figure 2.4: *OpenShift Console View*

Step 2: Installing the OpenShift Virtualization Operator

Using the Web Console

a. In the OpenShift Web Console, go to **`Operators → OperatorHub`**.

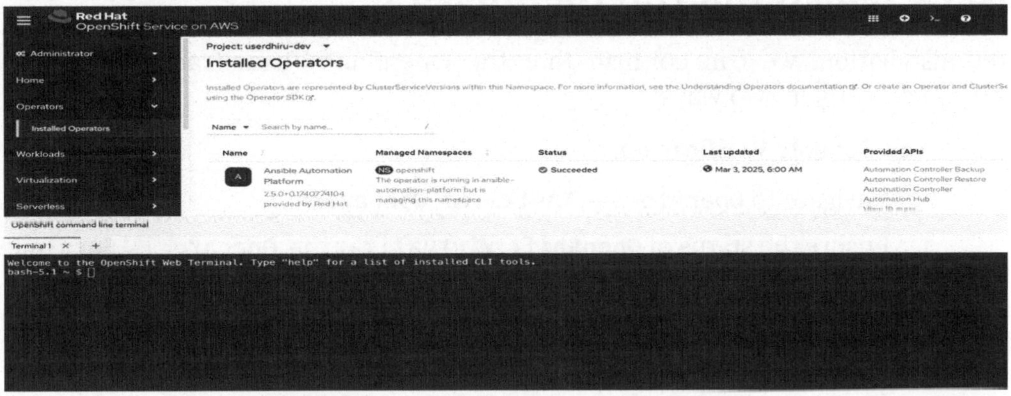

Figure 2.5: *OpenShift Operators from Console*

b. In the search **`bar.type`**, **`OpenShift Virtualization`** to locate the operator.

c. Click the **`OpenShift Virtualization Operator`**, and select **`Install`**.

d. Choose the following installation options:

   - **Installation Mode:** Cluster-wide (recommended)
   - **Update Approval:** Automatic or Manual (Automatic ensures that the operator stays updated without intervention)

e. Click **`Install`**, and wait for the installation to complete.

Using the CLI

For users, who prefer CLI-based installations, execute the following command to create a subscription to the OpenShift Virtualization Operator:

```
cat <<EOF | oc apply -f -
apiVersion: operators.coreos.com/v1alpha1
kind: Subscription
metadata:
  name: kubevirt-hyperconverged
  namespace: openshift-cnv
spec:
  channel: stable
  name: kubevirt-hyperconverged
```

```
  source: redhat-operators
  sourceNamespace: openshift-marketplace
EOF
```

This command ensures that the OpenShift Virtualization Operator is installed and managed by the Operator Lifecycle Manager.

Step 3: Verifying the Installation

After installation, we can confirm that the OpenShift Virtualization Operator is running correctly in two ways:

1. **Web Console Verification:**
   - Navigate to **`Operators`** → **`Installed Operators`**.
   - Ensure the status of **`OpenShift Virtualization Operator`** is "**`Succeeded`**".
2. **CLI Verification:** Run the following command to check the status of the operator:

   ```
   oc get pods -n openshift-cnv
   ```

   The output should display pods running for the OpenShift Virtualization Operator.

Step 4: Enabling OpenShift Virtualization

Once the operator is installed, one needs to enable OpenShift Virtualization:

a. Go to **`Virtualization`** → **`Overview`** in the web console.

b. Click **`Enable OpenShift Virtualization`** and confirm.

c. Wait for the necessary components to be deployed, including KubeVirt, CDI (Containerized Data Importer), and networking components.

Verify the successful deployment by running the following command:

```
oc get pods -n openshift-cnv
```

Step 5: Configuring Storage and Networking

To ensure seamless VM operations, configure appropriate storage and networking:

a. Set up a **`PersistentVolume` (PV)** and **`Storage Class`** to provide persistent storage for virtual machines.

b. Verify the available storage classes:

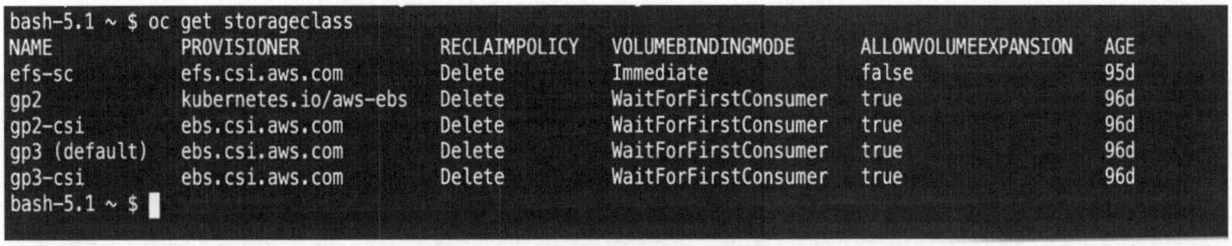

```
bash-5.1 ~ $ oc get storageclass
NAME            PROVISIONER             RECLAIMPOLICY   VOLUMEBINDINGMODE      ALLOWVOLUMEEXPANSION   AGE
efs-sc          efs.csi.aws.com         Delete          Immediate              false                  95d
gp2             kubernetes.io/aws-ebs   Delete          WaitForFirstConsumer   true                   96d
gp2-csi         ebs.csi.aws.com         Delete          WaitForFirstConsumer   true                   96d
gp3 (default)   ebs.csi.aws.com         Delete          WaitForFirstConsumer   true                   96d
gp3-csi         ebs.csi.aws.com         Delete          WaitForFirstConsumer   true                   96d
bash-5.1 ~ $
```

Figure 2.6: *StorageClass*

Assign a default storage class for virtualization workloads, if necessary.

- Ensure that the **`Multus CNI Plugin`** is available for advanced networking features.
- Configure a dedicated network attachment definition, if required:

  `oc get network-attachment-definitions -n openshift-cnv`

Real-World Example: Deploying a Virtual Machine

After successful installation, let us create a simple virtual machine:

```
cat <<EOF | oc apply -f -
apiVersion: kubevirt.io/v1
kind: VirtualMachine
metadata:
  name: fedora-apricot-iguana
  namespace: default
spec:
  running: true
  template:
    metadata:
      labels:
        kubevirt.io/domain: test-vm
    spec:
      domain:
        devices:
          disks:
            - name: rootdisk
              disk:
                bus: virtio
        resources:
          requests:
            memory: 2Gi
      volumes:
        - name: rootdisk
          containerDisk:
            image: quay.io/kubevirt/cirros-container-disk
EOF
```

Check the VM status with:

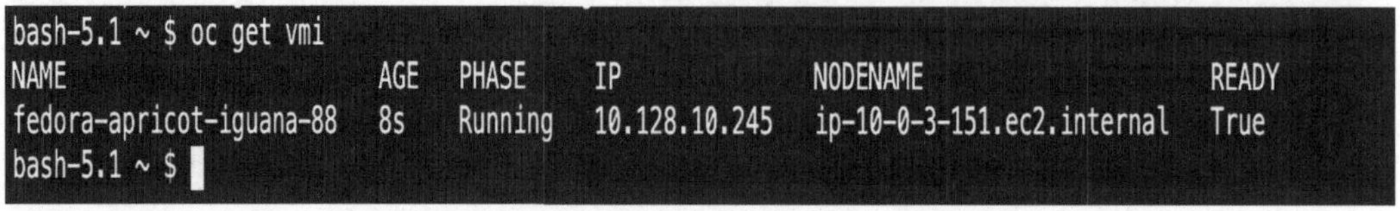

Figure 2.7: *Command to Get Details about VM*

Configuring Cluster Resources for Virtualization

Virtualization in OpenShift with KubeVirt enables the seamless execution of virtual machines alongside containerized workloads. However, to ensure optimal performance, scalability, and resource efficiency, configuring cluster resources properly is essential. This chapter provides an in-depth guide on setting up cluster resources tailored for virtualization workloads, covering compute, memory, storage, and networking configurations in an OpenShift environment.

Understanding Resource Allocation in OpenShift Virtualization

KubeVirt leverages Kubernetes' declarative resource management capabilities to allocate resources for VMs efficiently. Unlike traditional hypervisors, which operate outside Kubernetes, KubeVirt integrates virtualization workloads into the Kubernetes control plane, allowing them to benefit from dynamic resource allocation, and policy enforcement.

Key Considerations:

- **Compute resources:** CPU and memory reservations, limits, and NUMA affinity.
- **Storage provisioning:** Persistent storage backends such as Ceph, NFS, and OpenShift Data Foundation (ODF).
- **Networking:** Configuring Multus for multiple network interfaces.
- **Scaling and scheduling policies:** Node selectors, taints, and tolerations to optimize VM placement.

Configuring Compute Resources

Compute resources are crucial for VM performance, and must be managed efficiently to avoid resource contention. Kubernetes provides mechanisms such as **CPU requests and limits** to allocate compute resources effectively.

Setting CPU and Memory Requests

```
apiVersion: kubevirt.io/v1
kind: VirtualMachine
metadata:
  name: example-vm
spec:
  running: true
  template:
    spec:
      domain:
        cpu:
          cores: 4
        resources:
          requests:
            memory: 8Gi
            cpu: 4
          limits:
            memory: 16Gi
            cpu: 8
```

Best Practices:

- Set CPU requests, based on the expected VM load, and ensure that it does not exceed the node capacity.
- Use CPU pinning and NUMA-aware scheduling for performance-intensive applications.
- Ensure that memory over commitment policies align with workload demands to avoid OOM (Out of Memory) errors.

Storage Configuration for Virtualization

Persistent storage is necessary for VMs, and KubeVirt supports multiple storage backends. Configuring storage correctly ensures high availability and performance.

Using OpenShift Data Foundation (ODF) for Persistent Storage

ODF provides a scalable storage backend for VMs in OpenShift.

Example: Creating a `PersistentVolumeClaim` (PVC) for VM Disk

```
apiVersion: v1
kind: PersistentVolumeClaim
metadata:
  name: vm-disk-pvc
spec:
```

```
    accessModes:
      - ReadWriteOnce
    resources:
      requests:
        storage: 50Gi
    storageClassName: ocs-storagecluster-ceph-rbd
```

Best Practices

- Use Ceph RBD for block storage to improve VM disk performance.
- Enable snapshot and cloning capabilities for backup and disaster recovery.
- Ensure that the storage class is properly configured to support dynamic provisioning.

Networking for Virtualization

VM networking in KubeVirt can be configured using default pod networking or advanced configurations with Multus to enable multiple network interfaces.

Example: Configuring Multus for Additional Network Interface

```
# partial example - kept short for brevity
apiVersion: kubevirt.io/v1
kind: VirtualMachine
spec:
  template:
   spec:
      domain:
        devices:
          interfaces:
          - name: default
            masquerade: {}
          - name: bridge-net
            bridge: {}
      networks:
      - name: default
        pod: {} # Stock pod network
      - name: bridge-net
        multus: # Secondary multus network
          networkName: linux-bridge-net-ipam #ref to NAD name
```

Best Practices:

- Use `Multus` to provide VMs with direct access to external networks.
- Configure SR-IOV for high-performance network interfaces.
- Implement network policies to secure VM traffic.

Scaling and Scheduling Policies

Proper VM placement enhances cluster performance. Kubernetes provides scheduling mechanisms to optimize workload distribution.

Using Node Selectors and Taints

```
apiVersion: kubevirt.io/v1
kind: VirtualMachineInstance
metadata:
  name: example-vmi
spec:
  affinity:
    nodeAffinity:
      requiredDuringSchedulingIgnoredDuringExecution:
        nodeSelectorTerms:
          - matchExpressions:
              - key: kubernetes.io/hostname
                operator: In
                values:
                  - worker-node-1
```

Best Practices:

- Use **node selectors** to deploy VMs on specific hardware.
- Apply **taints and tolerations** to isolate VMs from regular workloads.
- Enable **Horizontal Pod Autoscaler (HPA)** for dynamic scaling, based on demand.

Networking Setup and Integration

Networking plays a crucial role in integrating KubeVirt workloads within an OpenShift environment. Proper networking setup ensures seamless communication between virtual machines, pods, and external services, while maintaining security, high availability, and performance. This chapter delves into the key networking components, configurations, and best practices to optimize KubeVirt's network integration within OpenShift.

KubeVirt Networking Overview

KubeVirt extends Kubernetes networking to support virtualized workloads. Unlike traditional Kubernetes workloads that rely on pod networking (CNI-based), KubeVirt VMs require additional networking considerations such as:

- **Multiple interfaces:** VMs need additional interfaces beyond the default Kubernetes pod network.

- **Bridged networking:** Direct network access for workloads that require low latency and predictable MAC/IP addresses.
- **Service exposure:** Methods for exposing VMs to external clients, using NodePorts, Load Balancers, or ingress solutions.
- **Security and isolation:** Policies to control VM-to-VM and VM-to-pod communication securely.

Key Components

- **Multus CNI**: Enables multiple network interfaces per VM.
- **SR-IOV**: Provides near-native performance for network-intensive workloads.
- **MACVLAN/Bridge Mode**: Supports direct L2 access, and enables VM communication on the same subnet as physical servers.
- **OpenShift SDN**: Manages networking between Kubernetes pods and KubeVirt VMs.
- **Network Policies**: Ensures security by defining ingress/egress rules.

Networking Setup in OpenShift with KubeVirt

Default Pod Network: By default, KubeVirt assigns VMs a single interface attached to the OpenShift SDN. This approach allows seamless pod-to-VM communication, without requiring additional network configuration. However, for workloads needing L2 access or external connectivity, additional configurations are necessary.

Example YAML for a VM with a default pod network:

```yaml
apiVersion: kubevirt.io/v1
kind: VirtualMachine
metadata:
  name: test-vm
spec:
  running: false
  template:
    spec:
      domain:
        devices:
          interfaces:
          - name: default
            masquerade: {}
      networks:
      - name: default
        pod: {}
```

Multus CNI for Multiple Network Interfaces

Multus CNI allows assigning additional interfaces to VMs which is useful for scenarios requiring dedicated networks, VLAN segmentation, or external connectivity.

Steps to configure Multus:

1. Install and configure **`Multus CNI`** in OpenShift.
2. Define a **`NetworkAttachmentDefinition`** (NAD) for the additional network.
3. Attach the network to the VM.

Example NAD definition:

```
apiVersion: k8s.cni.cncf.io/v1
kind: NetworkAttachmentDefinition
metadata:
  name: macvlan-net
  namespace: default
spec:
  config: '{
    "cniVersion": "0.3.1",
    "type": "macvlan",
    "master": "eth0",
    "mode": "bridge",
    "ipam": {
      "type": "static",
      "addresses": [
        {"address": "192.168.1.100/24", "gateway": "192.168.1.1"}
      ]
    }
  }'
```

Example VM attachment:

```
apiVersion: kubevirt.io/v1
kind: VirtualMachine
metadata:
  name: test-vm-multus
spec:
  template:
    spec:
      domain:
        devices:
          interfaces:
          - name: default
            masquerade: {}
          - name: macvlan-net
```

```
        bridge: {}
  networks:
  - name: default
    pod: {}
  - name: macvlan-net
    multus:
      networkName: macvlan-net
```

SR-IOV for High-Performance Networking

Single Root I/O Virtualization (SR-IOV) provides near-native network performance by bypassing the software stack. This is ideal for workloads such as NFV (Network Function Virtualization) and high-frequency trading.

SR-IOV Setup Steps

1. Enable SR-IOV in the host BIOS and kernel.
2. Configure the OpenShift SR-IOV Network Operator.
3. Create an SR-IOV NetworkAttachmentDefinition.
4. Attach the SR-IOV interface to a VM.

Example SR-IOV NetworkAttachmentDefinition:

```
apiVersion: k8s.cni.cncf.io/v1
kind: NetworkAttachmentDefinition
metadata:
  name: sriov-net
spec:
  config: '{
    "cniVersion": "0.3.1",
    "type": "sriov",
    "deviceID": "0000:03:00.0",
    "ipam": { "type": "dhcp" }
  }'
```

Security Considerations

- **Network Policies:** Enforce isolation between VMs and other workloads.
- **Firewalls and ACLs:** Restrict inbound/outbound traffic.
- **TLS and Encryption:** Use TLS for sensitive data transmission.
- **Monitoring:** Use OpenShift monitoring tools to track network performance and security threats.

Verifying and Troubleshooting the Installation

Ensuring the successful installation of KubeVirt on OpenShift requires a structured verification, and troubleshooting process. Given the complexity of KubeVirt's integration with OpenShift's virtualization layer, issues may arise due to configuration mismatches, resource constraints, or operator failures. This chapter provides a systematic approach to verifying the installation and resolving common issues, ensuring a stable and functional deployment.

Verifying Installation

Checking Operator and Custom Resource Deployment

After installing KubeVirt using the OpenShift Operator Lifecycle Manager (OLM) or manual deployment, the first step is to confirm that the required resources are active and healthy.

Verifying the KubeVirt Operator

Check the status of the KubeVirt operator by running:

```
oc get pods -n kubevirt
```

Expected Output:

```
NAME                                READY   STATUS    RESTARTS   AGE
kubevirt-operator-6b8f55c4d7-xyz   1/1     Running   0          5m
```

If the operator is not running, describe the pod:

```
oc describe pod/kubevirt-operator-6b8f55c4d7-xyz -n kubevirt
```

Check events for scheduling errors, image pull issues, or permission-related failures.

Verifying the KubeVirt Custom Resource (CR)

Once the operator is active, confirm the KubeVirt CR is correctly applied:

```
oc get kubevirt -n kubevirt
```

Expected output:

```
NAME       AGE   PHASE
kubevirt   5m    Deployed
```

If the status is not "**Deployed**," check the logs:

```
oc logs deployment/kubevirt-operator -n kubevirt
```

Confirming Virtualization Components

Verify the installation of essential components such as the Virtualization API and handlers.

Checking Virtualization API Availability

```
oc get apiservices | grep kubevirt
```

Expected output:

```
v1alpha3.subresources.kubevirt.io   True        kubevirt-apiserver
```

If **`unavailable.restart`** the API service:

```
oc delete pod -l kubevirt.io=virt-api -n kubevirt
```

Checking KubeVirt Components

```
oc get pods -n kubevirt
```

All relevant pods, such as **`virt-controller, virt-api, and virt-handler`**, should be in a "**`Running`**" state.

Troubleshooting Common Installation Issues

Operator Deployment Failures

If the operator does not deploy, check for the following:

- **Insufficient permissions**: Ensure that the service account has the necessary cluster roles.
- **Image pull failures**: Verify the image registry credentials and connectivity.
- **Node scheduling issues**: Use **`oc describe node`** to check taints and labels.

Virtualization API Not Responding

If the API service is not running:

1. Restart the **`virt-api`** pods.
2. Check **`oc logs deployment/virt-api -n KubeVirt`** for errors related to authentication or connectivity.

Virtual Machines Failing to Start

If VMs fail to launch, verify:

- **Networking:** Ensure that Multus is correctly configured.
- **Storage:** Check **`PersistentVolumeClaims`** (PVCs) are bound.
- **Node Resources:** Ensure that adequate CPU and memory are allocated to worker nodes.

Example Debugging Steps

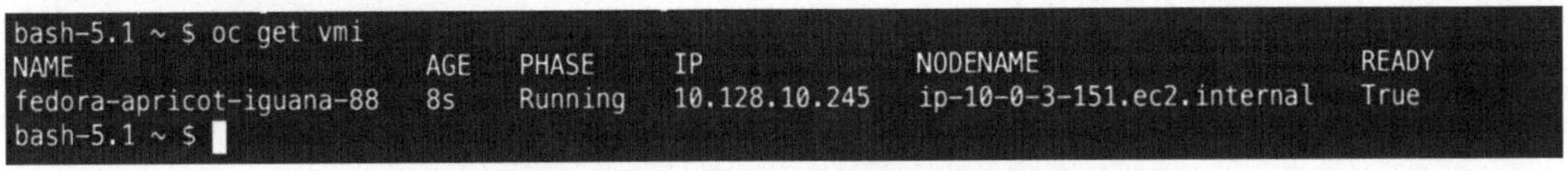

Figure 2.8: *Command to Get VM Status*

```
oc describe vmi my-vm -n my-namespace
oc logs -l kubevirt.io=virt-launcher -n my-namespace
```

Cluster Configuration Issues

Figure 2.9: *Check OpenShift cli Version*

```
oc get nodes
```

Ensure that OpenShift is at a supported version, and nodes have necessary virtualization extensions (for example, **`kvm`** enabled in **`lscpu`**).

Tools for Environment Preparation

Deploying and managing virtualized workloads efficiently on OpenShift with KubeVirt requires a well-prepared environment. This involves setting up infrastructure, configuring dependencies, and ensuring optimal performance. Various tools facilitate environment preparation, covering aspects such as infrastructure provisioning, network configuration, security enforcement, and resource optimization. This chapter explores the key tools used to establish a robust and scalable environment for KubeVirt-based workloads.

Infrastructure Provisioning Tools

- **Terraform:** Terraform is an Infrastructure-as-Code (IaC) tool that enables declarative provisioning of cloud and on-premises resources. It supports major cloud providers such as AWS, Azure, and GCP, along with on-prem solutions such as OpenShift Virtualization.

Key Features:

- Declarative syntax with HCL (HashiCorp Configuration Language).
- State management for tracking infrastructure changes.
- Provider ecosystem for multi-cloud compatibility.
- Automated dependency resolution.

Example: A Terraform configuration to provision an OpenShift cluster on AWS:

```
provider "aws" {
  region = "us-west-2"
}

resource "aws_instance" "ocp_node" {
  ami           = "ami-12345678"
  instance_type = "m5.large"
}
```

- **Ansible**: Ansible is an agentless configuration management tool that automates infrastructure provisioning and deployment.

Key Features:

- YAML-based playbooks for easy automation.
- SSH-based execution, without agent installation.
- Built-in modules for OpenShift and Kubernetes.

Example: Deploying OpenShift with Ansible:

```
- name: Install OpenShift Cluster
  hosts: masters
  tasks:
    - name: Install OpenShift CLI
      yum:
        name: openshift-client
        state: present
```

Kubernetes Cluster Management Tools

- **OpenShift Installer**: The OpenShift Installer (**`openshift-install`**) is used for automated cluster deployment on supported platforms.

Key Features:

  - Supports full-stack automated deployments
  - Integrated Ignition configuration for node setup
  - Predefined machine sets for scalability

- **Kubeadm:** Kubeadm is a lightweight Kubernetes bootstrapping tool that can be used to set up OpenShift clusters in custom environments.

Example: Initializing a Kubernetes control plane:

```
kubeadm init --apiserver-advertise-address=<IP> --pod-network
-cidr=192.168.0.0/16
```

Networking and Load Balancing Tools

- **MetalLB**: MetalLB provides a network load-balancing solution for bare-metal Kubernetes clusters, offering Layer 2 and BGP-based routing.

Key Features:

  - Supports external IP allocation for services
  - BGP integration for advanced networking
  - Seamless integration with OpenShift Virtualization

- **Cilium:** Cilium is an eBPF-based networking tool that enhances security and observability in Kubernetes environments.

Example: Installing Cilium:

```
helm install cilium cilium/cilium --namespace kube-system
```

Storage Management Tools

- **OpenShift Container Storage (OCS)**: OCS provides scalable, software-defined storage for OpenShift workloads, integrating with Ceph and Rook.

Key Features:

  - Dynamic provisioning with PersistentVolumeClaims (PVCs)
  - High availability with Ceph replication
  - Supports block, file, and object storage

- **Longhorn**

Longhorn is a lightweight, cloud-native storage solution for Kubernetes, offering snapshot and backup capabilities.

Example: Deploying Longhorn:

```
kubectl apply -f https://raw.githubusercontent.com/longhorn/long-
horn/master/deploy/longhorn.yaml
```

Security and Compliance Tools

- **OpenSCAP:** OpenSCAP is an automated compliance-checking tool used to ensure security configurations align with industry standards.

Example: Running a compliance scan:

```
oscap xccdf eval --profile xccdf_org.ssgproject.content_profile_cis
/usr/share/xml/scap/ssg/content/ssg-rhel8-ds.xml
```

- **Falco:** Falco is a runtime security tool that monitors system calls for potential security threats.

Example: Installing Falco

Conclusion

Setting up the environment for KubeVirt in OpenShift requires meticulous planning, covering hardware compatibility, networking configurations, storage provisioning, and security enforcement. Need to ensure that worker nodes have virtualization support, configuring the OpenShift Virtualization Operator, and setting up essential components such as Multus, CDI, and SR-IOV are critical steps in enabling a robust and scalable virtualization platform. With these configurations, OpenShift can effectively orchestrate both containerized and virtual machine workloads within a unified infrastructure.

By following the structured approach outlined in this chapter, administrators can create an optimized environment that meets the demands of modern enterprise workloads. Proper resource allocation, policy enforcement, and integration with OpenShift's ecosystem will ensure reliability, performance, and security in virtualized workloads. With verification and troubleshooting methodologies in place, any deployment challenges can be addressed efficiently, leading to a seamless operational experience.

The next chapter will offer a detailed look into KubeVirt's architecture, covering its core components, virtualization stack, and integration with Kubernetes networking and storage—equipping readers to effectively deploy VMs in OpenShift.

We can try KubeVirt from the following links:

- KubeVirt on Killercoda: https://killercoda.com/kubevirt
- KubeVirt on Minikube: https://kubevirt.io/quickstart_minikube/
- KubeVirt on Kind: https://kubevirt.io/quickstart_kind/
- KubeVirt on Cloud Providers: https://kubevirt.io/quickstart_cloud/

CHAPTER 3
Understanding the KubeVirt Architecture

Introduction

This chapter provides a comprehensive overview of KubeVirt's architecture, beginning with an introduction to its fundamental components: virt-controller, virt-handler, virt-launcher, and virt-api. These components work together to manage the lifecycle of virtual machines, with virt-api, providing a RESTful interface for interaction.

The chapter will explain the roles of libvirt and QEMU which enable virtualization within KubeVirt. Libvirt acts as the underlying management layer for VMs, while QEMU functions as the hypervisor. The interaction between these tools and Kubernetes is explored, demonstrating KubeVirt's ability to merge established virtualization technologies with Kubernetes' flexibility.

Networking and storage are also key topics in this chapter. You will learn how KubeVirt integrates with Kubernetes' networking plugins, and storage interfaces for seamless VM integration. Concepts such as DataVolumes and Multus will be introduced to show how KubeVirt manages data and connectivity for virtualized workloads.

By the end of the chapter, readers will have a solid understanding of KubeVirt's internal operations, strengths, and limitations, providing a strong foundation for using KubeVirt effectively in OpenShift environments.

Structure

In this chapter, we will be covering the following topics:

- The Core KubeVirt Components
- KubeVirt CRDs
- The Vital Role of Libvirt and QEMU in KubeVirt

The Core Components

The core components of the KubeVirt project can be mostly broken down to:

Component	Description
`virt-api-server`	The HTTP API server that handles virtualization requests, and manages CRDs.
`virt-controller`	A Kubernetes controller that monitors VMI objects, and manages the associated pods.
`virt-handler`	A DaemonSet running on each node that interacts with libvirt to launch and manage VMs.
`virt-launcher`	A specialized pod that runs for each VMI. It provides the necessary namespaces and cgroups to host the VM process, starts the VM using a local libvirtd instance, monitors the VM process, and terminates, once the VM exits.

Table 3.1: *KubeVirt Core Components*

Apart from this, there is also another important piece that fits the puzzle, and would be one of the most lower level components, which is - **`libvirtd`**. While not a component that is developed and maintained as part of the KubeVirt project itself, it is a separate, upstream project. It is an external dependency that KubeVirt relies on.

We will dive into each of these components, their functions, responsibilities, and interactions among them in this section, also looking at the architecture diagram along the way.

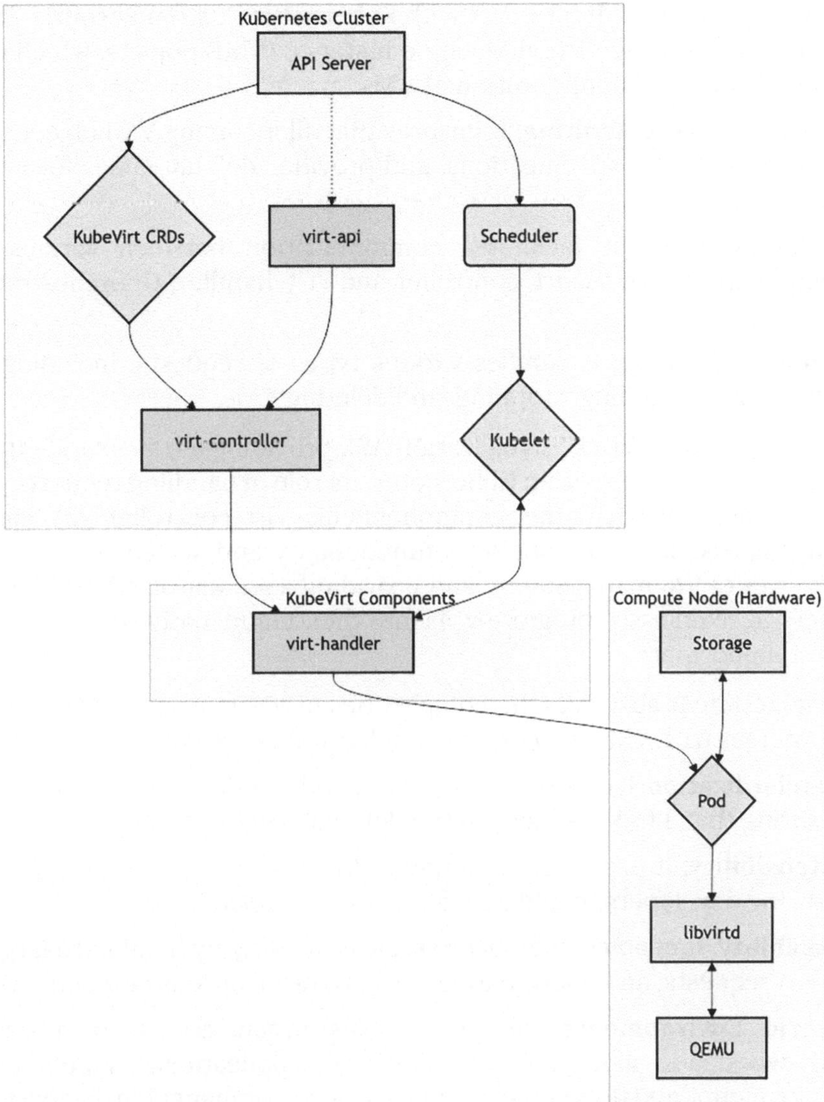

Figure 3.1: *KubeVirt Architecture Diagram*

`virt-api`: The Central API Server for KubeVirt

This is the core of KubeVirt's Virtualization API. It acts as the entry point for all virtualization-related requests, and plays a crucial role in managing the lifecycle of virtual machines within the Kubernetes cluster. Think of it as the control center for KubeVirt's VMs, responsible for:

- **API Endpoint:** It serves as an HTTP API server, handling all incoming requests related to VM management.

- **CRD Management:** It interacts with Kubernetes Custom Resource Definitions (CRDs), specifically Virtual Machine Instance (VMI) objects, which define the desired state and configuration of VMs.
- **Validation and Defaulting:** It ensures that all incoming VMI object definitions adhere to the API specifications, and provides default values for any missing parameters.
- **Communication:** It facilitates communication between various KubeVirt components, such as virt-controller and virt-handler, to orchestrate the VM lifecycle.
- **Request Handling:** It handles various types of requests, including creating, scheduling, launching, stopping, and deleting VMs.

The cornerstone of KubeVirt's Virtualization API, providing a robust and efficient way to manage virtual machines within Kubernetes. Its role in handling requests, managing CRDs, and coordinating with other components like virt-controller, virt-handler, and virt-launcher is essential for KubeVirt's functionality and scalability. By abstracting the complexities of VM management, and providing a standardized interface, virt-api enables users to seamlessly integrate VMs into their cloud-native environments. Here is why it is so important:

- **Abstraction:** It abstracts the complexities of VM management, allowing users to interact with VMs through the familiar Kubernetes API.
- **Standardization:** It enforces consistency and standardization in VM definitions, ensuring that all VMs adhere to the defined specifications.
- **Extensibility:** It provides a foundation for extending KubeVirt's functionality, allowing developers to add new features and capabilities.
- **Scalability:** It enables KubeVirt to scale efficiently by handling a large number of VM requests, and coordinating the actions of various components.
- **Hybrid Environments:** virt-api enables organizations to run traditional VM workloads alongside containerized applications, supporting hybrid deployments, and providing a unified platform for managing diverse workloads.
- **Legacy Application Migration:** It helps organizations preserve the existing VM investments, and migrate legacy applications to Kubernetes, facilitating a smooth transition to a modern, containerized environment.

`virt-controller`: The Core Control Plane Component

The **`virt-controller`** is a Kubernetes Operator responsible for managing the lifecycle of VMs, within a KubeVirt environment. It operates at the cluster level, monitoring VirtualMachineInstance (VMI) custom resources, and ensuring the creation and management of associated pods. Essentially, it acts as the brain behind VM orchestration, making sure that VMs are properly provisioned, scheduled, and maintained. The primary responsibilities of the virt-controller include:

- **Monitoring VMIs:** The `virt-controller` continuously monitors VMI objects within the Kubernetes API server. These objects define the desired state of a VM, including its specifications such as CPU, memory, and disk configuration.
- **Creating and Managing Pods:** When a new VMI is created, the virt-controller creates a corresponding pod to host the VM[2]. It manages the lifecycle of this pod, ensuring that it remains in the desired state throughout the VM's lifecycle.
- **Scheduling VMs:** The virt-controller works in conjunction with the Kubernetes scheduler to determine the optimal node for running the VM pod[3]. It considers factors like resource availability, node affinity, and taints to make informed scheduling decisions.
- **Handling VM Lifecycle Events:** The virt-controller responds to various VM lifecycle events such as starting, stopping, restarting, and migrating VMs. It coordinates with other KubeVirt components to ensure smooth transitions during these operations.
- **Updating VM Status:** The virt-controller keeps track of the VM's status, and updates the VMI object accordingly. This includes information about the VM's state (running, stopped, paused), its IP address, and any relevant events.

The virt-controller manages the entire VM lifecycle, from creation to deletion. It handles various operations, including:

- **Power On/Off:** When a VM is started, the `virt-controller` initiates the process of powering on the VM by interacting with the `virt-handler` and `virt-launcher`. Similarly, it handles the shutdown and graceful termination of VMs.
- **Live Migration:** The virt-controller orchestrates the live migration of VMs between nodes. It coordinates the transfer of VM state and resources between the source and destination nodes, ensuring minimal downtime during the migration process.
- **Handling VM Failures:** If a VM fails, the `virt-controller` will recreate it, similar to how Kubernetes handles pod failures. This ensures high availability and resilience for VM workloads.
- **Run Strategies:** The virt-controller supports different run strategies for managing VM replicas. These strategies determine how VM instances are created and maintained. Some of the supported modes include:
    - **`RerunOnFailure`:** The VM will be recreated only if it fails, not if it is stopped manually.

  - **`Always`:** The VM will always run, regardless of whether it fails or is stopped.
  - **`Manual`:** The user has to manually start, stop, and restart the VM.
  - **`Halted`:** The VM will be created, but not started automatically. The user needs to manually start it.
- **VM Scheduling:** When a new VM object is posted to the API server, the virt-controller takes notice, and creates the pod in which the VM will run. When the pod is scheduled on a particular node, the virt-controller modifies the VM object with the node name, and transfers further responsibilities to the virt-handler.

Apart from this, it is also responsible for leveraging Kubernetes' resource management capabilities to allocate resources to VMs. It ensures that VMs receive the requested CPU, memory, and storage resources. It also enforces resource limits to prevent VMs from consuming excessive resources, and impacting other workloads.

The virt-controller also monitors the health and status of VMs. It collects metrics and events related to VM performance, resource usage, and any errors encountered. This information is reported back to the Kubernetes API server, allowing users to monitor their VMs, and troubleshoot any issues.

`virt-handler`: The Agent on Each Node

The virt-handler is a node-level agent in KubeVirt that acts as a bridge between the Kubernetes cluster and the underlying virtualization infrastructure. It is responsible for managing the lifecycle of VMs on each node where it is deployed. Think of it as the Kubernetes kubelet, but specifically designed for virtual machines.

Here is a breakdown of its key responsibilities:

- **VM Lifecycle Management:** The virt-handler handles the creation, starting, stopping, pausing, unpausing, and deletion of VMs on its node. It ensures that the VMs adhere to the desired state defined in their Virtual Machine Instance specifications.
- **Synchronization with Kubernetes:** It monitors changes to Virtual Machine Instance objects in the Kubernetes API, and takes necessary actions to keep the VMs in sync with their desired configurations.
- **Collaboration with Kubelet:** The virt-handler works closely with the Kubelet, Kubernetes' node agent, to manage the pod in which the VM runs. This collaboration ensures that the VM has the necessary resources and environment to operate correctly.
- **Domain Management:** It interacts with libvirtd, a virtualization management tool, to create and manage the libvirt domains that represent the VMs.

- **Networking and Storage:** The virt-handler invokes node-centric plugins to fulfill the networking and storage requirements specified in the Virtual Machine Instance specifications. It ensures that the VMs have access to the appropriate network interfaces and storage volumes. KubeVirt supports various network configurations, including masquerade, bridge, and slirp interface types.
- **Monitoring and Reporting:** It monitors the state of the VMs, and reports back to the Kubernetes cluster, providing information about their status, resource usage, and any errors encountered.
- **Node Health Reporting:** The virt-handler also plays a vital role in node health reporting. It periodically updates the node's status with a heartbeat, indicating its availability to schedule new VMIs.

Node Health Monitoring

In addition to its core responsibilities, the virt-handler plays a crucial role in monitoring the health of the nodes where it is deployed. It uses a heartbeat mechanism to detect node issues, and prevent the scheduling of new VMIs on unhealthy nodes.

The virt-handler periodically updates the kubevirt.io/schedulable label and the kubevirt.io/heartbeat annotation on its node. The scheduler uses the kubevirt.io/schedulable label to determine if a node is available for scheduling VMIs. If the virt-handler fails to update the heartbeat within a certain timeframe, the node controller marks the node as unschedulable, preventing new VMIs from being placed on that node. This mechanism ensures that VMIs are only scheduled on healthy nodes capable of running them.

Architecture and Communication Flow

The virt-handler operates as a DaemonSet, meaning it runs a single instance on each node in the Kubernetes cluster that is designated for running VMs. It communicates with other KubeVirt components, and the Kubernetes API server to perform its tasks.

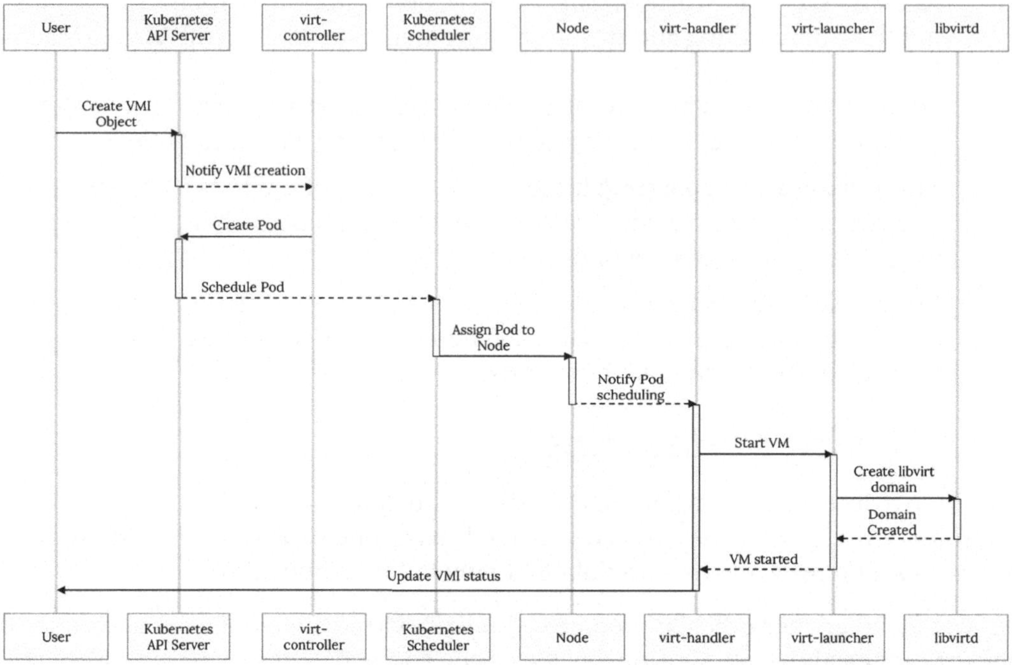

***Figure* 3.2:** *Creating a* VM

Here is a simplified overview of the communication flow involved in creating a VM:

- **VMI Creation:** A user creates a VirtualMachineInstance (VMI) object in the Kubernetes API, defining the desired configuration of the VM.
- **Pod Creation:** The virt-controller, a cluster-level KubeVirt component, observes the VMI creation, and creates a corresponding pod to host the VM.
- **Scheduling:** Kubernetes schedules the pod on a node with the necessary resources and labels.
- **`virt-handler` Activation:** The virt-handler on the selected node detects the scheduled VMI, and initiates the VM creation process.
- **`virt-launcher` Interaction:** The virt-handler interacts with the virt-launcher, a component running within the VM's pod, to start the VM. It does this by passing the VMI's CRD object to virt-launcher, which then uses libvirtd to start the VMI.
- **Domain Creation:** libvirtd creates a **`libvirt`** domain which represents the running VM.
- **Lifecycle Management:** The virt-launcher monitors the VM process, and terminates once the VMI has exited. If Kubernetes tries to shut down the **`virt-`**

`launcher` pod before the VM has exited, virt-launcher forwards signals from Kubernetes to the VM process, and attempts to delay the pod's termination until the VM has shut down successfully.

- **Status Updates:** The virt-handler monitors the VM's state, and updates the VMI object in the Kubernetes API accordingly.

It is important to note that KubeVirt leverages Kubernetes' existing infrastructure for networking and storage. This means that VMs can utilize the same resources and APIs as pods, simplifying management and integration with other Kubernetes workloads. Additionally, KubeVirt prioritizes a Kubernetes-native approach, ensuring that features work seamlessly for both containers and VMs.

`virt-launcher`: The per-VMI Process Manager

The virt-launcher is a crucial component in the KubeVirt architecture. It is responsible for launching and managing the VM process within a pod. Here is a breakdown of its key functions:

- **Launching the VM:** When a VM is scheduled to a node, the virt-handler signals the virt-launcher to start the VM. The virt-launcher uses a local libvirtd instance within its container to initiate the VM process.
- **Monitoring the VM:** Once the VM is running, the virt-launcher monitors its state, and reports any changes back to the virt-handler. This includes monitoring the VM's lifecycle events, such as starting, stopping, and pausing.
- **Managing Resources:** The virt-launcher ensures that the VM has the necessary resources such as CPU, memory, and storage. It leverages the Kubernetes resource management system to allocate these resources to the VM, providing the same granular control as for containers. It also manages the VM's network connectivity.
- **Handling Termination:** When a VM is terminated, the virt-launcher gracefully shuts down the VM process, and cleans up any associated resources. If Kubernetes tries to terminate the virt-launcher pod before the VM process is complete, virt-launcher forwards signals to the VM process, and attempts to delay the pod's termination until the VM has shut down successfully.

A key aspect of virt-launcher is its use of namespaces and cgroups to isolate the VM process. This ensures that the VM runs in a secure and controlled environment, preventing interference with other processes or containers in the cluster. The virt-launcher pod provides the necessary cgroups and namespaces to host the VM process, similar to how containers provide isolation for applications.

`virt-launcher` works in conjunction with other KubeVirt components to ensure the smooth operation of VMs in the cluster. Here is how it interacts with other components:

- **`virt-handler`:** The virt-handler acts as the intermediary between the virt-controller and the virt-launcher. It instructs the virt-launcher to start or stop VMs, and receives updates on the VM's state.
- **`libvirtd`:** The virt-launcher uses libvirtd to interact with the underlying virtualization technology (KVM). libvirtd provides a low-level interface for managing VM lifecycle and resources.

Apart from these components, there is another very critical component which is **`libvirtd`**, but since it is not a part of KubeVirt core itself, and is used in a critical manner as an external component - we will discuss it in a bit more detail in a later section of this book. For now, let us talk about another crucial conjunction point of Kubernetes and KubeVirt which is the use of CRDs by KubeVirt for various aspects.

KubeVirt CRDs: A Prioritized Overview

This section provides a prioritized overview of Custom Resource Definitions (CRDs) in KubeVirt, based on the KubeVirt documentation. Understanding these CRDs is crucial for effectively managing Virtual Machines (VMs) within a Kubernetes cluster, using KubeVirt.

KubeVirt extends the Kubernetes API by introducing CRDs that represent various aspects of VM management. These CRDs allow you to define and manage VMs in a declarative manner, leveraging Kubernetes' capabilities for orchestration, scaling, and self-healing. Some of the key benefits of using CRDs for managing VMs in Kubernetes include:

- **Declarative Configuration:** Define the desired state of your VMs in YAML files, and KubeVirt ensures that the actual state matches the desired state.
- **Self-Healing:** KubeVirt automatically restarts or reschedules VMs, if they fail or if the underlying node experiences issues.
- **Integration with Kubernetes Ecosystem:** Manage VMs using familiar Kubernetes tools like kubectl, and integrate with other Kubernetes features like namespaces, resource quotas, and role-based access control.

While the KubeVirt documentation does not explicitly list all CRDs in a single location, we can infer a comprehensive list from various sections within the user guide and API reference. The following table presents the identified CRDs in a prioritized order, considering factors such as frequency of use, core functionality versus advanced features, and necessity for basic KubeVirt operations:

`VirtualMachineInstance` (VMI)

The VirtualMachineInstance is the most crucial CRD in KubeVirt. It represents a running virtual machine within your Kubernetes cluster. When you create a VMI, KubeVirt schedules it on a node with sufficient resources, and launches a pod that hosts the VM. The VMI defines all aspects of the VM, including:

- **Compute Resources:** CPU and memory allocation for the VM.
- **Storage:** Disks and volumes attached to the VM, including persistent volumes, container disks, and cloud-init disks.
- **Network Interfaces:** Network configuration for the VM, including network type, MAC address, and IP address.
- **Guest Operating System:** The operating system running inside the VM.
- **Virtual Hardware:** Virtual devices such as network cards, serial ports, and video cards.

You can manage VMIs using kubectl commands, just like any other Kubernetes resource. For example, you can use:

- `` `kubectl get vmi` `` to list all VMIs in your cluster,
- `` `kubectl describe vmi <vmi-name>` `` to view details about a specific VMI, and
- `` `kubectl delete vmi <vmi-name>` `` to delete a VMI.

`VirtualMachine` (VM)

The **`VirtualMachine`** CRD provides a higher-level abstraction for managing VMs in KubeVirt. It represents the desired state of a VM, rather than a running instance. This means that a VM can exist even when it's not running. The VM CRD is responsible for managing the lifecycle of the VM, including:

- **Starting and Stopping:** You can start and stop a VM using the **`virtctl`** command-line tool, or by updating the VM's status in Kubernetes.
- **Restarting:** KubeVirt automatically restarts a VM if it crashes or if the underlying node fails.
- **Live Migration:** You can migrate a running VM to another node in the cluster without any downtime.

VMs are useful for managing stateful applications that need to persist data across restarts. They also provide a more user-friendly way to manage VMs, as you don't need to worry about the underlying VMI.

The relationship between VirtualMachine and VirtualMachineInstance is crucial to understand. A VirtualMachine defines the desired state of the VM, while the

VirtualMachineInstance represents the actual running instance. When you create a VirtualMachine, KubeVirt creates a corresponding VirtualMachineInstance to run the VM. The VirtualMachine controller ensures that the VirtualMachineInstance is running and matches the desired state defined in the VirtualMachine spec.

DataVolume

The DataVolume CRD, belonging to the cdi.kubevirt.io API group, plays a vital role in managing VM disks in KubeVirt. It allows you to define and manage disks independently of VMs, enabling features like disk sharing and cloning.

DataVolumes provide a way to import and manage VM disk images, which can then be attached to VMIs. They can be backed by various storage sources, including:

- **Persistent Volumes:** Use existing persistent volumes in your Kubernetes cluster as the storage for your DataVolumes.
- **Container Disks:** Import disk images from container registries like Docker Hub or Quay.io.
- **Cloud-Init Disks:** Create disks with cloud-init configurations for automating VM provisioning.

By decoupling disk management from VMs, DataVolumes offer flexibility and efficiency in managing VM storage. You can create a DataVolume once and use it for multiple VMs, or clone a DataVolume to create a new disk with the same data.

VirtualMachineInstanceReplicaSet (VMIRS)

The VirtualMachineInstanceReplicaSet is similar to Kubernetes ReplicaSets for pods. It allows you to manage multiple VMIs with the same configuration. This is useful for scaling applications and ensuring high availability. When you create a VMIRS, KubeVirt creates the specified number of VMIs and ensures that the desired number of replicas are always running. If a VMI fails, the VMIRS automatically creates a new one to replace it.

For example, you could use a VMIRS to deploy three replicas of a web server VM. If one of the VMs fails, the VMIRS will automatically create a new VM to maintain the desired number of replicas, ensuring that your web application remains available.

VMIRS are defined using a template that specifies the configuration of the VMIs. This template includes the same information as a VMI, such as compute resources, storage, and network interfaces. You can update the VMIRS template to change the configuration of all the VMIs in the set.

`instancetype`

The instancetype CRD, a part of the **`instancetype.kubevirt.io`** API group, allows users to define reusable instance types with predefined compute resources (CPU, memory, and GPUs). This simplifies VM deployments by providing standardized configurations.

Instead of specifying the compute resources for each VMI individually, you can create an instancetype that defines a specific combination of resources. Then, you can reference this instancetype in your VM or VMI specifications. This promotes consistency, and reduces duplication in your VM deployments.

Less Common CRDs

While the CRDs already discussed are the most frequently used, KubeVirt provides several other CRDs for more specialized use cases. These include:

- **`VirtualMachineInstancePreset`:** Allows you to define reusable configurations for VMIs such as common security settings or network configurations.
- **`VirtualMachineSnapshot and VirtualMachineSnapshotContent`:** Enables you to capture and manage VM snapshots for backup and recovery purposes.
- **`VirtualMachineRestore`:** Facilitates restoring a VM from a previously taken snapshot.
- **`VirtualMachineFlavor and VirtualMachineClusterFlavor`:** Define specific sets of compute resources for VMs at the VM or cluster level.
- **`VirtualMachinePreference and VirtualMachineClusterPreference`:** Allow users or administrators to specify preferences for VM deployments such as preferred node types or CPU topology.

These less common CRDs provide advanced functionalities for managing VMs in KubeVirt. While they might not be essential for basic KubeVirt operations, they offer valuable features for specific use cases and scenarios.

The Vital Role of `libvirt` and QEMU in KubeVirt

libvirt and QEMU are the two key components that play vital roles in KubeVirt's architecture. This section delves into the role of libvirt and QEMU in KubeVirt, exploring their functionalities, and how they contribute to the platform's capabilities. Let us first try to understand a bit more about what libvirt and QEMU are, and the functionalities they provide.

`libvirt`: The Virtualization API

Libvirt is an open-source API, daemon, and management tool that provides a common interface for managing various virtualization technologies. It acts as an abstraction layer, allowing users to interact with different hypervisors, such as KVM, Xen and VMware ESXi through a consistent set of APIs. Libvirt offers several functionalities that are crucial for managing VMs:

- VM Management
- Remote Machine Support
- Storage Management
- Network Interface Management
- Virtual NAT and Routed Networking
- Debugging and Customization

QEMU: The Virtual Machine Emulator and Virtualizer

QEMU is an open-source machine emulator and virtualizer. It can emulate a wide range of hardware, including processors, memory, and peripherals, allowing it to run operating systems and applications designed for different architectures. When combined with a hypervisor like KVM and QEMU can provide near-native performance for virtualized workloads. QEMU offers several key features that make it a versatile tool for virtualization:

- **Full System Emulation:** QEMU can emulate an entire machine, including the processor, memory, and various peripherals. This allows users to run operating systems and applications designed for different hardware architectures on a single physical machine.
- **User-Mode Emulation:** QEMU can also run processes compiled for one CPU on another CPU. This is particularly useful for cross-platform development and testing.
- **Hardware Virtualization:** QEMU can leverage hardware virtualization extensions such as Intel VT-x and AMD-V to improve performance. When used with KVM, QEMU can run VMs with near-native speed.
- **Snapshotting:** QEMU supports snapshotting, allowing users to save the state of a VM, and restore it later. This is useful for testing, development, and backup purposes.
- **Live Migration:** QEMU can perform live migration of VMs, allowing users to move running VMs from one host to another, with minimal downtime. This is essential for maintaining high availability in production environments.

- **Versatile Disk Image Formats:** QEMU supports various disk image formats, including raw, qcow2, and VMDK. This flexibility allows users to choose the best format for their needs.

Side note: There have been few abbreviations in the preceding sections, and it might be informative to talk about a few of them for the sake of the reader's knowledge.

- **QEMU:** Quick Emulator
- **KVM:** Kernel-based Virtual Machine

Apart from that, let us quickly talk a bit about two more important – storage formats and their capabilities:

- RAW
  - Direct Access
  - Simple Structure
  - Storage Inefficiency
  - Limited Snapshotting
- **Qcow2:** short form of QEMU Copy-On-Write version 2 - specifically designed for QEMU and offers the following:
  - Storage Efficiency
  - Snapshots, live migration and online resizing
  - Backup Integration (with KVM and OpenStack backup solutions)

The Interplay of `libvirt`, QEMU, and KubeVirt

Figure 3.3 depicts the interaction between **`libvirt`**, QEMU, and KubeVirt.

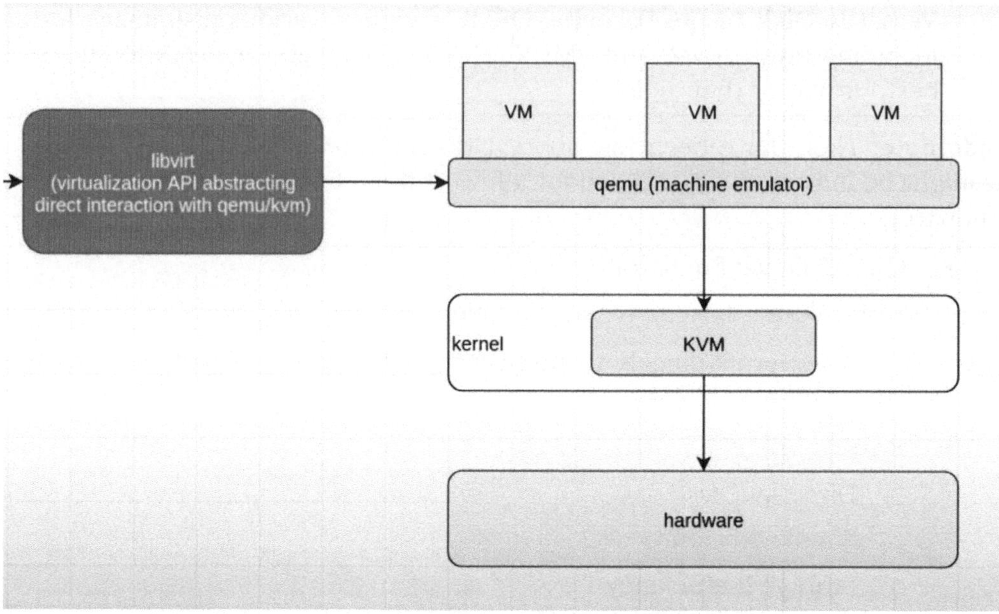

Figure 3.3: *Interaction between libvirt, QEMU and KubeVirt*

KubeVirt leverages libvirt and QEMU to provide a seamless virtualization experience within Kubernetes. Libvirt acts as the virtualization API, abstracting away the complexities of different hypervisors, while QEMU provides the underlying emulation and virtualization capabilities. Here's how these components work together to manage VMs in KubeVirt:

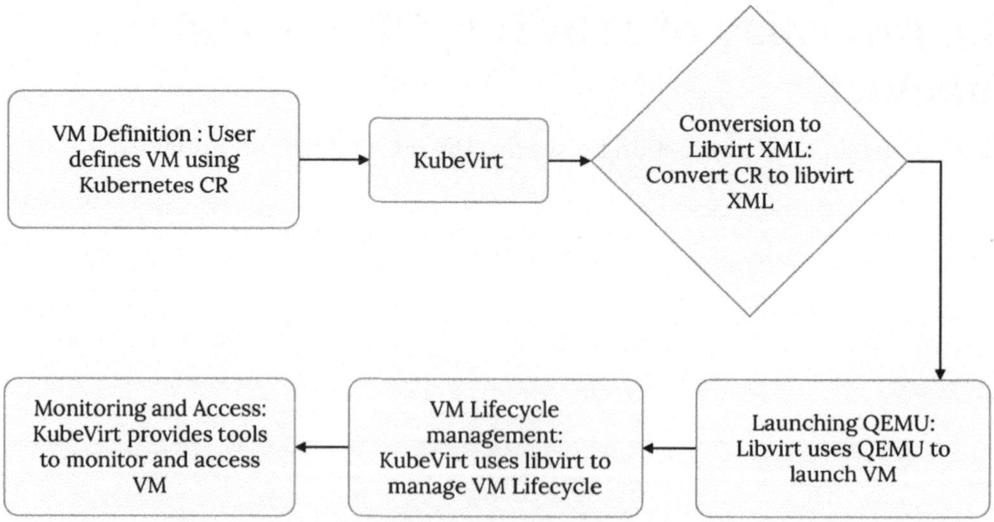

Figure 3.4: *Flowchart of the Whole Process*

1. **VM Definition:** Users define VMs in KubeVirt using Kubernetes Custom Resources (CRs) which describe the desired state of the VM, including specifications such as the virtual hardware, networking, and storage.
2. **Conversion to libvirt XML:** KubeVirt converts the CRs into libvirt's XML format which is used to configure and manage VMs.
3. **Launching QEMU:** Libvirt uses QEMU to launch and manage the VM instances. QEMU emulates the necessary hardware, and provides the environment for the guest operating system to run.
4. **VM Lifecycle Management:** KubeVirt uses libvirt to manage the VM lifecycle, including starting, stopping, pausing, and migrating VMs.
5. **Monitoring and Access:** KubeVirt provides tools and APIs to monitor VM health, access consoles, and interact with the VMs.

Conclusion

This chapter provided a thorough exploration of KubeVirt's architecture, detailing the roles of its core components: virt-controller, virt-handler, virt-launcher, and virt-api. It highlighted how KubeVirt integrates established virtualization technologies such as libvirt and QEMU with Kubernetes, ensuring seamless VM management within a cloud-native environment. By understanding its internal operations, including networking, storage, and the function of crucial CRDs, readers gain a strong foundation for effectively deploying and managing virtualized workloads on OpenShift. The next chapter explains how to manage virtual machines.

CHAPTER 4
Managing Virtual Machines (VMs)

Introduction

In this chapter, we will cover VM customization, including configuring CPU, memory, and storage requirements. The use of templates to standardize VM specifications is explored, enabling organizations to deploy consistent and reusable VM configurations. You will also understand how to attach and manage data volumes, using Kubernetes PersistentVolumeClaims (PVCs) and DataVolumes, ensuring VMs have the storage resources they need.

The chapter begins by introducing the concept of managing VMs as Kubernetes-native objects through KubeVirt's Custom Resource Definitions (CRDs). you will learn how to define and deploy VMs using YAML manifests or the OpenShift Console, making VM management intuitive and accessible for developers and operators alike.

The chapter will also address VM scheduling, demonstrating how to leverage Kubernetes' native scheduling mechanisms to place VMs on specific nodes based on resource availability, node labels, or affinity rules. Advanced scheduling techniques, such as anti-affinity and topology-aware scheduling, are introduced for optimizing workload distribution.

Structure

In this chapter, we will cover the following topics:

- Defining Virtual Machines (VMs) Manifests
- Configuring Machine Specifications
- Managing VM Templates and Replicas
- VM Replicas in KubeVirt
- DataVolumes for VM Storage
- Lifecycle Management

Defining Virtual Machines (VMs) Manifests

A YAML manifest for a VM provides a clear and concise way to specify its configuration, including the operating system image, resource allocation, storage, and networking. This declarative approach simplifies VM management by allowing you to define the "**what**" rather than the "**how**," leaving Kubernetes to handle the underlying implementation details.

To simplify the creation of these manifests, you can use the virtctl command-line utility. This tool provides commands for generating and managing VM manifests, making it easier to define and deploy VMs in your Kubernetes cluster. We will talk about virtctl later, but let us focus more on creating a simple VM manifest itself to create the VM first.

```
apiVersion: kubevirt.io/v1
kind: VirtualMachine
metadata:
  name: ubuntu-vm
spec:
  running: false
  template:
    metadata:
      labels:
        kubevirt.io/vm: ubuntu-vm
    spec:
      domain:
        devices:
          disks:
          - disk:
              bus: virtio
              name: rootfs
          - disk:
              bus: virtio
              name: cloudinit
          interfaces:
          - name: default
            masquerade: {}
        resources:
          requests:
            memory: 64M
      networks:
      - name: default
        pod: {}
      volumes:
```

```
    - name: rootfs
      containerDisk:
        image: kubevirt/ubuntu-cloud-init
    - name: cloudinit
      cloudInitNoCloud:
        userDataBase64: SGkuXG4=
```

A well-defined VM YAML manifest requires several key components to ensure proper functionality and configuration. These components provide Kubernetes with the necessary information to create and manage the VM effectively. Here is a breakdown of the essential elements:

- **Image:** The image field specifies the container image that will be used as the base for the VM's operating system. This image should contain the necessary operating system files and configurations.
- **Resources:** The resources field defines the compute resources allocated to the VM such as CPU and memory. This ensures that the VM has sufficient resources to run its applications. You can specify requests and limits for resources to control how much CPU and memory, the VM can consume.
- **Storage:** The volumes and disks fields specify the storage resources attached to the VM. This can include persistent volumes, container disks, or config maps. You can define different types of disks, such as virtio or scsi, and specify their size and storage class.
- **Networking:** The networks and interfaces fields define the VM's network configuration, including network interfaces, network attachments, and IP addresses. You can configure different types of network interfaces such as bridge or masquerade, and specify network policies to control traffic flow.
- **Cloud-init:** The cloudInitNoCloud field allows you to provide user data and configuration scripts to customize the VM during startup. This can include setting up users, installing packages, and configuring network settings. You can provide the user data as plain text or in base64-encoded format.
- **RunStrategy:** The RunStrategy field defines how the VM should be started and stopped. It offers different options such as Halted, Always, and RerunOnFailure, allowing you to control the VM's lifecycle and behavior in case of failures.

Configuring VM Specifications

One of the key aspects of managing VMs is the ability to configure their specifications such as CPU, memory, and storage. KubeVirt achieves this through Custom Resource Definitions (CRDs).

Configuring CPU

In KubeVirt, you can configure the CPU resources for a VM using the spec.template.spec.domain.cpu field in the VirtualMachine configuration. This field allows you to specify the number of virtual CPUs (vCPUs), CPU topology (sockets, cores, threads), CPU model, and CPU features.

Number of vCPUs

The number of vCPUs assigned to a VM determines its processing power. You can specify the desired number of vCPUs using the cores, sockets, and threads fields within the cpu object. The total number of vCPUs is calculated by the following formula: cores * sockets * threads. For example, to configure a VM with 4 vCPUs, you can use the following configuration:

```
apiVersion: kubevirt.io/v1
kind: VirtualMachine
spec:
  ...
  template:
    spec:
      domain:
        cpu:
          cores: 2
          sockets: 2
          threads: 1
  ...
```

CPU Topology

The CPU topology defines how the vCPUs are presented to the guest operating system. It involves understanding the relationship between sockets, cores, and threads. A socket is a physical CPU package that can contain one or more cores. Each core can execute multiple threads concurrently through technologies like hyper threading.

You can configure the topology by adjusting the cores, sockets, and thread fields in the VirtualMachine configuration. By default, KubeVirt presents vCPUs as sockets. However, you can change this behavior by using the **`preferredCPUTopology`** field in a **`VirtualMachinePreference`** CRD. For example, to present vCPUs as cores, you can create a VirtualMachinePreference with the following configuration:

```
apiVersion: instancetype.kubevirt.io/v1beta1
kind: VirtualMachinePreference
metadata:
  name: example-preference-cpu-topology
spec:
```

```
  cpu:
      preferredCPUTopology: cores
```

Then, reference this preference in your VirtualMachine configuration:

```
apiVersion: kubevirt.io/v1
kind: VirtualMachine
spec:
  ...
  preference:
      name: example-preference-cpu-topology
  ...
```

CPU Model

The CPU model determines the type of CPU emulated for the VM. By default, KubeVirt selects a CPU model that is closest to the one used on the node where the VM is running. You can explicitly set the CPU model using the model field in the **`VirtualMachine`** configuration. For example, to use the Conroe CPU model, you can use the following configuration:

```
apiVersion: kubevirt.io/v1
kind: VirtualMachine
spec:
  ...
  template:
    spec:
      domain:
        cpu:
          model: Conroe
  ...
```

CPU Features

You can configure specific CPU features for the VM using the features field in the **`VirtualMachine`** configuration. This field allows you to enable or disable individual CPU features, potentially influencing compatibility and performance within the guest operating system. For example, to enable the apic feature, you can use the following configuration:

```
apiVersion: kubevirt.io/v1
kind: VirtualMachine
spec:
  ...
  template:
    spec:
      domain:
```

```
            cpu:
              features:
              - name: apic
                policy: require
    ...
```

Configuring Memory

You can configure the memory resources for a VM using the **spec.template.spec.domain.memory** field in the **VirtualMachine** configuration. This field allows you to specify the amount of memory allocated to the VM.

Memory Allocation

The guest field within the memory object specifies the amount of memory allocated to the VM. You can specify the memory size using standard Kubernetes units such as **Gi** or **Mi**. For example, to allocate 2 GB of memory to a VM, you can use the following configuration:

```
apiVersion: kubevirt.io/v1
kind: VirtualMachine
spec:
  ...
  template:
    spec:
      domain:
        memory:
          guest: 2Gi
  ...
```

Configuring Storage

KubeVirt provides various options for configuring storage for VMs. You can use PersistentVolumeClaims (PVCs) to attach storage to your VMs.

PersistentVolumeClaims

PVCs are the standard way to provision persistent storage in Kubernetes. You can use PVCs to attach persistent disks to your VMs. To use a PVC, you need to create a PVC object, and then reference it in the **spec.template.spec.domain.devices.disks** field of the **VirtualMachine** configuration. For example:

```
apiVersion: kubevirt.io/v1
kind: VirtualMachine
spec:
```

```
...
template:
  spec:
    domain:
      devices:
        disks:
        - name: mypvcdisk
          disk:
            bus: virtio
          volumeName: mypvc
    volumes:
    - name: mypvc
      persistentVolumeClaim:
        claimName: myclaim
...
```

A Consolidated Example

Here is an example of a complete KubeVirt CRD file that configures CPU, memory, and storage for a VM:

```
apiVersion: kubevirt.io/v1
kind: VirtualMachine
metadata:
  name: example-vm
spec:
  running: false
  template:
    spec:
      domain:
        cpu:
          cores: 2
        memory:
          guest: 1Gi
        devices:
          disks:
            - name: mydisk
              disk:
                bus: virtio
              volumeName: mypvc
      volumes:
        - name: mypvc
          persistentVolumeClaim:
            claimName: myclaim

...
```

This configuration creates a VM with 2 vCPUs, 1 GB of memory, and a persistent disk attached from a PVC called myclaim.

Managing VM Templates and Replicas

In KubeVirt, a VM template is a blueprint for creating Virtual Machines (VMs). It defines the basic characteristics of a VM such as the operating system, workload type, and resource allocation (CPU, memory). These templates serve as a foundation for quickly deploying VMs with predefined specifications, ensuring consistency, and reducing manual configuration efforts. A template is essentially a master copy of a VM, including the guest OS, virtual disks, software, and configuration files, but it cannot be run directly. Instead, it is used to create instances of VMs, known as replicas.

KubeVirt controllers utilize these templates to create new objects in Kubernetes, specifically VirtualMachineInstances (VMIs). VM templates are fully pre-installed and pre-configured, simplifying the process of creating similar VMs. They are master copies used for cloning, allowing for efficient and consistent VM deployments.

Benefits of Using VM Templates

VM templates offer several advantages:

- **Standardization:** They ensure consistency across VM deployments, reducing configuration errors, and simplifying management.
- **Efficiency:** Templates streamline the VM deployment process, saving time and efforts, compared to manual configuration.
- **Scalability:** They facilitate rapid scaling of virtual environments by enabling quick creation of multiple VMs from a single template.
- **Simplified Management:** Templates reduce the complexity associated with manual VM creation and maintenance.

Creating VM Templates

In the context of KubeVirt CRDs, VM templates can be created just like any other CRD. The kind is **`VirtualMachineTemplate`**. Here is an example:

```
apiVersion: kubevirt.io/v1
kind: VirtualMachineTemplate
metadata:
  name: my-vm-template
spec:
  template:
    metadata:
      labels:
```

```
        app: my-app
    spec:
      domain:
        resources:
          requests:
            memory: 1Gi
        devices:
          disks:
          - name: containerdisk
            disk:
              bus: virtio
      volumes:
      - name: containerdisk
        containerDisk:
          image: 'fedora:latest'
```

Managing VM Templates

VM templates in KubeVirt are managed as Custom Resource Definitions (CRDs). You can use kubectl to interact with these CRDs, and perform various management tasks.

- **Create:** To create a VM template, you can define the template in a YAML file and apply it using **kubectl apply -f <template-file.yaml>**.
- **Read:** To view the details of a VM template, you can use kubectl get vmtemplate **<template-name> -o yaml**.
- **Update:** To update an existing VM template, you can modify the YAML definition, and apply the changes using **kubectl apply -f <template-file.yaml>**.
- **Delete:** To delete a VM template, you can use kubectl delete vmtemplate **<template-name>**.

VM Replicas in KubeVirt

VM replicas in KubeVirt are instances of VMs created from a template. They ensure high availability and fault tolerance by maintaining a specified number of identical VMs running at any given time. The replicas field in the YAML definition specifies the number of VM instances to be created. KubeVirt provides two main resources for managing VM replicas:

- **VirtualMachineInstanceReplicaSet (VMIRS):** Similar to Kubernetes ReplicaSets for pods, VMIRS ensures that a specified number of VirtualMachineInstance (VMI) replicas are running. These VMIs are generally ephemeral, meaning that they do not persist data after termination, unless persistent volumes are used.

- **`VirtualMachinePool` (VMP):** VMP ensures that a specified number of VirtualMachine (VM) replicas are running. These VMs are stateful, meaning that they persist data even after termination.

Creating VM Replicas

```
apiVersion: kubevirt.io/v1
kind: VirtualMachineInstanceReplicaSet
metadata:
  name: my-vmirs
spec:
  replicas: 3 # Desired number of replicas
  selector:
    matchLabels:
       app: my-vm
  template:
    metadata:
       labels:
         app: my-vm
    spec:
       domain:
         devices:
           disks:
              - name: containerdisk
               disk:
                 bus: virtio
              - name: cloudinitdisk
               disk:
                 bus: virtio
         resources:
           requests:
             memory: 1Gi
      volumes:
       - name: containerdisk
         containerDisk:
           image: quay.io/kubevirt/cirros-container-disk-demo
       - name: cloudinitdisk
         cloudInitNoCloud:
           userData: |
              #cloud-config
              users:
               - name: cirros
                 groups: sudo
                 shell: /bin/bash
                 sudo: ['ALL=(ALL) NOPASSWD:ALL']
      terminationGracePeriodSeconds: 0
```

DataVolumes for VM Storage

This section delves into the utilization of DataVolumes for addressing the storage requirements of Virtual Machines within KubeVirt. DataVolumes serve as an abstraction layer built upon PersistentVolumeClaims (PVCs) and the Containerized Data Importer (CDI). They streamline the management of VM storage by monitoring and orchestrating the import, upload, and cloning of data into PVCs.

Understanding the Containerized Data Importer (CDI)

The Containerized Data Importer (CDI) is a key component in KubeVirt's storage ecosystem. Its primary function is to populate PVCs with data, making them ready for use as VM disks. CDI achieves this by managing the lifecycle of importer pods that handle the data transfer and conversion processes. CDI offers several functionalities that simplify VM storage provisioning.

CDI enables the import of disk images from various sources such as:

- **HTTP/HTTPS URLs:** You can import disk images directly from web servers or object storage services like Amazon S3 and Google Cloud Storage (GCS). This is useful for provisioning VMs with publicly available operating system images, or pre-built application images.
- **Container registries:** CDI can import images stored in container registries, allowing you to leverage existing containerized workflows for VM provisioning.
- **ImageIO endpoints:** For users with oVirt installations, CDI supports importing disk images from oVirt imageio endpoints. This provides a seamless way to migrate VMs from oVirt to KubeVirt.
- **Cloning PVCs:** CDI allows the cloning of the existing PVCs to create new DataVolumes. This is an efficient way to replicate VM disks for tasks such as scaling deployments, creating backups, or setting up development environments. CDI offers different cloning strategies to optimize resource usage and performance which can be customized through storage profiles.
- **Uploading disk images:** CDI supports the direct upload of local disk images to DataVolumes. This simplifies the process of provisioning VMs with pre-existing disk images that may not be readily available from online sources.

Alternative Storage Options

While DataVolumes are a common choice for persistent VM storage in KubeVirt, several alternative options are available:

- **PersistentVolumeClaims (PVCs):** You can directly use PVCs to provide storage for VMs. This approach offers more flexibility and control over storage provisioning, but requires more manual configuration, and may not provide the same level of abstraction as DataVolumes.
- **Container disks:** Container disks are ephemeral storage provided by KubeVirt, suitable for temporary or non-persistent data. They are useful for storing temporary files, logs, or application data that does not need to be preserved across VM restarts.
- **Host disks:** Host disks allow VMs to access disks on the host node. However, this can pose security risks, and is generally not recommended for production environments.
- **ConfigMaps and secrets:** ConfigMaps and secrets can be used to provide configuration data or sensitive information to VMs. This is useful for injecting configuration files, environment variables, or credentials into VMs, without directly embedding them in the disk image.

The choice of storage option depends on the specific needs of your VM workloads, and the overall storage infrastructure.

Using DataVolumes with KubeVirt

To use DataVolumes with KubeVirt, you typically define them within a VirtualMachine (VM) or **`VirtualMachineInstance`** (VMI) specification. Here is a basic example of how to use a DataVolume to provision a VM with a disk image from a web server:

```
apiVersion: kubevirt.io/v1
kind: VirtualMachine
metadata:
  name: ubuntu-golden-image
  namespace: default # Adjust namespace as needed
spec:
  running: false # Start manually when needed
  template:
    metadata:
      labels:
        kubevirt.io/vm: ubuntu-golden-image
    spec:
      domain:
        devices:
```

```
          disks:
            - name: rootdisk
              disk:
                bus: virtio
        resources:
          requests:
            memory: 2Gi
      volumes:
        - name: rootdisk
          dataVolume:
            name: ubuntu-golden-dv # DataVolume to be created by
CDI
  dataVolumeTemplates:
    - metadata:
        name: ubuntu-golden-dv
      spec:
        source:
          http:
            url: "https://cloud-images.ubuntu.com/releases/jammy/
release/ubuntu-22.04-server-cloudimg-amd64.img" # Replace with
desired Ubuntu version.
        pvc:
          accessModes:
            - ReadWriteOnce
          resources:
            requests:
              storage: 20Gi # Adjust storage size as needed
          storageClassName: "your-storage-class" # Replace with
your storage class
```

How it Works (CDI Cloning)

1. **Create the VirtualMachine:** Apply this YAML file to your Kubernetes cluster using **`kubectl apply -f your-file.yaml`**.
2. **CDI Action:** CDI will detect the dataVolumeTemplates section, and automatically create a DataVolume as well as a corresponding PVC.
3. **Image Download:** CDI will download the Ubuntu image from the specified URL, and store it in the PVC.
4. **Ready DataVolume:** Once the download is complete, the DataVolume will be marked as ready.
5. **Golden Image:** The PVC now contains your golden Ubuntu image which you can use for creating other VMs.

DataVolume Features and Considerations

DataVolumes offer several features and considerations that are important to understand, when using them with KubeVirt:

- **Storage API:** CDI provides a storage API that simplifies the definition of DataVolumes by automatically computing virtualization-specific defaults for optional fields. This reduces the amount of manual configuration required, and helps ensure optimal storage provisioning. For example, when using Ceph RBD, the accessModes is automatically set to ReadWriteMany, which enables live migration, and volumeMode is set to block to maximize performance.
- **Block volume mode:** DataVolumes support block volume mode, allowing you to import, clone, and upload disk images to raw block persistent volumes. This can be beneficial for performance-sensitive applications that require direct access to block devices. Think of it like this: Instead of accessing a file on a file system, the VM can interact directly with the storage device, similar to how a physical machine accesses its hard drive.
- **Content types:** DataVolumes can handle various content types, including KubeVirt (virtual disk images) and archive (tar archives). CDI automatically detects the content type and performs the necessary conversions or extractions. For instance, if the content type is KubeVirt, CDI treats the source as a virtual disk image, converts it to raw format, and sizes it appropriately. If the content type is archive, CDI treats it as a tar archive, and extracts its contents into the DataVolume.
- **Conditions and status:** DataVolumes have conditions that reflect their status such as Ready, Bound, and Running. These conditions provide insights into the progress of data provisioning, and can be used to monitor the health of DataVolumes.
- **Ready:** Indicates whether the DataVolume is ready for use. It will be False, while the data is being imported, cloned, or uploaded, and will transition to True, once the process is complete.
- **Bound:** Shows whether the DataVolume is bound to a PVC. It becomes True, when a PVC is successfully created and associated with the DataVolume.
- **Running:** Indicates whether the import, clone, or upload process is actively running. It is True, while the operation is in progress and transitions to False upon completion or failure.

Uploading Disk Images with `virtctl image-upload`

KubeVirt provides a command-line tool called virtctl that includes a useful command for uploading disk images to DataVolumes: virtctl image-upload. This command simplifies the process of uploading local disk images to your Kubernetes cluster for use with KubeVirt VMs.

Here is a basic example of how to use virtctl image-upload to create a new DataVolume, and upload an image to it:

```
virtctl image-upload dv my-datavolume --size=10Gi --image-path=/
path/to/my-image.qcow2
```

Practical Use Cases for DataVolumes

DataVolumes offer a versatile solution for various VM storage needs in KubeVirt. Here are some practical examples of how DataVolumes can be used:

- **Provisioning VMs with operating system images:** DataVolumes simplify the process of provisioning VMs with operating system images from various sources such as public image repositories, private container registries, or object storage services.
- **Creating data disks for applications:** You can use DataVolumes to create separate data disks for applications running within your VMs. This allows you to isolate application data from the operating system disk, and provides flexibility in managing data persistence and backups.
- **Cloning VMs for scaling or disaster recovery:** DataVolumes facilitate the cloning of VMs by efficiently replicating their disks. This is useful for scaling deployments, creating backups, or setting up disaster recovery environments.

Benefits and Limitations of DataVolumes

Using DataVolumes with KubeVirt offers several benefits:

- **Simplified storage management:** DataVolumes abstract away the complexities of PVC management, making it easier to provision, and manage storage for VMs.
- **Improved efficiency:** CDI's data import and cloning capabilities can significantly improve the efficiency of VM provisioning, especially when dealing with large disk images or frequent cloning operations [3].
- **Enhanced portability:** DataVolumes can be easily moved or copied between Kubernetes clusters, enhancing the portability of VM workloads. This is because DataVolumes encapsulate the source of the data and the storage requirements, making it easy to recreate the same storage configuration in different environments.

However, there are also some limitations to consider:

- **Dependency on CDI:** DataVolumes rely on CDI which adds another layer of complexity to the storage infrastructure.
- **Performance considerations:** The performance of DataVolumes can be affected by factors such as the underlying storage provider, and the network connectivity.

Lifecycle Management

In this section, we will specifically focus on lifecycle management, encompassing actions such as starting, stopping, pausing, and restarting VMs. There are mainly two interfaces for managing KubeVirt Virtual Machine lifecycle:

- **`kubectl`:** This is the standard Kubernetes command-line tool used for interacting with the Kubernetes API. In the context of KubeVirt, you can use kubectl to start/stop VMs. You can also use kubectl to manage the lifecycle of Virtual Machines by patching the **`spec.running`** field or the **`spec.runStrategy`** field.
- **`virtctl`:** This is the official KubeVirt cli, and provides subcommands for all the given operations:
  - **`virtctl start`**
  - **`virtctl stop`**
  - **`virtctl pause`**
  - **`virtctl unpause`**

You might notice that we have not included the **`pause/unpause`** operations in the **`kubectl`** section. Here is a breakdown of why and what limitations exist:

Why `virtctl` is Necessary for Pause/Unpause:

- **Libvirt Interaction:**
  - The pause/unpause functionality relies on interacting with the underlying libvirt hypervisor.
  - virtctl sends commands to libvirt to suspend or resume the execution of the virtual machine's process.
  - This level of runtime control is not exposed through simple CRD field modifications.
- **Runtime State:**
  - Pausing is a runtime operation that affects the execution state of a running VirtualMachineInstance (VMI).
  - CRDs primarily define the desired state, not the transient runtime state.

While there exists a third way of achieving this using the KubeVirt client-go library. We will go over this and some other powerful patterns in a later chapter of this book which deals with automating all these operations and interactions, using a Golang based HTTP or similar service. Before closing this section, let us also go through the details of the type of **`spec.runStrategy`** available, and their meaning as well as use cases:

Run Strategy	**Description**	**Use Cases**
Always	The system ensures that the VM is always running by restarting it, if it terminates for any reason (controlled or uncontrolled).	Suitable for critical VMs that require high availability.
RerunOnFailure	Similar to **`"Always"`**, but the VM is only restarted if it terminates in an uncontrolled way due to an infrastructure issue (for example, node crash).	Useful for VMs where you want to control the shutdown process from within the guest OS.
Once	The VM will run once and not be restarted upon completion, regardless of whether it succeeds or fails.	Suitable for tasks that need to be executed only once.
Manual	The system does not automatically start or stop the VM. You manually control the VM's state using virtctl commands.	Provides complete control over the VM's lifecycle.
Halted	The system ensures that the VM is not running by stopping any associated VMI.	Useful for temporarily stopping a VM or for situations where you want to prevent the VM from running.

Table 4.1: *List of Strategies and Their Use Cases*

Conclusion

This chapter provided a comprehensive guide to managing Virtual Machines within a Kubernetes environment using KubeVirt. We explored essential aspects such as customizing VM specifications for CPU, memory, and storage, and learned how to leverage templates for consistent deployments. The chapter also covered advanced topics like VM scheduling, managing VM replicas with VMIRS and VMP, and utilizing DataVolumes for streamlined storage provisioning. Finally, we delved into VM lifecycle management using `**kubectl**` and `**virtctl**`, highlighting the different `**runStrategy**` options available. The next chapter will explore networking in OpenShift Virtualization.

CHAPTER 5
Networking in OpenShift Virtualization

Introduction

Networking is a critical component of any virtualization platform, and in OpenShift Virtualization powered by KubeVirt, it plays a crucial role in connecting Virtual Machines (VMs) to other workloads and external systems. This chapter will delve into the networking architecture, features, and best practices for managing VM networking within OpenShift Virtualization.

The chapter will begin with an overview of KubeVirt's networking model, explaining how VMs are treated as Kubernetes-native objects with networking capabilities that align with containerized workloads. We will understand how KubeVirt leverages Kubernetes networking plugins to integrate VMs seamlessly into the cluster network.

By the end of this chapter, we will have a comprehensive understanding of networking in OpenShift Virtualization. We will be equipped to design, implement, and troubleshoot networking solutions for VMs, ensuring seamless integration with the broader Kubernetes ecosystem.

Structure

In this chapter, we will cover the following topics:

- An Overview of KubeVirt's Networking Architecture
- Configuring Multus for Advanced Networking
- Connecting VMs to Kubernetes Services
- Bridged and NAT Networking Models

- Troubleshooting Network Connectivity Issues
- Security Considerations for Network Isolation

An Overview of KubeVirt's Networking Architecture

KubeVirt extends Kubernetes to manage virtual machines alongside container workloads, creating a unified compute platform. One of the most vital aspects of this integration is networking, as VMs traditionally rely on different networking paradigms, compared to containerized applications. KubeVirt's networking architecture enables seamless connectivity between VMs and Kubernetes-native workloads, while ensuring compatibility with the existing enterprise network infrastructures. This chapter will provide an in-depth technical overview of KubeVirt's networking components, configurations, and real-world deployment considerations.

KubeVirt Networking Fundamentals

KubeVirt leverages Kubernetes' Container Network Interface (CNI) for networking, but introduces additional abstractions to accommodate VM-specific requirements. Unlike containers, which rely on a pod's network namespace, VMs require direct access to network interfaces, often with specific VLANs, static IPs, or advanced routing configurations.

KubeVirt provides multiple networking models to support diverse workloads:

- **Bridge Networking:** Connects VMs to the host's network, using a Linux bridge, allowing them to appear as native network devices.
- **Masquerade Networking:** Uses Network Address Translation (NAT) to enable VM communication within the Kubernetes cluster.
- **Multus CNI Integration:** Supports multiple network interfaces per VM, enabling complex networking topologies.
- **SR-IOV (Single Root I/O Virtualization):** Provides high-performance and direct access to NICs for latency-sensitive applications.

https://kubevirt.io/user-guide/network/interfaces_and_networks/#interfaces

Each model has specific use cases depending on performance, security, and compatibility requirements. As a reader, we should know the basic understanding of all the above-mentioned concepts.

OpenShift Virtualization Networking Glossary

- **Container Network Interface (CNI):** A Cloud Native Computing Foundation project is focused on container network connectivity. OpenShift Virtualization uses CNI plugins to build upon the basic Kubernetes networking functionality.
- **Multus:** A "`meta`" CNI plugin that allows multiple CNIs to exist so that a pod or virtual machine can use the interfaces it needs.
- **Custom Resource Definition (CRD):** A Kubernetes API resource that allows you to define custom resources, or an object defined by using the CRD API resource.
- **Network Attachment Definition (NAD):** A CRD introduced by the Multus project that allows to attach pods, virtual machines, and virtual machine instances to one or more networks.
- **UserDefinedNetwork (UDN):** A Custom Resource Definition (CRD) scoped to a namespace, provided by the user-defined network API, enables the creation of a tenant-specific network that ensures isolation from other namespaces.
- **ClusterUserDefinedNetwork (CUDN):** The user-defined network API offers a cluster-scoped Custom Resource Definition (CRD) that enables administrators to configure a shared network accessible by multiple namespaces, within the cluster.

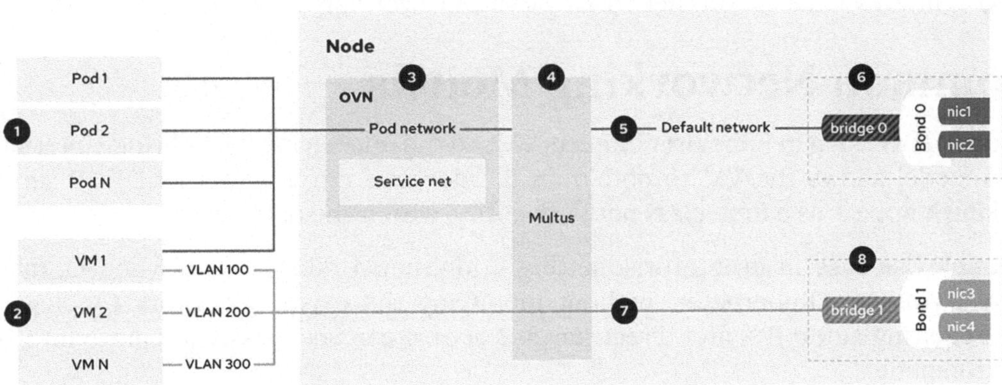

Figure 5.1: *Networking Components in KubeVirt*

Virtual Network Interface Controller (vNIC)

KubeVirt assigns a Virtual Network Interface Controller (vNIC) to each VM which is then connected to a Kubernetes CNI-compliant network. These vNICs interact with the existing Kubernetes networking constructs such as Services and NetworkPolicies.

Pod Network

Each VM in KubeVirt runs inside a Kubernetes pod. The pod's primary network interface can be shared with the VM (bridge mode) or exposed separately via additional network attachments (Multus). The pod network ensures that the VMs can communicate with other Kubernetes workloads, without additional network configuration.

KubeVirt's Network Binding Mechanism

The **virt-launcher pod**, responsible for running a VM, binds the VM's network interfaces at runtime. KubeVirt employs a **binding mechanism** that determines how a VM is connected to the host network:

- **Bridge Binding:** The VM's network interface is directly connected to a Linux bridge.
- **Masquerade Binding:** The VM is assigned an internal IP, with NAT applied for external connectivity.
- **Passthrough Binding:** The VM is assigned a direct physical NIC, commonly used for SR-IOV configurations.

https://docs.redhat.com/en/documentation/red_hat_openshift_service_on_aws/4/html/virtualization/networking#virt-networking

Common Networking Models

Bridge networking in KubeVirt connects VMs to the underlying host's bridge interface. This model allows the VM to obtain an IP address from an external DHCP server, making it appear as a first-class network entity, within the data center.

Example Use Case: In an enterprise setting, bridge networking is useful when migrating legacy VMs into Kubernetes, without modifying the existing network topology. A VM requiring static IPs, and direct Layer 2 access can seamlessly integrate into the environment.

https://kubevirt.io/user-guide/network/interfaces_and_networks/#bridge

Masquerade Networking (NAT)

This is the default networking mode in KubeVirt, where VMs use the pod's IP for communication. A NAT rule is applied to the route traffic between the VM and external networks.

Example Use Case: Masquerade networking is ideal for development and test environments, where full network exposure is unnecessary. It provides a simple and secure way to connect VMs, without requiring complex network configurations.

https://kubevirt.io/user-guide/network/interfaces_and_networks/#multus

Multus CNI for Multi-Network Attachments

Multus CNI enables a VM to have multiple network interfaces, each connected to a different network. This allows VMs to interact with Kubernetes Services, while maintaining separate external connections.

Example Use Case: In a telco 5G core deployment, Multus can be used to assign separate interfaces for control and data plane traffic, ensuring isolation and adherence to network policies.

https://developers.redhat.com/blog/2020/11/18/using-multus-and-datavolume-in-kubevirt#

SR-IOV for High-Performance Networking

SR-IOV enables VMs to achieve near-native network performance by bypassing the virtualization layer, and directly accessing a physical network device.

Example Use Case: A financial trading application requiring ultra-low latency can leverage SR-IOV to ensure direct access to a high-speed NIC, minimizing packet processing overhead.

https://kubevirt.io/user-guide/network/hotplug_interfaces/#sr-iov-interfaces

Networking Considerations and Best Practices

When deploying KubeVirt in production, networking design must consider performance, security, and integration with the existing infrastructure. The following are the key considerations:

- **IP Management:** DHCP or static IPs should be carefully planned, especially when using bridge networking.
- **Security:** NetworkPolicies should be enforced to restrict VM communication, where necessary.
- **High Availability:** Use multiple network interfaces with Multus for redundancy and load balancing.

- **Performance Optimization:** Enable SR-IOV or DPDK for workloads demanding low-latency, and high-throughput networking.
- **Service Discovery:** Kubernetes Services can be leveraged to expose VMs to external applications, ensuring seamless interaction between containerized and virtualized workloads.

Real-World Deployment Scenario

Considering an enterprise running a hybrid workload that includes both containerized applications and VMs hosting legacy applications. The networking architecture could be designed as follows:

- **Containerized workloads** use the default CNI network for communication.
- **VMs running databases** use bridge networking for direct access to the enterprise VLAN.
- **High-performance workloads** leverage SR-IOV for minimal latency.
- **Multus CNI** is used to provide multiple interfaces for applications requiring segmented traffic.

Configuring Multus for Advanced Networking in OpenShift Virtualization

As cloud-native environments evolve, the need for advanced networking capabilities in Kubernetes-based platforms such as OpenShift has grown significantly. Multus, a Container Network Interface (CNI) plugin, enables multiple network interfaces per pod, allowing for complex networking use cases such as Network Function Virtualization (NFV), Software-Defined Networking (SDN), and high-performance data plane configurations.

Understanding Multus in OpenShift Virtualization

Multus functions as a meta-plugin for Kubernetes, enabling pods to attach to multiple networks beyond the primary cluster network. In OpenShift Virtualization, this capability is crucial for workloads that require dedicated interfaces for storage, high-throughput applications, or security isolation.

Key Benefits of Multus

- **Multi-Network Support:** Attach multiple networks to virtual machines and pods.

- **Custom Network Isolation:** Implement dedicated VLANs or VRFs for different workloads.
- **Enhanced Performance:** Utilize high-performance networking solutions such as SR-IOV and DPDK.
- **Flexible IPAM:** Integrate different IP Address Management (IPAM) solutions for each interface.

Installing and Configuring Multus in OpenShift

Before configuring Multus, one needs to ensure that the prerequisites are met:

- OpenShift Virtualization is installed and configured.
- A functional OpenShift cluster with administrative privileges.
- OpenShift Networking Operator is deployed.
- Understanding of OpenShift CNI and networking components.

Step 1: Deploying the Multus CNI Plugin

Multus is enabled by default in OpenShift 4.x. However, if a custom configuration is required, one needs to follow these steps:

1. Need to Verify Multus is installed:
   ```
   oc get pods -n openshift-multus
   ```
2. If missing, deploy the Multus daemonset manually:
   ```
   oc apply -f https://raw.githubusercontent.com/
   k8snetworkplumbingwg/multus-cni/master/deployments/multus-
   daemonset.yml
   ```

Step 2: Configuring Additional Network Attachments

To attach additional networks using Multus, define a NetworkAttachmentDefinition (NAD) in OpenShift.

Example: Creating a Bridge Network Attachment

```
apiVersion: k8s.cni.cncf.io/v1
kind: NetworkAttachmentDefinition
metadata:
  name: custom-bridge-net
  namespace: default
spec:
  config: '{
    "cniVersion": "0.3.1",
    "type": "bridge",
```

```
        "bridge": "br0",
        "isGateway": true,
        "ipam": {
          "type": "static",
          "addresses": [{
            "address": "192.168.1.100/24",
            "gateway": "192.168.1.1"
          }]
        }
      }'
```

Apply the configuration:

```
oc apply -f bridge-network.yaml
```

Step 3: Attaching a Network to a Virtual Machine

Once the NAD is created, reference it in a KubeVirt VirtualMachine definition.

Example: Assigning Multiple Networks to a VM

```
apiVersion: kubevirt.io/v1
kind: VirtualMachine
metadata:
  name: vm-multus-example
  namespace: default
spec:
  template:
    metadata:
      annotations:
        k8s.v1.cni.cncf.io/networks: '[{"name": "custom-
bridge-net"}]'
    spec:
      domain:
        devices:
          interfaces:
          - name: default
            masquerade: {}
          - name: custom-bridge-net
            bridge: {}
      networks:
      - name: default
        pod: {}
      - name: custom-bridge-net
        multus:
          networkName: custom-bridge-net
```

Apply the configuration:

```
oc apply -f vm-multus.yaml
```

Step 4: Verifying Multus Network Configuration

After deploying the VM, need to verify the network interfaces:

```
oc exec -it <vm-pod-name> -- ip a
```

The output should display multiple network interfaces, confirming the successful attachment.

Real-World Use Cases

1. **High-Performance Network Functions:** Multus enables NFV workloads in OpenShift Virtualization by providing multiple interfaces with dedicated bandwidth.
2. **Storage Network Isolation:** VMs running databases can use a separate storage network, reducing congestion on the primary network.
3. **Security and Compliance:** Sensitive workloads can be assigned to isolated VLANs for regulatory compliance.

Troubleshooting Multus Issues

Issue 1: Secondary Interface Not Visible in VM

- Need to verify that the NetworkAttachmentDefinition is applied correctly.
- Need to check Multus logs:

```
oc logs -n openshift-multus daemonset/multus
```

Issue 2: Network Latency or Packet Loss

- Use `ethtool` to check interface performance inside the VM.
- Ensure correct MTU settings are applied across the network.

Connecting VMs to Kubernetes Services

As organizations adopt Kubernetes for container orchestration, many still rely on virtual machines for legacy workloads, specialized applications, or stateful services. **KubeVirt, an extension for Kubernetes**, allows users to manage VMs alongside containerized workloads, leveraging the same declarative API and operational paradigms. However, integrating VMs with Kubernetes-native services requires careful networking considerations to ensure seamless connectivity, service discovery, and workload interoperability.

In *Chapter 2, Setting Up the Environment*, we have already explained most of the things such as ClusterIP, NodePort, LoadBalancer, and ExternalName services. We will cover the advanced connectivity, using Multus, Istio, and hybrid network policies. More details, can be read from the following link:

https://kubevirt.io/user-guide/network/service_objects/

Networking Strategies for VM and Kubernetes Service Connectivity

Multus CNI for Multi-Network Attachments: By default, Kubernetes uses a single network interface per Pod. **Multus CNI** enables additional interfaces, allowing VMs to have both a Kubernetes-native interface, and a traditional network interface.

Implementation:

```
apiVersion: "k8s.cni.cncf.io/v1"
kind: NetworkAttachmentDefinition
metadata:
  name: macvlan-net
spec:
  - config: '{ "cniVersion": "0.3.1", "type": "macvlan", "master":
"eth0", "ipam": { "type": "dhcp" } }'
```

The VM attaches to `macvlan-net`, while maintaining a Kubernetes interface.

Istio for VM Service Mesh Integration

For advanced traffic control, security, and observability, **Istio enables VMs** need to participate in Kubernetes service meshes.

Process:

1. Need to deploy the **Istio CNI**.
2. Configure a **sidecar proxy** for the VM.
3. Define Istio `ServiceEntry` for VM discovery.

Example:

```
apiVersion: networking.istio.io/v1beta1
kind: ServiceEntry
metadata:
  name: vm-external-service
spec:
  hosts:
    - vm-app.internal
```

```
    addresses:
      - 10.10.10.100/32
    location: MESH_EXTERNAL
    ports:
      - number: 443
        name: https
        protocol: HTTPS
  - resolution: NONE
This will allow Kubernetes services to communicate with the VM as
if it were a Pod.
```

Hybrid Network Policies

To enforce security between VMs and Kubernetes services, **NetworkPolicies** and **Cilium CNI** offer granular controls.

Example Policy: Allowing only specific VMs to access a Kubernetes service.

```
apiVersion: networking.k8s.io/v1
kind: NetworkPolicy
metadata:
  name: allow-vm-access
spec:
  podSelector:
    matchLabels:
      app: backend
  ingress:
    - from:
        - ipBlock:
            cidr: 192.168.1.0/24
      ports:
        - protocol: TCP
          port: 80
```

Here, only VMs in the **`192.168.1.0/24`** range can access the backend service.

Bridged and NAT Networking Models

Networking plays a crucial role in virtualization, influencing performance, security, and accessibility of workloads. In the context of **KubeVirt on OpenShift Virtualization**, understanding different networking models is essential for designing an efficient and scalable architecture. Among the widely used models, **Bridged Networking** and **Network Address Translation (NAT)** provide distinct approaches to managing network connectivity for virtualized workloads. This section will explore these models, their implementation in **KubeVirt**, and real-world use cases that highlight their relevance.

Bridged Networking

Bridged networking connects virtual machines directly to the physical network as if they were separate physical hosts. The VM receives an IP address from the same subnet as the host machine, allowing it to communicate with other machines, without additional network address translation.

How It Works

1. The hypervisor creates a **network bridge** (for example, `br0`) which acts as a virtual switch.
2. The physical network interface (for example, `eth0`) is added to this bridge, forwarding packets between VMs and the external network.
3. Each VM is assigned a unique MAC address and an IP address by the external DHCP server.
4. The VM can communicate with external devices, using standard networking protocols, without NAT overhead.

Benefits

- **Performance:** Minimal overhead, since packets are sent directly between the VM and the network.
- **Seamless Integration:** VMs appear as physical hosts, simplifying interactions with network devices such as routers and firewalls.
- **Support for Advanced Networking:** Ideal for scenarios requiring broadcast, multicast, or VLAN segmentation.

Challenges

- **Security:** Exposes VMs directly to external traffic, increasing the attack surface.
- **Administrative Overhead:** Requires proper VLAN and MAC filtering configurations to prevent unauthorized access.
- **Network Dependency:** If the physical network is down, all bridged VMs lose connectivity.

Use Case in OpenShift Virtualization

Bridged networking is particularly useful in **telco-grade workloads** where VMs need low-latency connections to physical appliances. In **KubeVirt**, administrators can configure a bridge using **Multus CNI** to assign VMs direct network access, while maintaining OpenShift's security controls.

NAT Networking

NAT (Network Address Translation) networking provides a private network for VMs, where outbound traffic is routed through the host's IP address. In this model, VMs are assigned private IPs, and they communicate with external networks via the hypervisor's NAT mechanism.

How It Works

1. The hypervisor creates an internal virtual network (for example, **`virbr0`**), typically using **Libvirt's NAT-based networking**.
2. Each VM receives a private IP from this virtual subnet.
3. Outbound traffic is translated at the hypervisor level, making it appear as if it originated from the host machine's external IP.
4. Incoming traffic requires port forwarding or explicit NAT rules for external access.

Benefits

- **Enhanced Security:** VMs are isolated from direct exposure to the external network, reducing attack risks.
- **Simplified Management:** No need for external DHCP or IP address configuration.
- **Efficient IP Utilization:** Useful when public IP addresses are scarce.

Challenges

- **Performance Overhead:** Additional processing required for NAT translations can introduce latency.
- **Limited Inbound Connectivity:** VMs cannot be reached externally, unless explicit port forwarding rules are defined.
- **Complicated Network Policies:** Additional configurations are needed to control outbound and inbound traffic.

NAT networking is useful for **developer environments and CI/CD pipelines**, where VMs require outbound internet access, but do not need inbound connections. In **KubeVirt**, default NAT configurations via PodNetwork allow seamless Internet access for VMs, without requiring complex networking setups.

Feature	Bridged Networking	NAT Networking
Performance	High (direct connectivity)	Moderate (NAT overhead)
Security	Lower (exposed to network)	Higher (isolated by default)
Setup Complexity	Requires external DHCP, VLANs	Simple, built-in with Libvirt
Inbound Access	Fully accessible	Requires port forwarding
Outbound Access	Unrestricted	Routed through host

Figure 5.2: *Choosing the Right Model in KubeVirt*

In **OpenShift Virtualization**, the choice depends on the workload's networking requirements. If a VM needs to function as an independent server, **bridged networking** is preferable. Conversely, for **isolated environments** like CI/CD runners, **NAT networking** provides a secure and easy-to-manage alternative.

Troubleshooting Network Connectivity Issues in KubeVirt for OpenShift Virtualization

Networking is a fundamental component of any cloud-native environment, and in **KubeVirt for OpenShift Virtualization**, ensuring seamless network connectivity is crucial for maintaining optimal performance, security, and reliability. However, network issues can arise due to misconfigurations, resource constraints, or component failures. This guide provides a structured approach to diagnosing and resolving common network connectivity issues in KubeVirt-based environments, ensuring minimal disruption to workloads.

Common Network Connectivity Challenges in KubeVirt

- Pod-to-Pod Communication Failures
- Node-to-Pod and External Connectivity Issues
- Service and Load Balancer Inaccessibility
- Network Policies Blocking Traffic
- DNS Resolution Failures
- Misconfigured Virtual Machine Interfaces (VMIs)

- MTU and Packet Fragmentation Issues
- Performance Bottlenecks and Packet Loss

More details: https://kubevirt.io/2018/KubeVirt-Network-Deep-Dive.html

Step-by-Step Troubleshooting Approach

1. **Verify Network Configuration and Interface Status:** Begin by checking the network interfaces and their configurations on both the host node and the Virtual Machine Instance (VMI):

```
ip a  # Need to Check assigned IP addresses
ip route  #Need to  Verify routing table
nmcli dev status  # Need to Check interface status in OpenShift
nodes
```

For VMIs, ensure that the correct network attachment is defined in the **`NetworkAttachmentDefinition`**:

```
oc get network-attachment-definitions.k8s.cni.cncf.io -n
<namespace>
```

Ensure that the VMI has a properly configured interface:

```
virtctl console <vmi-name>
```

Inside the VM, run:

```
ip a
ping <target-IP>
```

If the network interface does not appear or lacks an IP, check the **Multus CNI configuration** and the associated bridge plugin settings.

Debugging Pod-to-Pod Connectivity Issues

Checking Network Policies: Misconfigured **NetworkPolicies** can block traffic between workloads. List the network policies in effect:

```
oc get networkpolicies -n <namespace>
```

If policies exist, verify whether they are too restrictive:

```
apiVersion: networking.k8s.io/v1
kind: NetworkPolicy
metadata:
  name: allow-all-internal
spec:
  podSelector: {}
  policyTypes:
  - Ingress
```

```
    - Egress
    ingress:
    - from:
      - podSelector: {}
```

Need to apply a permissive policy temporarily to test if network policies are the root cause.

Checking OpenShift SDN or OVN-Kubernetes: Depending on the configured network plugin, need to check the status of the network components:

```
oc get pods -n openshift-sdn # For OpenShift SDN
```

Logs can provide insights into failures:

```
oc logs <sdn-pod-name> -n openshift-sdn
```

Troubleshooting Service and Load Balancer Issues

If a service is unreachable, check its endpoints:

```
oc get svc -n <namespace>
oc describe svc <service-name> -n <namespace>
```

Need to Ensure that the **Endpoints** object exists:

```
oc get endpoints -n <namespace>
```

For LoadBalancer services, check the external IP assignment:

```
oc get svc -o wide
```

DNS Resolution Debugging

If a VMI fails to resolve DNS, check the DNS configuration:

```
cat /etc/resolv.conf
```

Use the following commands to validate DNS resolution inside a pod or VMI:

```
nslookup <service-name>.<namespace>.svc.cluster.local
```

If DNS resolution fails, check the CoreDNS pods:

```
oc get pods -n openshift-dns
oc logs <coredns-pod> -n openshift-dns
```

Identifying MTU and Packet Fragmentation Issues

If large packets fail to transmit, adjust the **MTU** settings:

```
ip link set eth0 mtu 1450
```

Check if lowering the MTU resolves intermittent connectivity issues.

Performance and Packet Loss Troubleshooting

If there are latency issues or packet loss, use **iperf3** to measure the network throughput:

```
iperf3 -s  # On server VM
iperf3 -c <server-IP>  # On client VM
```

For dropped packets, check the **iptables** or **OVS** rules:

```
iptables -L -v -n
ovs-ofctl dump-flows br-int  # For OVN-Kubernetes
```

https://kubevirt.io/user-guide/network/istio_service_mesh/#troubleshooting

Security Considerations for Network Isolation

Network isolation is a critical security aspect in multi-tenant and cloud-native environments. In OpenShift Virtualization powered by KubeVirt, securing workloads across virtual machines and containers requires a robust strategy to mitigate unauthorized access, data exfiltration, and lateral movement of threats. This chapter delves into the key security considerations for network isolation, addressing best practices, technical controls, and real-world implementation approaches.

Understanding Network Isolation in KubeVirt

KubeVirt enables the coexistence of VMs and containers within Kubernetes clusters, introducing complex network segmentation challenges. Network isolation ensures that different workloads—whether containerized applications or VMs—do not unintentionally interact or expose the sensitive data.

Key Network Isolation Models

- **Namespace-based Isolation:** Kubernetes namespaces provide logical separation between workloads. Applying NetworkPolicies at the namespace level can prevent unauthorized cross-namespace communication.
- **NetworkPolicy Enforcement:** Kubernetes **NetworkPolicies** define ingress and egress rules to restrict the traffic flow. In OpenShift, **OVN-Kubernetes** provides advanced policy-based isolation to ensure workloads only communicate as intended.
- **Multi-Tenant Network Segmentation:** OpenShift's **Multus CNI** enables multiple network interfaces per pod, facilitating strict segmentation between control, data, and storage networks.

Example: Running VM management traffic on an isolated control network, while keeping application traffic on a separate VLAN.

- **Service Mesh Integration: Istio or OpenShift Service Mesh** enhances isolation by controlling service-to-service communication, using **mutual TLS (mTLS)** and authorization policies.

  Example: Enforcing zero-trust communication between workloads to mitigate unauthorized lateral movement.

Security Risks in Network Isolation

East-West Traffic Exposure

- Without adequate isolation, internal traffic between workloads may be exposed to malicious insiders or compromised applications.
- **Mitigation:** Need to enforce `NetworkPolicies` to restrict communication only to trusted services.

Misconfigured Multus Networks

- Improper configuration of secondary networks in Multus can lead to unintended cross-tenant access.
- **Mitigation:** Need to implement **Role-Based Access Control (RBAC)** to limit who can attach workloads to secondary networks.

External Attack Surface Expansion

- Exposing services, without proper security controls increases the risk of external threats.
- **Mitigation:** Need to use **Ingress Controllers with TLS termination**, and enforce **EgressPolicies** to prevent unauthorized outbound connections.

Container and VM Coexistence Risks

- Mixed workloads may inadvertently share sensitive network segments.
- **Mitigation:** Need to assign VMs and containers to distinct network zones, using **Kubernetes. NetworkPolicy** and **OpenShift SecurityContextConstraints (SCCs).**

Best Practices for Securing Network Isolation

Implement Strict Network Policies

- Define **default-deny** policies, and explicitly allow only the required traffic.

  https://kubevirt.io/user-guide/network/networkpolicy/#create-networkpolicy-to-deny-all-traffic

Example Policy:

```
apiVersion: networking.k8s.io/v1
kind: NetworkPolicy
metadata:
  name: allow-web-to-db
  namespace: app-namespace
spec:
  podSelector:
    matchLabels:
      app: database
  policyTypes:
    - Ingress
  ingress:
    - from:
        - podSelector:
            matchLabels:
              app: web
      ports:
        - protocol: TCP
          port: 5432
```

Use Private Networking for Sensitive Traffic

- Utilize **PrivateLink or VPN tunnels** to restrict external access to critical services.
- **Example**: Configuring a private VLAN for database traffic in an OpenShift Virtualization environment.

Implement Layer 7 Security Controls

- Deploy **API gateways and Web Application Firewalls (WAFs)** to monitor and filter HTTP traffic.
- **Example**: OpenShift's built-in **HAProxy Ingress Controller** can enforce application-level security policies.

Secure DNS and Service Discovery

- Restrict internal DNS queries to prevent unauthorized service enumeration.
- Need to use **CoreDNS with policy-based filtering** to control resolution within specific namespaces.

Continuous Monitoring and Auditing

- Leverage **OpenShift Logging and Monitoring Stack (Prometheus, Grafana, Loki)** for real-time network anomaly detection.
- Need to use **eBPF-based security tools (Cilium)** to enforce deeper network observability and runtime protection.

Real-World Use Case: Securing Multi-Tenant OpenShift Virtualization

Consider a financial services company running an OpenShift Virtualization cluster with multiple tenants:

- **Challenge:** Need to isolate workloads for different departments, while ensuring secure interconnectivity.
- **Solution:**
  1. Need to use **Namespaces with Role-Based Access Control (RBAC)** to segment departments.
  2. Need to deploy **Multus CNI** for dedicated per-department networking.
  3. Need to enforce **strict NetworkPolicies** to restrict traffic between environments.
  4. Need to implement **Service Mesh with mTLS** for controlled service-to-service communication.

Conclusion

Network isolation is a critical security aspect in OpenShift Virtualization powered by KubeVirt, ensuring that both Virtual Machines (VMs) and containers remain secure from unauthorized access. Kubernetes-native features such as **Namespaces, NetworkPolicies**, and **Role-Based Access Control (RBAC)** enable strict segmentation, reducing the risk of lateral movement in case of a breach. Advanced mechanisms like Multus CNI for multiple network interfaces and service meshes such as Istio with mutual TLS (mTLS) further strengthen isolation, and secure service-to-service communication.

The primary risks lie in misconfigurations which may expose internal traffic or enable unintended cross-tenant access. To mitigate these, organizations should adopt a zero-trust model, enforce least-privilege network policies, and secure ingress with private networking, API gateways, and TLS termination.

Continuous monitoring through OpenShift's observability tools, including Prometheus, Grafana, and Loki, provides real-time visibility into network activity and threats. Ultimately, a multi-layered approach that combines segmentation, policy enforcement, encryption, and monitoring is necessary to protect OpenShift Virtualization environments against evolving security challenges.

The next chapter will provide a deep dive into **KubeVirt's storage architecture**, highlighting how OpenShift Virtualization leverages Kubernetes-native solutions such as PVs, PVCs, and DataVolumes to deliver scalable and persistent storage for virtual machines.

CHAPTER 6
Storage Integration

Introduction

Storage is a cornerstone of virtualized environments, and in OpenShift Virtualization, integrating reliable and scalable storage for Virtual Machines (VMs) is critical for achieving operational excellence. This chapter focuses on the storage architecture of KubeVirt, exploring how it seamlessly integrates with Kubernetes storage solutions to meet the needs of modern workloads.

The chapter begins with an introduction to Kubernetes' PersistentVolume (PV) and PersistentVolumeClaim (PVC) framework which KubeVirt utilizes to provide storage for VMs.

A key focus would be on **DataVolumes and Containerized Data Importer**, a KubeVirt-specific abstraction that simplifies VM storage management. Topics include importing, cloning, and resizing DataVolumes to support flexible and reusable storage configurations. The chapter also examines how to handle stateful workloads by attaching storage that persists beyond the lifecycle of a VM.

By the end of this chapter, you will have a strong foundation in configuring and managing storage for VMs, enabling seamless integration of persistent and ephemeral storage with OpenShift Virtualization.

Structure

In this chapter, we will cover the following topics:

- Persistent Storage for Virtual Machines
- Flexible Storage Provisioning with CDI and Kubernetes Primitives
- CSI Drivers for Enhanced Storage Support
- Managing Storage Performance and Scalability
- Troubleshooting Common Storage Issues
- Best Practices for Storage Integration

Persistent Storage for Virtual Machines

KubeVirt leverages the inherent storage primitives of Kubernetes, namely PersistentVolumes (PVs) and PersistentVolumeClaims (PVCs), and introduces its own concepts, including container disks. Furthermore, the Containerized Data Importer (CDI) project plays a crucial role in facilitating persistent storage for virtual machines managed by KubeVirt. This section will delve into these various persistent storage options available within the KubeVirt ecosystem, outlining their respective functionalities, and elucidating how they collectively contribute to providing durable storage for virtual machines.

Traditional Storage Solutions

Historically, virtual machines have predominantly relied on traditional storage solutions to meet their persistence requirements. These solutions encompass Direct-Attached Storage (DAS), where storage is directly connected to the server hosting the virtual machine; Storage Area Networks (SANs) that provide a dedicated high-speed network for accessing shared block-level storage; and Network-Attached Storage (NAS) which offers file-level access over a network. These traditional storage paradigms often necessitate intricate provisioning processes, involve dedicated hardware infrastructure, and can present considerable challenges in terms of scalability and management, particularly within the dynamic and rapidly evolving landscape of cloud-native environments.

KubeVirt endeavors to simplify these storage-related operations by harnessing the power of Kubernetes' inherent automation, and declarative configuration mechanisms. The traditional separation between the compute layer and the storage infrastructure often necessitates managing them as distinct entities. In contrast, KubeVirt integrates storage management directly within the Kubernetes orchestration framework, thereby enabling automation, and providing a unified control plane for both virtual machines and their underlying storage.

Kubernetes Foundational Storage Elements

A PersistentVolume (PV) in Kubernetes serves as a foundational element for providing persistent storage within the cluster. It is a resource that represents a provisioned piece of storage, the lifecycle of which is independent of any individual Pod that might consume it. Kubernetes supports a diverse range of volume plugins for PVs, allowing integration with various storage backends, including cloud provider-specific storage solutions, Network File System (NFS), Internet Small Computer Systems Interface (iSCSI), and local storage directly attached to nodes.

Complementary to PVs are PVCs. A PVC represents a request for storage made by a user, specifying the desired capacity, access modes (such as ReadWriteOnce,

ReadOnlyMany, or ReadWriteMany), and optionally a StorageClass. PVCs act as an abstraction layer, shielding users from the underlying storage implementation details. Developers can request storage resources, without needing to be concerned with the specific type or configuration of the storage hardware. When a PVC is created, Kubernetes attempts to find a matching PV with sufficient capacity and compatible access modes. If a StorageClass is specified in the PVC, and no suitable static PV exists, Kubernetes can dynamically provision a new PV, using the configured StorageClass to satisfy the claim. This dynamic provisioning capability significantly simplifies the process of obtaining persistent storage for applications running in Kubernetes.

KubeVirt's Utilization of these Foundational Elements

KubeVirt seamlessly integrates with the Kubernetes storage subsystem, enabling virtual machines to utilize PVs and PVCs in the same manner as containerized applications. When a VirtualMachineInstance (VMI) requires persistent storage, it defines a volume within its specification, setting the source to **`PersistentVolumeClaim`**, and specifying the **`ClaimName`** of an existing PVC. Kubernetes then ensures that the PersistentVolume (PV) bound to the referenced PVC is made accessible to the VMI's pod.

KubeVirt, in turn, exposes this storage to the virtual machine as a virtual disk. This mechanism guarantees that the data residing on the PV persists, even if the VMI or the underlying pod is restarted, rescheduled onto a different node, or otherwise undergoes lifecycle changes. The process of attaching a PVC to a VMI involves defining volumes in the **`spec.volumes`** section of the VMI or VirtualMachine (VM) specification, and then referencing these volumes by name within the **`spec.domain.devices.disks`** section. This is presented in the following example:

```
apiVersion: kubevirt.io/v1
kind: VirtualMachine
metadata:
  name: my-vm-template
spec:
  template:
    metadata:
      labels:
        app: my-vm
    spec:
      domain:
        devices:
          disks:
          - name: rootdisk
            disk:
```

```
            bus: virtio
        - name: datadisk
          disk:
            bus: virtio
          volumeName: my-data-volume
      resources:
        requests:
          memory: 2Gi
          cpu: "2"
    volumes:
    - name: rootdisk
      persistentVolumeClaim:
        claimName: my-root-pvc
    - name: my-data-volume
      persistentVolumeClaim:
        claimName: my-data-pvc
```

Storage Modes

KubeVirt provides the flexibility to utilize PVs and PVCs in both **filesystem** and **block** modes. In filesystem mode, when a filesystem-backed PV/PVC is used, KubeVirt expects a disk image file named disk.img to be located at the root of the filesystem. This image is required to be in a raw format, and must be owned by the user ID 107, which corresponds to the qemu user within the VMI's pod, to prevent any permission-related issues. If the disk.img file does not already exist on the PV, KubeVirt can automatically create an empty file with the size specified in the PVC.

In block mode, KubeVirt can directly consume raw block devices provided by PVs/PVCs. This mode offers lower-level access to the storage device, and can be advantageous for certain performance-sensitive workloads such as databases. To utilize block mode PVs/PVCs with KubeVirt, it is necessary to enable the BlockVolume feature gate within the KubeVirt configuration.

Table 6.1 highlights the various volume types, their use cases, the relevant data source and feature gates related to them:

Volume Type	Persistence	Data Source	Use Cases	Feature Gates
`PersistentVolumeClaim`	Yes	Existing Kubernetes PVC	Persistent storage for VM disks, ensuring data survives VM restarts and deletions. Suitable for stateful applications.	**`BlockVolume`** (for block mode), ExpandDisks

`data Volume`	Yes	HTTP URL, Container Registry, PVC, Client Upload, Blank, oVirt, and VMware	Automates the creation and population of PVCs with VM disk images or other data. Simplifies importing images for persistent VM storage.	CDI must be installed
`container Disk`	No	Container Image in a Registry	Rapid deployment of VMs with pre-configured OS and applications. Creating standardized, immutable VM images for testing or stateless workloads.	None
`ephemeral`	No	Backed by a PVC (currently)	Local copy-on-write images for scenarios where disk persistence is not required. Changes are discarded when the VM stops.	None
`emptyDisk`	No	Dynamically allocated empty qcow2 disk	Provides temporary storage for application dependencies and data within the VM that does not need to persist across VM re-creations.	None
`hostDisk`	Potentially	File or directory on the host node	Using or creating disk images directly on the node's filesystem. Use with caution; PersistentVolume is generally preferred.	HostDisk
`configMap`	No	Kubernetes ConfigMap	Injecting configuration data into the VM as an ISO disk or a filesystem.	`EnableVirtioFs ConfigVolumes` (for filesystem mode)

`secret`	No	Kubernetes Secret	Injecting sensitive information into the VM as an ISO disk or a filesystem.	**`EnableVirtioFs ConfigVolumes`** (for filesystem mode)
`service Account`	No	Kubernetes ServiceAccount information	Mounting ServiceAccount credentials into the VM as an ISO disk or a filesystem.	**`EnableVirtioFs ConfigVolumes`** (for filesystem mode)
`downward Metrics`	No	VM and host metrics	Exposing VM and host metrics to the guest via a raw block volume, or a virtio-serial port.	**`Downward Metrics`**

Table 6.1: *Volume Types, Data Sources and Feature Gates*

Flexible Storage Provisioning with CDI and Kubernetes Primitives

KubeVirt leverages Kubernetes' robust storage capabilities through tight integration with PersistentVolumeClaims (PVCs). To streamline the process of importing and managing virtual machine disk images and data, KubeVirt commonly utilizes the Containerized Data Importer (CDI). CDI introduces the DataVolume custom resource which simplifies the creation and population of PVCs, specifically for virtual machines. By abstracting the complexities of data import from various sources (such as container registries, HTTP, or existing PVCs), DataVolumes provide a user-friendly way to prepare storage for KubeVirt VMs, ultimately relying on the underlying flexibility and persistence offered by Kubernetes PVCs.

Containerized Data Importer (CDI) Project

The CDI project is a Kubernetes add-on that has been specifically developed to streamline the process of importing and managing virtual machine disk images for utilization with KubeVirt. Its primary objective is to offer a declarative method for the creation and population of PersistentVolumeClaims (PVCs) with virtual machine disk images, thereby making them readily available for consumption by KubeVirt virtual machines.

CDI operates as an extension to Kubernetes, leveraging Custom Resource Definitions (CRDs) and associated controllers to orchestrate data import as well as cloning operations. Notably, CDI is designed to be storage device agnostic, meaning it can seamlessly integrate with any storage backend that is capable of provisioning PVCs within a Kubernetes cluster. Beyond its primary focus on KubeVirt, CDI can also be employed for the initialization of standard Kubernetes Volumes with data.

The DataVolume Custom Resource

CDI introduces a CustomResourceDefinition (CRD) known as DataVolume which serves as an abstraction layer over the standard Kubernetes PVCs. DataVolumes enable users to declaratively define the source of the data such as a URL, a container registry, an existing PVC, or an upload stream, along with the desired storage characteristics. CDI then automates the creation of the underlying PVC, and the subsequent population of data into it. Utilizing DataVolumes is the recommended approach for interacting with CDI due to its enhanced functionality and superior integration with KubeVirt.

CDI supports importing virtual machine disk images and other data from a diverse range of sources.

HTTP/HTTPS URL Imports

This includes the ability to download images directly from HTTP or HTTPS URLs, facilitating the import of publicly accessible or internally hosted virtual machine images. CDI also supports basic authentication via secrets, and the specification of custom TLS certificates through ConfigMaps for secure downloads.

```
apiVersion: cdi.kubevirt.io/v1beta1
kind: DataVolume
metadata:
  name: ubuntu-http-import
  namespace: default # Specify your desired namespace if not
default
spec:
  pvc:
    accessModes:
      - ReadWriteOnce
    resources:
      requests:
        storage: 20Gi # Adjust the size based on the image
  source:
    http:
      url: "http://cloud-images.ubuntu.com/releases/jammy/
release/ubuntu-22.04-server-cloudimg-amd64.img"
       # Optional:
       # secretRef:
       #   name: my-http-auth-secret # Secret for basic
authentication
```

```
      # certConfigMapRef:
      # ConfigMap containing custom CA certificates
      #   name: my-custom-certs
  contentType: kubevirt # Recommended for VM disk images
```

Container Disk Imports from Container Registries

Furthermore, CDI can directly import Container Disks from container registries. For this source type, the contentType must be set to KubeVirt, and the image within the registry must be a valid Container Disk image.

```
...
spec:
  contentType: kubevirt
  source:
      registry:
      image: "docker.io/kubevirt/fedora-cloud-container-disk
-demo:latest"
      # optional:
      # imagePullSecretRef:
      #   name: my-registry-secret # Secret for registry
authentication
      # tlsClientConfig:
      # Set to true to skip TLS certificate verification
(not recommended for production)
      #   insecureSkipVerify: false
...
```

Efficient PVC Cloning

CDI also provides efficient cloning capabilities for the existing PVCs. If the underlying storage backend supports it, CDI will attempt a storage-level clone which is typically a very rapid operation. If a storage-level clone is not feasible, CDI will perform a data transfer between pods to accomplish the cloning process.

```
...
spec:
  source:
      pvc:
      name: existing-vm-disk-pvc
      # Specify the namespace if the source PVC is in a different
      # namespace
      namespace: default
```

Local Disk Image Uploads

Users can also upload local disk images to a PVC, using the **`virtctl image-upload`** command which is a part of the CDI toolkit. This involves creating a DataVolume with an upload source that initiates an upload proxy service. The virtctl command then securely transfers the image to the proxy which subsequently populates the PVC.

```
virtctl image-upload --uploadproxy-url=$(kubectl get service
cdi-uploadproxy -n kubevirt-cdi -o jsonpath='{.spec.clusterIP}') \
  --pvc-name=my-upload-pvc \
  --pvc-namespace=default \
  --image-path=/path/to/your/local/disk.img \
  --insecure
```

Creating Empty KubeVirt Virtual Machine Disks

CDI can also create an empty KubeVirt virtual machine disk on a PVC using the blank source. This is particularly useful for creating new, uninitialized persistent volumes for virtual machines. The contentType must be KubeVirt for this source, and CDI will utilize the entire available space on the PVC for the disk image.

```
apiVersion: cdi.kubevirt.io/v1beta1
kind: DataVolume
metadata:
  name: empty-vm-disk
  namespace: default # Specify your desired namespace if not
default
spec:
  pvc:
    accessModes:
      - ReadWriteOnce
  resources:
    requests:
      storage: 100Gi # Specify the desired size of the empty disk
  source:
    blank: {}
  contentType: kubevirt # Required for creating a KubeVirt VM
disk
```

Importing from oVirt Installations (`imageio` Source)

CDI offers the capability to import virtual machine disks from running oVirt installations, using the imageio source. This requires providing the necessary credentials to access the oVirt environment, enabling seamless migration of virtual machines from oVirt to KubeVirt.

```
apiVersion: cdi.kubevirt.io/v1beta1
kind: DataVolume
metadata:
  name: ovirt-vm-disk
  namespace: default # Specify your desired namespace if not
default
spec:
  pvc:
    accessModes:
      - ReadWriteOnce
    resources:
      requests:
        storage: 50Gi # Adjust based on the source VM's disk size
  source:
    imageio:
      url: "https://your-ovirt-server.com/ovirt-engine/api"
      credentialsSecret:
        name: ovirt-credentials
      vmName: "my-ovirt-vm"
      diskName: "disk/0" # Name of the disk within the oVirt VM
  contentType: kubevirt # Recommended for VM disk images
```

Importing from VMware Environments (vddk Source)

CDI can import disks from VMware environments, using the vddk source. This process involves using vCenter/ESX API credentials, and a user-provided image containing the non-redistributable VDDK library, facilitating migration from VMware to KubeVirt.

```
apiVersion: cdi.kubevirt.io/v1beta1
kind: DataVolume
metadata:
  name: vmware-vm-disk
  namespace: default # Specify your desired namespace if not
default
spec:
  pvc:
    accessModes:
      - ReadWriteOnce
  resources:
    requests:
      storage: 50Gi # Adjust based on the source VMDK size
  source:
    vddk:
      url: "https://your-vcenter.example.com/sdk"
```

```
      credentialsSecret:
        name: vcenter-credentials
      vmName: "MyVMwareVM"
      diskName: "Hard disk 1" # Name of the virtual disk in
VMware
      uuid: "503e170c-3a93-c797-a1c7-4b2b0b1f0000" # Optional:
UUID of the VM
      # Optional: vCenter certificate thumbprint
      thumbprint: "AA:BB:CC:DD:EE:FF:00:11:22:33:44:55:66:77:88:9
9:AA:BB:CC:DD"
      # insecureSkipVerify: true # Not recommended for production
      # Replace with your VDDK init image
      vddkInitImage: "registry.example.com/path/to/vddk-init:
latest"
  contentType: kubevirt # Recommended for VM disk images
```

Specialized Content Type Handling

CDI provides specialized handling for **KubeVirt** and **archive** content types.

When the contentType is set to KubeVirt, CDI automatically decompresses the image, if it is in **`gzip`** or **`xz`** format, converts it into the raw format required by KubeVirt, and resizes the disk to utilize the full capacity of the PVC.

For the archive content type, CDI will extract the contents of a tar archive into the volume which can be then used with regular pods or with KubeVirt's filesystem feature for virtual machines.

ContainerDisks in KubeVirt

Container disks in KubeVirt provide a method for storing and distributing virtual machine disk images as container images, within a container image registry. This approach leverages the existing container registry infrastructure and workflows for managing VM images. While stored similarly to container images, container disks offer ephemeral storage to VMs. Modifications within the running VM are not persisted back to the container image, and are lost upon VM termination. Therefore, container disks are best suited for scenarios where persistent data storage is not a primary concern, or is managed separately via PVCs.

Container disks excel in rapidly deploying multiple VMs with consistent OS and application stacks, as images can be efficiently pulled across the Kubernetes cluster. They facilitate the creation and management of standardized, immutable "golden images" for various VM workloads. Container disks are also beneficial in testing and development for achieving clean and consistent states upon each VM restart. Utilizing container registries enables efficient distribution and version control of VM images, similar to container image management, often leveraging features such as image layering and caching for optimized pull times.

To use a container disk, a VM disk image (RAW or QCOW2, with QCOW2 recommended for space efficiency) needs to be packaged into a container image. The disk image file is conventionally placed in the `/disk` directory within the container image. In the VirtualMachine or VirtualMachineInstance specification, a volume of type containerDisk is defined in spec.volumes. This volume specification includes the image field, pointing to the container image in the registry (including URL, repository, and tag) containing the VM disk. Subsequently, a disk is defined in spec.domain.devices. disks, referencing the containerDisk volume by name. For KubeVirt to access the disk image, it must be readable by the qemu user (**UID 107** inside the VMI's pod). Ensure appropriate file permissions are set on the disk image file, when creating the container image. KubeVirt also allows specifying a custom path to the disk image within the container image, using the path field under the containerDisk volume source if it is not at the default `/disk` path.

Container disks are well-suited for rapid deployment of numerous identical VMs such as scaling stateless application tiers. They are also appropriate for read-only root filesystems, or in testing/development where VM state persistence is not required. They are useful for distributing pre-packaged VM appliances or OS images.

Conversely, container disks are not suitable for VMs needing persistent modifications to their root filesystem or data that must survive VM termination. For stateful applications storing critical data on the primary disk, PVCs are the recommended approach.

CSI Drivers for Enhanced Storage Support

CSI is a standard API specification that serves as an extension mechanism, enabling arbitrary block and file storage systems to be seamlessly exposed to these containerized environments. This standardized interface allows third-party storage providers to develop and deploy plugins that facilitate the connection between their storage solutions and Kubernetes clusters, all without requiring any modifications to the core Kubernetes codebase.

CSI simplifies the overall storage management within containerized environments. By automating the creation of PVs, and reducing the need for manual intervention from administrators, CSI contributes to a more efficient operational model. This automation is largely driven by the dynamic provisioning capabilities that CSI facilitates, allowing storage volumes to be created on-demand, when applications request them, rather than requiring administrators to pre-allocate storage resources.

The architecture of CSI is designed to establish seamless communication between container orchestration systems, and the underlying storage infrastructure. This is achieved through a well-defined set of components that work in concert. The primary components of the CSI architecture are the Controller and Node plugins.

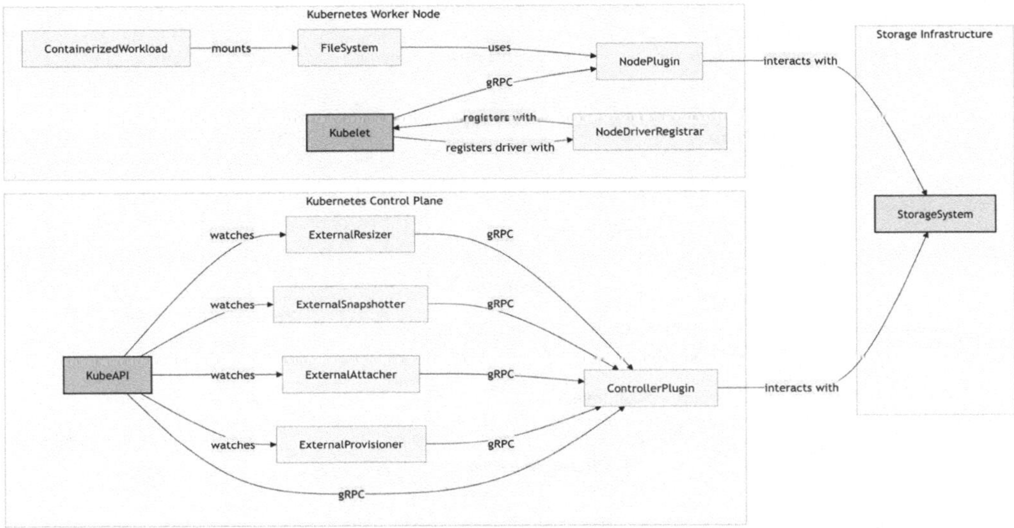

Figure 6.1: *CSI Driver Architecture*

Leveraging CSI Drivers in KubeVirt

KubeVirt's integration with Kubernetes storage primitives extends to a seamless utilization of Container Storage Interface (CSI) drivers. These drivers play a crucial role in providing dynamic and feature-rich storage for virtual machines managed by KubeVirt.

When a virtual machine in KubeVirt requests storage through a PVC that is backed by a CSI StorageClass, KubeVirt directly interacts with the corresponding CSI driver to provision the necessary volume. This interaction is facilitated by Kubernetes which acts as the intermediary between KubeVirt and the CSI driver. The StorageClass, as mentioned earlier, specifies the CSI driver that should be used to handle provisioning for claims requesting that class.

The integration with CSI drivers enables a wide range of advanced storage functionalities for KubeVirt VMs. These features, which are dependent on the capabilities implemented by the specific CSI driver, can include:

- **Snapshots:** Creating point-in-time copies of the virtual machine's disk volumes for backup and recovery purposes.
- **Cloning:** Rapidly creating new virtual machines by duplicating existing VM disk volumes.
- **Resizing:** Dynamically increasing or decreasing the size of the persistent volumes attached to running virtual machines.

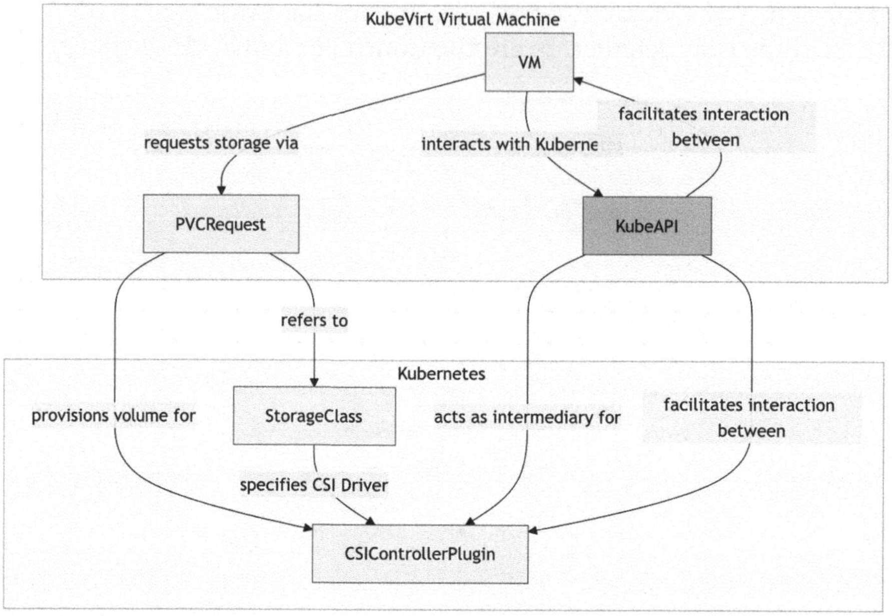

Figure 6.2: *KubeVirt VM Interaction with CSI Driver*

Enhanced Flexibility and Choice of Storage Backends

The CSI framework inherently supports a wide range of storage backends through the development and deployment of specific drivers. KubeVirt, by integrating with Kubernetes storage primitives, can leverage any CSI driver that is available within the Kubernetes cluster. This provides KubeVirt users with significant flexibility and choice, when it comes to selecting the most suitable storage solution for their virtual machine workloads.

This broad compatibility includes drivers for various types of storage, such as:

- **Cloud-based storage:** CSI drivers are available for major cloud providers, including AWS (EBS), Google Cloud (Persistent Disks), and Microsoft Azure (Managed Disks).
- **On-premise storage solutions:** CSI drivers exist for many on-premise storage systems such as Ceph, NFS, and various enterprise storage arrays from vendors such as NetApp and Dell EMC.

Popular CSI Drivers and KubeVirt Integration

In this section, we are going to talk about some popular CSI Drivers, and their integration with KubeVirt.

Cloud Provider CSI Drivers

For users running Kubernetes and KubeVirt on public cloud platforms, the cloud provider's CSI drivers offer seamless integration with their native storage services. Some of them are listed here.

- **AWS EBS CSI Driver:** The Amazon Elastic Block Store (EBS) CSI driver is designed to manage the lifecycle of AWS EBS volumes as storage for Kubernetes volumes. The driver can be used with KubeVirt on Amazon EKS (Elastic Kubernetes Service), providing persistent storage for virtual machines running within the EKS environment.
- **Google Persistent Disk CSI Driver:** The Google Compute Engine Persistent Disk CSI Driver provides a way to automatically deploy and manage Compute Engine persistent disks within Google Kubernetes Engine (GKE) clusters. Leveraging this driver enables KubeVirt users on Google Cloud to take advantage of the scalability and performance of Google's storage infrastructure for their virtualized workloads.
- **Azure Managed Disks CSI Driver:** The Azure Managed Disks CSI Driver is designed to manage the lifecycle of Azure Disk volumes for Kubernetes clusters deployed in Azure Kubernetes Service (AKS). This driver offers several advantages, including performance improvements during concurrent disk attach and detach operations. It supports various Azure Disk SKUs, including Premium SSD v1 and v2, as well as Zone-Redundant Storage (ZRS) disks for higher availability.

On-Premise CSI Drivers

For organizations that need to run KubeVirt in on-premise environments, several CSI drivers are available for popular storage solutions.

- **Ceph CSI Driver (Rook):** Rook is an open-source cloud-native storage orchestrator for Kubernetes that provides an operator to manage Ceph, a distributed storage system. Rook integrates with Ceph to provide block storage (via RBD), file storage (via CephFS), and an experimental NFS option to Kubernetes through CSI drivers. These drivers support dynamic and static provisioning, allowing for flexibility in how storage is managed. Volume expansion is also supported, enabling the resizing of persistent volumes. For block storage, RBD mirroring is available for enhanced data availability.
- **NFS CSI Driver:** The NFS CSI Driver allows Kubernetes clusters to access the existing NFS (Network File System) servers for dynamic provisioning of persistent volumes. This driver supports both NFSv3 and NFSv4, and requires an already configured NFS server to be accessible by the Kubernetes cluster. Once installed, the NFS CSI driver enables the dynamic creation of Persistent

Volumes via Persistent Volume Claims by creating new subdirectories under the NFS server's exported share.

It allows organizations to utilize their current NFS investments for KubeVirt workloads, without requiring the adoption of new or unfamiliar storage technologies. The driver supports basic storage operations such as provisioning and mounting NFS shares as persistent volumes for VMs.

Managing Storage Performance and Scalability

This section delves into the considerations for achieving optimal storage performance, and the ability to scale storage resources effectively, when using CSI drivers with KubeVirt. Understanding potential bottlenecks and limitations related to latency, connection constraints, and storage topology is crucial for designing a performant and scalable virtual machine infrastructure. Some of the points for consideration are mentioned in the following sections.

Latency in Volume Operations

Using CSI drivers with external storage arrays can introduce latency in volume operations (provisioning, attaching, detaching, snapshotting) due to network communication outside the Kubernetes cluster. For example, cloning of DataVolumes as Golden VM images can take significantly longer than using containerDisks for the same purpose. Factors that can affect this:

- **Underlying Storage Backend:** The storage backend's inherent performance characteristics are fundamental. Different storage technologies (HDDs vs. SSDs/NVMe) have vastly different latency profiles. SSDs/NVMe offer lower latency. Shared storage (NAS, cloud) can be affected by the overall system load. Cloud storage latency varies by region and service.
- **Container Storage Interface (CSI) Driver:** The CSI driver mediates communication between Kubernetes, and the storage backend. Driver efficiency and implementation quality directly impact latency. Poorly written drivers introduce overhead. Selecting a well-maintained, performant CSI driver for the chosen storage backend is crucial.
- **Network Latency (for Network-Attached Storage):** Network latency between KubeVirt nodes, and the storage backend is critical. Network hops, congestion, and bandwidth affect storage operation delays. Thus, low-latency and high-bandwidth network connections are essential.

- **KubeVirt Volume Types:** Different volume types (PVCs, DataVolumes, and containerDisks) can have slight variations in provisioning/access, affecting latency. The containerDisk may introduce latency during VM startup due to image pull.
- **Disk Cache Mode:** The configured disk cache mode for the VM's disk influences perceived and actual latency. KubeVirt supports **`none`**, **`writeback`**, and **`writethrough`** modes.
    - **`none`** (no host caching) is recommended for high I/O guests for lower write latency.
    - **`writeback`** (host caching) improves read latency but risks data loss without proper flushing.
    - **`writethrough`** (host caching with immediate write to media) balances read performance and data safety. The optimal mode depends on workload characteristics and performance/consistency trade-offs.
- **KubeVirt I/O Optimization Features:** KubeVirt provides features such as **`IOThreads`** and Virtio Block Multi-Queue to optimize I/O and reduce latency.

    IOThreads dedicate threads to disk I/O, improving scalability and latency on multi-CPU systems.

    Virtio Block Multi-Queue allows parallel I/O request processing across multiple vCPUs, enhancing performance for high-parallelism workloads.
- **Quality of Service (QoS) Limits:** QoS limits at the storage class level can affect latency. While necessary for resource contention management, overly restrictive limits increase latency for performance-sensitive VMs.

Identifying and Measuring Storage Latency

Identifying and measuring storage latency in KubeVirt environments is crucial for diagnosing performance issues. Kubernetes monitoring tools and KubeVirt-specific metrics provide valuable insights. KubeVirt exposes metrics like **`kubevirt_vmi_storage_read_times_seconds_total`** and **`kubevirt_vmi_storage_write_times_seconds_total`**.

Tools such as Prometheus and Grafana can query and visualize these metrics. Guest OS tools such as **`iostat`** (Linux) or **`Performance Monitor`** (Windows) offer granular latency views.

Specialized AI tools such as Hawkeye analyze and correlate storage latency with other performance metrics.

Host Connection Limits and Connection Pressure

External storage systems might have limitations on concurrent connections or volumes per host. A large number of VMs with multiple disks in a KubeVirt cluster can potentially exceed these limits, leading to performance degradation or failures. There is also a limitation of max kubernetes pods per node, based on the size of the CIDR ranges provided to the specific node for ServiceIPs and PodIPs.

Kubernetes nodes establish connections to storage backends (**`iSCSI`**, **`NFS`**, and cloud storage). Nodes, like OSes, have limits on concurrent connections to external resources. These limits significantly impact storage performance for KubeVirt VMs, especially in high-density environments.

Connection pressure arises from a large number of VMs, each with potential multiple disks, on a KubeVirt cluster. Each virtual disk requires a connection from the host to the storage backend. Increased VMs/disks on a node increase the total storage connections from that node. This can lead to the host approaching or exceeding connection limits, resulting in performance degradation and instability. Examples: `iSCSI` initiator sessions, and `NFS` server client mounts.

Strategies to Mitigate

Optimize VMs per node based on storage capabilities and connection limits.

Plan VM density considering storage requirements (disk count and access patterns) and storage infrastructure connection limits.

Monitor active storage connections originating from each Kubernetes node to identify potential bottlenecks.

Utilize storage solutions designed for high connection concurrency. Choose storage backends and CSI drivers known to handle many concurrent connections efficiently. Use distributed storage solutions that scale connection handling horizontally. Employ techniques such as volume sharing where appropriate to reduce overall storage connections.

Use **ReadOnlyMany** (ROX) PersistentVolumes for multiple VMs requiring read-only access to the same data.

Consider shared file systems via **ReadWriteMany** (RWX) PersistentVolumes (with careful data consistency management).

Scalability Considerations with Local and Topology-Constrained Storage

Using local storage or storage constrained by topology (for example, availability zones) with the KubeVirt CSI driver can present scalability issues related to VM scheduling, and the driver's ability to manage volumes across different topology domains.

Local Storage Scalability Challenges

Local storage (devices within compute nodes) offers high performance due to direct attachment and reduced latency. However, it introduces challenges for scalability in KubeVirt.

- **Data Locality and Node-Specific Failures:** If a KubeVirt VM relies on local storage on a node, the data becomes inaccessible, if that node fails. This impacts VM availability. Achieving high availability requires application-level data replication, adding complexity.
- **Live Migration Limitations:** Live migration (moving a running VM between nodes without downtime) typically requires shared storage. With local storage, migration necessitates moving potentially large volumes of data. This is time-consuming and disruptive, becoming a cold migration, rather than a seamless live migration.

Topology-Constrained Storage Scalability Considerations

Topology-constrained storage (for example, zonal storage) offers a balance by placing storage closer to compute resources within the same availability zone. This reduces network latency, and improves performance. However, it also introduces scalability considerations. While aligning storage and compute in the same zone enhances performance, it can create limitations and complexities in cross-zone or cross-region live migration.

Migrating a KubeVirt VM across different availability zones or regions can introduce significant network latency. This might negatively impact the migration process and post-migration VM performance. Ensuring data consistency across different zones or regions often requires storage replication mechanisms, increasing complexity and cost.

Kubernetes Features for Managing Topology: Kubernetes provides features to manage VM and storage placement based on topology. Topology spread constraints and **node affinity/anti-affinity** can be used. These features define rules to influence

VM scheduling. The goal is to place VMs in the same zone as their storage to minimize latency.

Solutions and Best Practices

`VolumeBindingMode: WaitForFirstConsumer`: Kubernetes feature in **`StorageClass`**. Enables topology-aware volume provisioning. Delays PV binding/provisioning until a pod (hosting the KubeVirt VM) is scheduled. Allows the Kubernetes scheduler to consider pod topology constraints.

Local Storage Provisioners: For example, **`HostPath`** Provisioner. Manages local disks on nodes. Creates **`PersistentVolumes`** that are aware of the node's topology. Automates local storage resource management within the KubeVirt cluster.

Storage Solutions with Built-in Replication and High Availability: The most effective solution. Software-defined storage (SDS) solutions like Portworx and IOMesh. These provide Kubernetes-native capabilities. They pool local storage resources from multiple nodes. They also replicate data across nodes. This offers high availability and data resilience even with node failures.

Many support **`ReadWriteMany` (RWX)** access mode.

RWX is essential for facilitating live migration of KubeVirt VMs with local or topology-constrained storage.

Impact of Access Modes on Live Migration

The access modes of underlying storage (for example, RWO) can influence the feasibility of live migration for KubeVirt VMs. RWO volumes, being single-node mount, typically prevent direct live migration, without specific storage migration mechanisms or RWX volumes.

Storage Access Modes Defined

Kubernetes defines storage access modes for **`PersistentVolumes`** (PVs) and **`PersistentVolumeClaims`** (PVCs). These modes dictate how storage can be accessed by pods. The three primary access modes are:

- **`ReadWriteOnce` (RWO):** Allows a volume to be mounted as read-write by a single node. Commonly used for workloads requiring exclusive storage access (for example, databases).
- **`ReadOnlyMany` (ROX):** Permits a volume to be mounted as read-only by many nodes simultaneously. Suitable for sharing data that should not be modified (for example, configuration files, static content).

- `ReadWriteMany` **(RWX):** Enables a volume to be mounted as read-write by many nodes concurrently. Often used for shared file systems or applications requiring collaborative storage access.

Impact of RWO on Live Migration

`RWO` typically prevents seamless live migration of KubeVirt VMs. Live migration requires both source and destination VMs to access storage during transition. `RWO` volumes can only be mounted read-write by a single node. The target node would not be able to access the volume, while it is still attached to the source node in read-write mode. KubeVirt offers a volume update strategy (with the Migration option) to facilitate moving storage from one `RWO` volume to another. However, this is not the same as seamless live migration of the VM's compute resources. The Migration Toolkit for Virtualization (MTV) also explicitly states that `RWO` access mode does not enable live virtual machine migration.

Impact of ROX on Live Migration

ROX might allow live migration in certain scenarios, as the target node only needs read access. However, the source VM typically needs to retain write access until migration completion. Ensuring a clean handover of storage responsibilities and maintaining data consistency between source and destination nodes can still present challenges with ROX volumes during live migration. While multiple nodes can read from an ROX volume, the primary limitation for live migration arises from the need for the source VM to potentially write to the storage, until the very end of the migration process.

Impact of RWX on Live Migration

RWX is generally the preferred and recommended mode for enabling seamless live migration of virtual machines in KubeVirt. RWX allows both source and destination nodes to concurrently read and write to the same storage volume. During live migration, the source VM continues to run, while its memory and state are copied to the target node. With RWX access, the target VM can also access the storage volume, ensuring that it has the necessary data to take over seamlessly, once the migration is complete.

Portworx, a storage solution often used with KubeVirt, explicitly requires `RWX` volumes for live migration. KubeVirt's own documentation also confirms that VMs using PVCs must have an `RWX` access mode to be live-migrated. In some cases, using `RWX` volumes with shared storage backends can even enable memory-only live migration which is faster and less resource-intensive than migrating the entire block device.

Access Mode	Description	Impact on Live Migration in KubeVirt	Typical Use Cases
`ReadWriteOnce` (RWO)	Read-write by a single node	Generally prevents live migration; volume migration strategies might offer alternatives.	Databases, and standalone applications with local data.
`ReadOnlyMany` (ROX)	Read-only by many nodes	May allow live migration with complexities in ensuring write access handover and data consistency.	Sharing configuration files, and static content.
`ReadWriteMany` (RWX)	Read-write by many nodes	Preferred mode for seamless live migration; enables concurrent access for source and destination VMs.	Shared file systems and collaborative applications.

Table 6.2: *Access Modes and Live Migration*

Troubleshooting Common Storage Issues

Integrating storage with KubeVirt Virtual Machines (VMs) is a critical aspect of managing virtualized workloads within a Kubernetes environment. However, this integration can sometimes present challenges. Understanding common issues and effective troubleshooting techniques is necessary for maintaining a stable and performant KubeVirt infrastructure.

Volume Mounting Failures

One of the primary challenges encountered when integrating storage with KubeVirt VMs involves failures in mounting storage volumes. These failures can stem from various underlying issues within the Kubernetes cluster, or the VM configuration itself.

Common Causes

Several factors can contribute to volume mounting failures, particularly incorrect configuration of the DataVolume specification.

Missing **`accessMode`** and **`volumeMode`** can prevent successful volume creation. This often arises due to default StorageProfile settings not aligning with the required volume attributes. Furthermore, issues at the Kubernetes node level such as the absence of necessary packages like **`nfs-common`** for NFS volumes, can lead to pods being stuck in a pending state. Stale volume attachments linked to non-existent nodes can also confuse the cluster and hinder the attachment process. Inconsistent states during volume migration, especially when cancellations occur prematurely, can leave VMs in a `ManualRecoveryRequired` state, preventing them from booting correctly.

Additionally, the guest operating system within the VM might lack support for certain filesystem types such as `virtiofs`, necessitating kernel version checks and potential workarounds.

Troubleshooting Steps

Diagnosing volume mounting failures requires a systematic approach. Examining the events of the affected pod, using `kubectl describe pod <pod-name>` can reveal initial error messages.

For issues related to stale volume attachments, identifying the associated PV name, and then checking the existing `VolumeAttachments`, using `kubectl get volumeattachment` is crucial.

Deleting any stale `VolumeAttachment` objects with `kubectl delete volumeattachment <volumeattachment_name>` can resolve the problem.

In cases of migration failures, reverting the VM specification to its original state can cancel the migration. If a VM is marked with `ManualRecoveryRequired`, users need to revert the volume set in the VM spec.

Ensuring the guest OS supports the required filesystem by checking for the `virtiofs` module, using `modprobe virtiofs`, and verifying the kernel version with `uname -r` is also important.

For Portworx environments, verifying the `RWX` access mode of PVCs with `kubectl get pvc -n <vm-namespace>` is recommended.

Examining the logs of the `virt-launcher` pod associated with the VM can also provide valuable insights into the mounting process.

Storage Performance Bottlenecks

Slow storage performance can significantly impact the responsiveness and usability of KubeVirt VMs. Identifying and resolving these bottlenecks is crucial for ensuring optimal workload operation.

Common Causes

Performance issues can arise from various points in the storage path. Running KubeVirt in emulation mode, instead of utilizing hardware virtualization can lead to significant performance degradation.

The choice of disk cache mode (**`none`**, **`writeback`**, **`writethrough`**) also plays a crucial role, with **`none`** generally being the best option for guests with large I/O requirements.

Insufficient filesystem overhead, particularly when using Portworx filesystem volumes, can cause errors when creating VMs from templates. Network latency in accessing network-based storage can also introduce bottlenecks. Additionally, limitations in the underlying storage infrastructure or misconfigurations in **`StorageClasses`** can contribute to slow performance. The type of disk interface used (IDE vs. VirtIO) also has a significant impact, with VirtIO generally offering superior performance.

Diagnosing and Resolving Bottlenecks

Diagnosing storage performance issues often involves monitoring various metrics. Tools such as `kubectl top pod` can provide the basic resource utilization, but more detailed analysis might require specialized monitoring solutions.

Examining the KubeVirt metrics related to storage I/O operations (IOPS, throughput, and latency) using Prometheus can provide valuable insights.

For Portworx environments, ensuring the **`portworx.io/app: KubeVirt`** annotation is added to PVC specs can optimize performance. Adjusting the filesystem overhead for Portworx volumes by editing the HyperConverged Operator (HCO) object might be necessary. Selecting the appropriate disk cache mode, generally **`none`** for high I/O workloads, can improve performance.

Ensuring that KubeVirt is running with hardware virtualization enabled is critical; this can be checked via the KubeVirt **`configmap`**. Utilizing the VirtIO interface for VM disks, if supported by the guest OS, is highly recommended for better I/O performance. In some cases, the underlying storage solution might be the bottleneck, and evaluating its performance and configuration might be necessary.

Data Corruption Issues

Ensuring data integrity within KubeVirt storage configurations is paramount for preventing data loss, and maintaining application reliability.

Identifying and Addressing Corruption

Data corruption can be a severe issue, potentially leading to application failures and data loss. While KubeVirt itself does not have built-in data corruption detection mechanisms at the storage level, understanding potential causes, and implementing preventative measures are crucial.

One potential cause of data corruption can be inconsistencies during live migrations, especially if a node loses connection to shared storage. Improper handling of volume updates, and cancellations during migration can also lead to inconsistent states. While the snippets do not detail specific methods for identifying data corruption within KubeVirt storage, standard practices for the guest operating system and the underlying storage provider should be followed.

Tools such as filesystem checks (**`fsck`** in Linux) within the guest VM can help detect and repair corruption. Implementing robust backup and restore strategies is essential for recovering from data corruption incidents. Ensuring that storage policies are correctly configured, and that appropriate access modes are used (for example, **`ReadWriteOnce`** for exclusive access when needed) can help prevent corruption due to concurrent writes. During VM migrations, ensuring that the VM is powered off to prevent data loss or corruption is a good practice.

Network Connectivity Problems

Network connectivity is essential for KubeVirt VMs to access storage, especially when using network-based storage solutions such as **`NFS`** or **`iSCSI`**.

Impact on Storage Access and Solutions

Network problems can manifest as an inability for VMs to access storage volumes, leading to boot failures or application errors. Common network issues affecting storage access include node connectivity problems, misconfigured network interfaces within the VM, and firewall restrictions. Solutions often involve verifying the network configuration of the KubeVirt nodes and the VMs, ensuring that the correct network binding plugins are configured, and checking firewall rules to allow traffic on the necessary ports.

Using tools such as **`ping`** and **`traceroute`** from within the VM or the KubeVirt node can help diagnose network reachability issues. For VMs requiring static IP addresses, configuring the network interface to use a bridge type, and utilizing **`cloud-init`** to set the static IP within the guest OS is a recommended approach.

In environments utilizing secondary networks with Multus, ensuring the correct **`NetworkAttachmentDefinition`** is specified for the VM is crucial. During live VMs migrations, especially those using bridge network mode, solutions such as Kube-OVN can provide network transparency, and minimize interruptions.

Best Practices for Storage Integration

Effective storage integration with KubeVirt involves careful planning and configuration to ensure performance, reliability, and scalability. In this section, we will be shedding light on some of the important points to consider as best practices.

Selecting Appropriate Storage Types

The choice of storage type significantly impacts the performance and capabilities of KubeVirt VMs. Selecting the right type, based on the workload requirements, is a key best practice.

Block, File, and Object Storage

KubeVirt primarily utilizes block and file storage. Block storage, accessed at the sector level, is generally preferred for high-performance workloads requiring low latency such as databases.

`PersistentVolumeClaims` in KubeVirt can be configured in "**`block`**" mode to consume raw block devices. File storage, accessed through a filesystem, offers more flexibility for general-purpose workloads.

`PersistentVolumes` can also be in "**`filesystem`**" mode, requiring the disk image to be named as **`disk.img`**.

Ephemeral storage options such as `containerDisk` and **`emptyDisk`** provide file-based storage that does not persist beyond the VM's lifecycle, suitable for temporary data or read-only images. While object storage is not directly used as a primary disk type, it can be accessed from within the VM if the guest OS supports it, often used for secondary storage such as backups or large data repositories.

Workload-Specific Recommendations

For workloads requiring persistent data, using **`PersistentVolumeClaims`** is essential. Ephemeral VMs that do not need to retain data after termination are well-suited for **`containerDisk`** or **`emptyDisk`**. Sharing data between the host and the VM or between VMs can be achieved using **`hostDisk,`** or by sharing **`PersistentVolumeClaims`**, respectively.

Configuration data can be injected into VMs using **`configMap`** and **`secret`** volumes. Generally, block storage is recommended for performance-sensitive applications, while file storage offers more versatility for other workloads.

Recommended Configurations for `StorageClasses` and `PersistentVolumes`

Properly configuring **`StorageClasses`** and **`PersistentVolumes`** is crucial for ensuring that KubeVirt VMs have access to the appropriate storage resources, with the desired characteristics.

StorageClass Configuration

Creating well-defined **StorageClasses** allows for dynamic provisioning of storage with specific performance characteristics and policies. Utilizing **volumeBindingMode: WaitForFirstConsumer** ensures that volumes are provisioned on nodes where the VM can be scheduled, improving efficiency.

Setting the **reclaimPolicy** to "**Delete**" or "**Retain**" as per the data retention requirements is important for managing the lifecycle of the underlying storage. For storage providers that support it, enabling **allowVolumeExpansion: true** allows for online resizing of volumes. Annotating a `StorageClass` with **storageclass.kubernetes.io/is-default-class: "true"** designates it as the default for PVCs that do not specify a StorageClass.

For Portworx, using the **sharedv4: "true"** and **sharedv4_mount_options: vers=3.0,nolock** parameters in the StorageClass is recommended for KubeVirt compatibility.

PersistentVolume and PersistentVolumeClaim Configuration

PersistentVolumes can be provisioned statically or dynamically via **StorageClasses**. **PersistentVolumeClaims** express the storage requirements (size, access modes) of the VM. Selecting the appropriate `accessModes` (**ReadWriteOnce**, **ReadOnlyMany**, **ReadWriteMany**) based on how the VM needs to access the storage is crucial.

Using `volumeMode` to specify whether the volume should be a filesystem, or a block device is also important. For importing existing VM images, the CDI provides the DataVolume CRD, which simplifies the process of creating PVCs with pre-populated data.

Guidelines on Monitoring

Proactive monitoring of storage usage and performance is vital for identifying potential problems, before they impact KubeVirt workloads.

Monitoring Tools and Metrics

KubeVirt exposes a rich set of metrics that can be monitored using tools such as Prometheus. Key metrics to track include:

- disk allocated size
- storage read/write times
- Traffic

- filesystem capacity
- I/O Operations Per Second (IOPS)

Grafana can be used to create dashboards for visualizing these metrics, providing insights into storage usage patterns and performance trends. OpenShift Virtualization also provides built-in cluster checkups for storage which can be run via the web console or the command line. Additionally, AI-powered tools such as Hawkeye can provide automated analysis, and correlation of the storage performance data.

Proactive Identification

By continuously monitoring these metrics, administrators can proactively identify potential issues such as low disk space, high latency, or excessive I/O wait times. Setting up alerts, based on predefined thresholds can notify administrators of potential problems before they escalate.

For example, an alert can be configured to fire, when the available disk space on a volume falls below a certain percentage. Analyzing trends in storage usage can also help with capacity planning, ensuring that sufficient storage resources are available for future needs. Regularly reviewing the status and events of **`PersistentVolumeClaims`** and **`PersistentVolumes`** can also help in identifying and resolving storage-related issues early on.

Conclusion

This chapter highlighted the critical role of storage integration in OpenShift Virtualization, emphasizing KubeVirt's seamless use of Kubernetes' PersistentVolume (PV) and PersistentVolumeClaim (PVC) framework. It delved into DataVolumes and the Containerized Data Importer (CDI) for simplified VM storage management, covering aspects such as importing, cloning, and resizing. Furthermore, the chapter explored CSI drivers for enhanced storage support, providing flexibility and advanced functionalities such as snapshots, cloning, and resizing. Finally, it covered crucial considerations for managing storage performance, scalability, and common troubleshooting techniques, along with the best practices for selecting appropriate storage types and monitoring.

The next chapter will delve into the security model of KubeVirt, exploring how VMs are isolated using Kubernetes features such as namespaces, RBAC, and pod security policies. It will also cover compliance requirements, including data security, encryption, and the use of tools such as SELinux and AppArmor for hardening VMs. The chapter will conclude with practical approaches for vulnerability management in VM environments.

Chapter 7
Security and Compliance

Introduction

In this chapter, we will begin by outlining the security model of OpenShift and KubeVirt , focusing on how Virtual Machines (VMs) are isolated from other workloads, using Kubernetes' built-in mechanisms like namespaces, Role-Based Access Control (RBAC), and pod security policies. We will also learn how these features can be extended to enforce stringent security measures for VMs. The cost of mistakes, when it comes to security-related tasks, are higher than most of the operations in clusters. Recently, data-breaches and hacks have cost companies millions of dollars.

The next chapter will cover compliance requirements, addressing the need to meet industry regulations such as Topics that include auditing VM activities, securing data at rest, and in transit, as well as implementing encryption mechanisms.

The role of tools such as SELinux, AppArmor, and OpenShift compliance operators in hardening VMs, and their associated workloads are also explored. The chapter emphasizes practical approaches to vulnerability scanning, monitoring, and patching for VM environments.

Structure

In this chapter, we will cover the following topics:

- Role-Based Access Control for Virtual Machines
- Using SELinux and Seccomp Profiles for Enhanced Security
- Configuring OpenShift Security Policies
- Auditing and Monitoring Virtual Machine Activity
- Kyverno: How It Can Help KubeVirt and OpenShift
- Real-World Security Challenges and Solutions

Role-Based Access Control for Virtual Machines

Role-Based Access Control (RBAC) is a critical security mechanism for managing user access in cloud environments. When working with Virtual Machines (VMs) in OpenShift Virtualization powered by KubeVirt, RBAC ensures that users and services have precisely the permissions they need–nothing more, nothing less. This structured approach enhances security, reduces administrative overhead, and aligns with enterprise governance policies.

Understanding RBAC in KubeVirt

RBAC is a policy-driven access control model that grants permissions, based on user roles rather than assigning permissions directly to individuals. This is particularly important in large-scale Kubernetes environments where multiple teams interact with virtualized workloads.

Core RBAC Components

- **`Roles` and `ClusterRoles`:** Define permissions within a namespace (Role) or cluster-wide (**`ClusterRole`**).
- **`RoleBindings` and `ClusterRoleBindings`:** Associate users, groups, or service accounts with **`Roles`** or **`ClusterRoles`**.
- **Subjects:** Users, groups, or service accounts assigned permissions.
- **Verbs:** Actions such as **`'get'`**, **`'list'`**, **`'create'`**, **`'delete'`**, and **`'patch'`**.
- **API Resources:** Objects like **`VirtualMachine`** (VM), **`VirtualMachineInstance`** (VMI), and **`PersistentVolumeClaim`** (PVC).

RBAC Implementation in KubeVirt

To implement RBAC for VMs in OpenShift Virtualization, administrators define **`Roles`** and **`RoleBindings`** that align with organizational policies.

Example 1: Defining a Role for VM Management

A cloud architect may want to create a Role allowing developers to start and stop VMs, but preventing them from deleting instances.

```
apiVersion: rbac.authorization.k8s.io/v1
kind: Role
metadata:
  name: vm-operator
  namespace: dev-vms
```

```
rules:
  - apiGroups: ["kubevirt.io"]
    resources: ["virtualmachines"]
    verbs: ["get", "list", "start", "stop"]
```

This **Role** grants developers' permissions to view and operate VMs, but restricts them from deletion or modification beyond start/stop actions. By default, the **Role** of cluster has been illustrated in the following diagram:

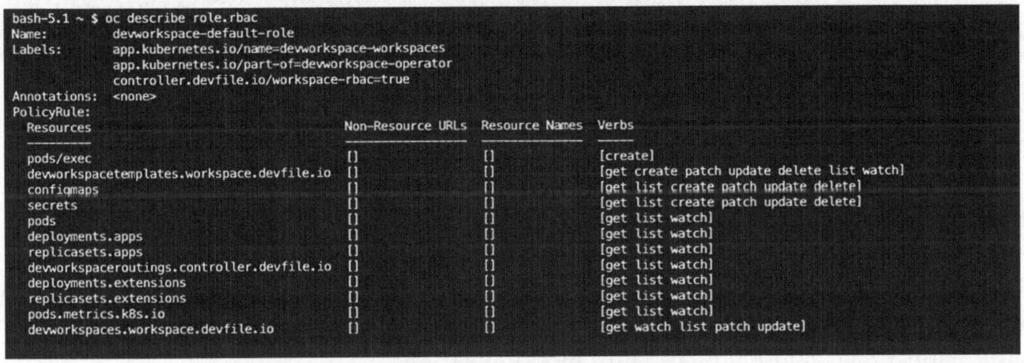

Figure 7.1: *Default Roles of OpenShift*

Example 2: Binding a Role to a User

Once the **Role** is defined, we need to assign it to a specific user or group using a **RoleBinding**:

```
apiVersion: rbac.authorization.k8s.io/v1
kind: RoleBinding
metadata:
  name: vm-operator-binding
  namespace: dev-vms
subjects:
  - kind: User
    name: developer1
    apiGroup: rbac.authorization.k8s.io
roleRef:
  kind: Role
  name: vm-operator
  apiGroup: rbac.authorization.k8s.io
```

This ensures that **deveoper1** can manage VMs within the **dev-vms** namespace, while following defined access restrictions.

Some of the default **RoleBindings** for **Openshift** cluster are listed as follows:

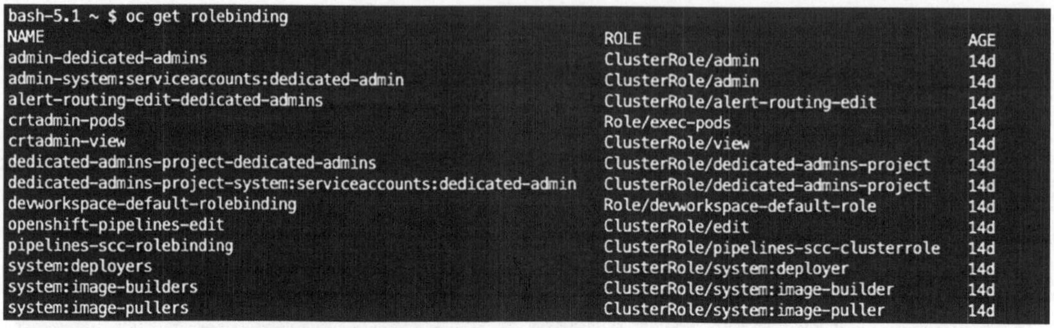

Figure 7.2: *Openshift Default Rolebinding*

Example 3: Cluster RoleBinding

Advanced RBAC Use Cases

Multi-Tenancy and Namespace Isolation: In multi-tenant environments, organizations need to restrict access to specific namespaces. This is accomplished using namespace-scoped **`Roles`** and **`RoleBindings`**.

Service Accounts for Automated VM Management: Instead of using human users, automation scripts and CI/CD pipelines can leverage service accounts bound to restricted roles.

```
apiVersion: v1
kind: ServiceAccount
metadata:
  name: vm-ci-bot
  namespace: ci-automation
```

Then, bind it to a **`Role`** allowing safe VM provisioning:

```
kind: RoleBinding
metadata:
  name: vm-ci-bot-binding
  namespace: ci-automation
subjects:
  - kind: ServiceAccount
    name: vm-ci-bot
    namespace: ci-automation
roleRef:
  kind: Role
  name: vm-creator
  apiGroup: rbac.authorization.k8s.io
```

Cluster-Wide VM Administrators: For platform engineers, who require permissions across multiple namespaces, a **ClusterRole** is more appropriate:

```
apiVersion: rbac.authorization.k8s.io/v1
kind: ClusterRole
metadata:
  name: vm-admin
rules:
  - apiGroups: ["kubevirt.io"]
    resources: ["virtualmachines", "virtualmachineinstances"]
    verbs: ["*"]
```

This **ClusterRole** provides unrestricted VM management capabilities across the entire OpenShift cluster.

Best Practices for RBAC in OpenShift Virtualization

To maintain security and efficiency, organizations should adhere to the following best practices:

1. **Follow the Principle of Least Privilege (PoLP):** Assign the minimum required permissions to each user, reducing the risk of unauthorized actions.
2. **Use Namespace-Based Roles:** Prevent accidental cross-namespace access by scoping roles appropriately.
3. **Leverage Groups Instead of Individual Users:** Simplify management by assigning roles to groups, rather than individual users.
4. **Audit and Review RBAC Policies Regularly:** Ensure that access controls align with the evolving organizational policies.
5. **Monitor and Log Access Events:** Use OpenShift logging and monitoring tools to track access patterns and detect anomalies.

Using SELinux and Seccomp Profiles for Enhanced Security

Security is a critical aspect of modern cloud environments, particularly when deploying virtualization solutions such as KubeVirt on OpenShift. With the increasing number of containerized workloads and virtualized applications, it is imperative to implement robust security mechanisms to prevent unauthorized access, privilege escalation, and system compromise. In this chapter, we explore how Security-

Enhanced Linux (SELinux) and Seccomp (Secure Computing Mode) profiles can be leveraged to strengthen security in KubeVirt-based deployments.

Introduction to SELinux and Seccomp

SELinux and Seccomp are two powerful security mechanisms used to enforce Mandatory Access Controls (MAC), and restrict system call access in Linux-based environments.

SELinux Overview

SELinux is a security module in the Linux kernel that provides fine-grained access controls by enforcing policies that define which actions users and processes can perform. Originally developed by the NSA, SELinux operates in three modes:

- **Enforcing:** Policies are actively enforced, and violations are blocked.
- **Permissive:** Violations are logged but not enforced, useful for debugging.
- **Disabled:** SELinux is turned off, making the system less secure.

Seccomp Overview

Seccomp is a kernel feature that limits the system calls a process can make, reducing the attack surface by restricting interactions with the kernel. It supports three modes:

- **Strict Mode:** Allows only read, write, exit, and `sigreturn` system calls.
- **Filter Mode:** Uses Berkeley Packet Filter (BPF) rules to selectively allow or deny system calls.
- **Disabled:** No restrictions are applied.

Thus, by combining SELinux and Seccomp, organizations can implement a defense-in-depth approach to security, ensuring that workloads are tightly controlled.

Real-World Use Cases

Implementing SELinux and Seccomp in KubeVirt environments provides tangible security benefits:

- **Preventing Unauthorized Resource Access:** SELinux ensures that KubeVirt pods and VMs do not access unauthorized files or directories.
- **Mitigating Kernel Exploits:** Seccomp prevents privilege escalation attacks by restricting unnecessary system calls.

- **Enhancing Multi-Tenancy Security:** By enforcing strict security contexts, cloud service providers can safely run multi-tenant workloads.

Configuring OpenShift Security Policies

Security is a critical aspect of any OpenShift deployment, especially when integrating KubeVirt for OpenShift Virtualization. OpenShift provides a robust security model that includes Role-Based Access Control (RBAC), Security Context Constraints (SCCs), network policies, and compliance enforcement mechanisms. This chapter delves into configuring OpenShift security policies to ensure a hardened cluster environment that aligns with enterprise security requirements.

OpenShift Cluster Access

Accessing an OpenShift cluster is a foundational operation that underpins nearly every lifecycle phase of application and infrastructure management—be it deploying KubeVirt virtual machines, configuring persistent storage, or orchestrating GitOps pipelines. Secure, efficient, and policy-driven access mechanisms are paramount in enterprise environments, where multi-tenancy, compliance, and observability are critical.

Overview of OpenShift Cluster Access

OpenShift builds on Kubernetes RBAC, and adds an opinionated security layer. Cluster access in OpenShift can be broadly categorized into three dimensions:

- **Authentication:** Identifying who is making the request.
- **Authorization:** Determining whether the authenticated identity is allowed to perform a specific action.
- **Access Pathways:** The interfaces used to interact with the cluster (CLI, web console, and APIs).

Real-World Use Case

Considering an enterprise managing both containerized workloads and VMs via KubeVirt. Different personas—DevOps engineers, VM admins, and platform SREs—require distinct levels of access. Efficient cluster access patterns ensure that each persona operates within their privilege scope, while maintaining operational security and auditability.

Authentication Mechanisms

OpenShift uses OAuth 2.0 tokens for authentication. When a user logs in via the web console or CLI (oc login), they are redirected to an OAuth server, integrated with an Identity Provider (IdP).

Supported IdPs include:

- LDAP/Active Directory
- GitHub/GitLab
- OpenID Connect (for example, Keycloak)
- Keystone
- Basic Authentication
- Request Header
- Google
- `HTPasswd` for local users (typically used for development)

```
identityProviders:
  - name: corp-ldap
    mappingMethod: claim
    type: LDAP
    ldap:
      url: "ldap://ldap.corp.com:389/ou=users,dc=corp,dc=com"
      bindDN: "cn=admin,dc=corp,dc=com"
      bindPassword:
        name: ldap-bind-password
      attributes:
        id: ["uid"]
        email: ["mail"]
        name: ["cn"]
```

This configuration is defined in the OAuth cluster resource which can be managed, using the `oc edit oauth` command.

CLI and Web Console Access

OpenShift CLI (oc): The oc command-line tool is a superset of kubectl, tailored for OpenShift. It allows administrators to manage resources, projects, RBAC, and cluster settings.

```
oc login --token=<OAuth_Token> --server=https://api.openshift.
example.com:6443
```

Tokens can be retrieved from the OpenShift web console or via API, and are usually short-lived for enhanced security.

Web Console: The web console provides a GUI-based access method, and is tightly integrated with authentication and RBAC. It allows for:

- Visualizing KubeVirt virtual machines
- Managing network policies and storage
- Accessing developer and administrator perspectives

The web console honors the same access controls as the CLI, enforcing consistency across interfaces.

Role-Based Access Control (RBAC)

RBAC governs permissions in an OpenShift cluster by defining which users or service accounts can perform specific actions on resources. The core components of RBAC include:

Roles and RoleBindings

Roles define permissions, while **`RoleBindings`** associate these roles with users or groups. OpenShift supports two types:

- **ClusterRoles:** Define permissions at the cluster level.
- **Roles:** Scoped to a specific namespace.

Example: Defining a `Role` and `RoleBinding` for a KubeVirt Administrator

```
apiVersion: rbac.authorization.k8s.io/v1
kind: Role
metadata:
  namespace: kubevirt
  name: kubevirt-admin
rules:
  - apiGroups: ["kubevirt.io"]
    resources: ["virtualmachines", "virtualmachineinstances"]
    verbs: ["get", "list", "create", "delete"]
---
apiVersion: rbac.authorization.k8s.io/v1
kind: RoleBinding
metadata:
  name: kubevirt-admin-binding
  namespace: kubevirt
subjects:
  - kind: User
    name: admin-user
    apiGroup: rbac.authorization.k8s.io
roleRef:
  kind: Role
```

```
    name: kubevirt-admin
    apiGroup: rbac.authorization.k8s.io
```

This configuration grants **admin-user** permissions to manage KubeVirt virtual machines within the **KubeVirt** namespace.

Security Context Constraints (SCCs)

SCCs define security policies for workloads, ensuring that pods run with appropriate privileges. OpenShift predefines several SCCs such as **restricted**, **anyuid**, and **privileged**.

Creating a Custom SCC for KubeVirt Workloads

```
apiVersion: security.openshift.io/v1
kind: SecurityContextConstraints
metadata:
  name: kubevirt-scc
allowPrivilegedContainer: false
runAsUser:
  type: MustRunAsRange
  uidRangeMin: 1000
  uidRangeMax: 2000
seLinuxContext:
  type: MustRunAs
fsGroup:
  type: MustRunAs
users:
  - system:serviceaccount:kubevirt:kubevirt-controller
```

This SCC restricts privileged execution, while ensuring that SELinux and file system policies are enforced.

Network Policies for Securing Virtualized Workloads

OpenShift uses **NetworkPolicy** resources to define how pods communicate. Network policies help secure KubeVirt workloads by isolating Virtual Machine Instances (VMIs) from unnecessary exposure.

Example: Restricting External Access to VMIs

```
apiVersion: networking.k8s.io/v1
kind: NetworkPolicy
metadata:
  name: restrict-vmi-access
  namespace: kubevirt
```

```
spec:
  podSelector:
    matchLabels:
      kubevirt.io: vmi
  policyTypes:
    - Ingress
  ingress:
    - from:
        - podSelector:
            matchLabels:
              app: frontend
      ports:
        - protocol: TCP
          port: 22
```

This policy ensures that only pods with the label **`app: frontend`** can communicate with VMIs over SSH (port 22).

Compliance and Auditing

Ensuring regulatory compliance is crucial for enterprises running OpenShift. This provides tools such as Compliance Operator and Audit Logs to enforce and track security policies.

Enabling the Compliance Operator

```
apiVersion: operators.coreos.com/v1alpha1
kind: Subscription
metadata:
  name: compliance-operator-sub
  namespace: openshift-compliance
spec:
  channel: stable
  name: compliance-operator
  source: redhat-operators
  sourceNamespace: openshift-marketplace
```

Once installed, the Compliance Operator scans the cluster against predefined security benchmarks such as CIS and NIST.

Auditing and Monitoring Virtual Machine Activity

In modern cloud-native environments, auditing and monitoring virtual machine activity is critical to ensuring security, compliance, and operational efficiency. KubeVirt, a Kubernetes-native virtualization solution, enables organizations to run VMs alongside containers, presenting unique challenges and opportunities for observability. This chapter delves into the methodologies, tools, and best practices for auditing and monitoring VM activity within OpenShift Virtualization powered by KubeVirt.

Importance of Auditing and Monitoring

Auditing and monitoring serve distinct but complementary roles:

- **Auditing** involves recording historical activities for compliance, forensic analysis, and anomaly detection.
- **Monitoring** focuses on real-time observability, detecting performance issues, and ensuring availability.

In regulated industries such as finance and healthcare, strict audit trails are necessary for compliance with standards like HIPAA and SOC 2. In high-availability environments, proactive monitoring ensures optimal resource utilization and uptime.

Logging VM Activity in KubeVirt

KubeVirt integrates seamlessly with Kubernetes logging mechanisms, allowing administrators to collect and analyze logs using:

- **Fluentd, Fluent Bit,** and **Logstash** for log aggregation.
- **Elasticsearch** and **Loki** for storage and querying.
- **Kibana** and **Grafana** for visualization.

Capturing VM Logs

KubeVirt VMs generate logs that can be retrieved, using `virtctl console` or `Kubernetes-native` logging commands:

```
kubectl logs -l kubevirt.io=virt-launcher -n <namespace>
```

These logs contain information about VM lifecycle events, disk activity, and network interactions.

Audit Logging for Security and Compliance

Kubernetes and OpenShift offer audit logging mechanisms that track API requests related to VM creation, deletion, modification, and access. To enable audit logging:

1. Configure the API server audit policy:

```
apiVersion: audit.k8s.io/v1
kind: Policy
```

```
rules:
  - level: RequestResponse
    resources:
    - group: kubevirt.io
      resources: ["virtualmachines", "virtualmachineinstances"]
```

2. Direct logs to a secure backend such as AWS CloudTrail, Azure Monitor, or an on-premises SIEM solution.
3. Set up alerts for unauthorized changes or unexpected VM operations.

Example: Detecting Unauthorized Access

Suppose an attacker gains unauthorized access to a KubeVirt VM, and modifies configurations. Audit logs will capture the API request metadata, including timestamps, user identities, and IP addresses. An alerting system integrated with Elasticsearch can flag anomalies, based on predefined security rules.

Monitoring VM Performance Metrics

KubeVirt exposes VM metrics via Prometheus, which can be visualized in Grafana. Key metrics include:

```
- CPU Usage: `kubevirt_vmi_vcpu_seconds_total`
- Memory Consumption: `kubevirt_vmi_memory_available_bytes`
- Disk I/O: `kubevirt_vmi_storage_read_traffic_bytes`
- Network Traffic: `kubevirt_vmi_network_receive_bytes_total`
```

Setting Up Prometheus for VM Monitoring

1. Deploy the Prometheus Operator in OpenShift:

   ```
   ```bash
   kubectl apply -f prometheus-operator.yaml
   ```

   https://operatorhub.io/operator/prometheus

2. Configure **ServiceMonitor** to scrape **KubeVirt** metrics:

   ```
   apiVersion: monitoring.coreos.com/v1
   kind: ServiceMonitor
   metadata:
     name: kubevirt-monitor
   spec:
     selector:
       matchLabels:
         prometheus.kubevirt.io: "true"
     endpoints:
     - port: metrics
   ```

3. Use Grafana dashboards to visualize trends and detect anomalies.
   ```

Example: Troubleshooting VM Performance

A sudden drop in **kubevirt_vmi_memory_available_bytes** indicates memory exhaustion, leading to potential OOM kills. Setting up alerts in Prometheus can notify administrators before service degradation.

Network Traffic Monitoring

KubeVirt relies on Kubernetes networking, making it crucial to monitor VM network activity. OpenShift provides:

- **Kubernetes Network Policies** to enforce traffic restrictions.
- **Service Mesh (Istio or OpenShift Service Mesh)** for enhanced observability.
- **eBPF-based tools like Cilium** for deep packet inspection.

Capturing Network Traffic Logs

Using **tcpdump** inside a VM:

```
kubectl exec -it <vm-pod> -- tcpdump -i eth0 -nn
```

Integrating Flow Logs with SIEM solutions enhances security monitoring.

Security Considerations

1. **Role-Based Access Control (RBAC):** Restricts access to VM logs and audit data.
2. **Encryption:** Ensure logs are encrypted at rest and in transit.
3. **Log Retention Policies:** Define appropriate retention periods, based on compliance requirements.

Kyverno: How It Can Help KubeVirt and OpenShift

Security and compliance are critical aspects of managing Kubernetes workloads, particularly in enterprise environments where regulatory requirements and organizational policies must be enforced. As OpenShift and KubeVirt enable virtualization within Kubernetes, ensuring policy adherence and workload security becomes even more vital. Kyverno, a policy engine designed for Kubernetes, provides a declarative way to enforce governance, security, and compliance policies within OpenShift and KubeVirt environments.

Kyverno is a Kubernetes-native policy engine that allows administrators to define and enforce policies, using Custom Resource Definitions (CRDs). Unlike traditional policy engines that require learning domain-specific languages (for example, Open Policy Agent's Rego), Kyverno leverages Kubernetes-native YAML constructs, making it intuitive for Kubernetes administrators and developers.

Key Features of Kyverno

- **Admission Control and Validation:** Enforces security and governance policies on Kubernetes objects at creation or modification.
- **Mutation:** Modifies Kubernetes resources dynamically to ensure compliance with predefined standards.
- **Generate Policies:** Automates resource creation, ensuring necessary configurations exist.
- **Policy Auditing and Reporting:** Monitors policy violations and provides compliance reporting.
- **Integration with Kubernetes-native RBAC and OpenShift Security Context Constraints (SCCs):** Enhances OpenShift and KubeVirt security configurations.

Applying Kyverno to KubeVirt

KubeVirt extends Kubernetes by enabling virtual machine workloads, and necessitating security policies beyond traditional container workloads. Kyverno can help enforce best practices in VM lifecycle management, security, and compliance.

1. **Enforcing VM Image Security:** Kyverno can validate and enforce the use of trusted VM images by defining policies that restrict unverified sources.

```
apiVersion: kyverno.io/v1
kind: ClusterPolicy
metadata:
  name: enforce-trusted-vm-images
spec:
  validationFailureAction: Enforce
  rules:
    - name: verify-vm-image-repo
      match:
        resources:
          kinds:
            - VirtualMachine
      validate:
        message: "Only images from trusted registry are allowed."
        pattern:
          spec:
            template:
              spec:
```

```
            domain:
              devices:
                disks:
                  - name: rootdisk
                    containerDisk:
                      image: "trusted-registry/*"
```

This policy ensures that only VM images from a trusted registry are deployed, preventing unauthorized workloads.

2. **Restricting VM Resource Consumption:** Administrators can enforce resource limits on virtual machines to prevent excessive CPU and memory consumption.

```
apiVersion: kyverno.io/v1
kind: ClusterPolicy
metadata:
  name: enforce-vm-resource-limits
spec:
  validationFailureAction: Enforce
  rules:
    - name: limit-vm-resources
      match:
        resources:
          kinds:
            - VirtualMachine
      validate:
        message: "VM resource requests must not exceed limits."
        pattern:
          spec:
            template:
              spec:
                domain:
                  resources:
                    requests:
                      cpu: "<=2"
                      memory: "<=4Gi"
```

This ensures fair resource allocation, and prevents resource exhaustion.

Enhancing OpenShift Security with Kyverno

OpenShift provides robust security features like Security Context Constraints (SCCs) and Role-Based Access Control (RBAC). Kyverno extends these capabilities with fine-grained policy enforcement.

Enforcing Network Policies

Kyverno can ensure that all deployed applications have predefined network policies, reducing the risk of unauthorized communication.

```
apiVersion: kyverno.io/v1
kind: ClusterPolicy
metadata:
  name: enforce-network-policies
spec:
  validationFailureAction: Enforce
  rules:
    - name: require-network-policy
      match:
        resources:
          kinds:
            - Pod
      validate:
        message: "All pods must have a NetworkPolicy."
        deny:
          conditions:
            - key: "{{request.object.metadata.namespace}}"
              operator: DoesNotHave
              value: networkPolicies
```

Enforcing OpenShift SCC Policies

Kyverno can validate that workloads comply with OpenShift's SCCs, ensuring that pods do not run with excessive privileges.

```
apiVersion: kyverno.io/v1
kind: ClusterPolicy
metadata:
  name: restrict-privileged-containers
spec:
  validationFailureAction: Enforce
  rules:
    - name: block-privileged-containers
      match:
        resources:
          kinds:
            - Pod
      validate:
        message: "Privileged containers are not allowed."
        pattern:
          spec:
```

```
          securityContext:
            privileged: "false"
```

Real-World Security Challenges and Solutions in KubeVirt and OpenShift Virtualization

As organizations adopt cloud-native architectures, securing virtualized workloads remains a top priority. KubeVirt extends Kubernetes to manage virtual machines alongside containers, but this introduces unique security challenges. OpenShift Virtualization, built on KubeVirt, provides an enterprise-grade solution, yet ensuring robust security across hybrid cloud environments that demand deep expertise. This chapter explores key security challenges in KubeVirt-based virtualization, and presents practical solutions.

Workload Isolation and Multi-Tenancy Risks

KubeVirt enables running VMs within Kubernetes clusters, but multi-tenancy introduces concerns over workload isolation. In shared environments, a compromised VM could exploit kernel vulnerabilities or leverage side-channel attacks (for example, Spectre, and Meltdown) to access the unauthorized data.

Solution: Kubernetes Namespace and SELinux Integration

- **Namespaces and RBAC (Role-Based Access Control):** Enforce strict namespace isolation to prevent unauthorized cross-tenant interactions.
- **SELinux and Seccomp:** Leverage SELinux policies and Seccomp profiles to restrict kernel-level access from VMs, and mitigate privilege escalation risks.
- **Pod Security Standards (PSS):** Adopt OpenShift's PSS to enforce secure workload configurations.

Network Security and East-West Traffic Protection

KubeVirt workloads rely on OpenShift networking, exposing them to threats such as lateral movement, ARP spoofing, and man-in-the-middle attacks.

Solution: NetworkPolicies and Service Mesh Security

- **Kubernetes NetworkPolicies:** Implement fine-grained controls to restrict inter-VM and pod communication based on security groups.
- **Istio Service Mesh:** Utilize Istio's mutual TLS (mTLS) to encrypt East-West traffic between workloads, ensuring data integrity and confidentiality.

- **Multus CNI for Isolated Networks:** Deploy Multus CNI to assign multiple interfaces per VM, and enforce network segmentation for security-sensitive workloads.

Storage Security and Data Protection

Storage in OpenShift Virtualization must be secured against unauthorized access and data breaches, particularly when dealing with Persistent Volumes (PVs) and block storage.

Solution: Encryption and Immutable Snapshots

- **Storage Encryption:** Enable in-transit and at-rest encryption, using OpenShift's support for LUKS and CSI-based encryption solutions.
- **Immutable Snapshots and Backup Policies:** Use OpenShift's Container Storage snapshots to create tamper-proof backups, preventing ransomware-induced data loss.
- **Data Integrity Monitoring:** Deploy OpenSCAP and AIDE to monitor file system integrity, and detect unauthorized modifications.

Supply Chain Security and Image Integrity

The increasing adoption of CI/CD pipelines for deploying VMs and containers introduces risks related to image tampering and software supply chain attacks.

Solution: Sigstore and Admission Control Policies

- **Sigstore and Cosign:** Implement Sigstore's Cosign to sign VM and container images, ensuring cryptographic verification before deployment.
- **Admission Controllers:** Use OpenShift's Gatekeeper (based on Open Policy Agent) to enforce security policies, preventing unverified images from running.
- **Continuous Scanning:** Integrate vulnerability scanners such as Trivy or Clair to assess VM images before deployment.

Identity and Access Management (IAM)

Managing authentication and authorization for virtualized workloads in OpenShift requires robust IAM mechanisms to prevent unauthorized access.

Solution: OpenID Connect and Fine-Grained RBAC

- **OpenID Connect (OIDC):** Integrate OpenShift authentication with enterprise IAM solutions like Keycloak, Okta, or Active Directory.
- **Fine-Grained RBAC:** Define granular roles and permissions for developers, operators, and security teams to enforce least privilege access.

- **Short-Lived Credentials:** Use OpenShift's service accounts with short-lived tokens to minimize the risk of credential compromise.

Best Practices for Securing OpenShift Virtualization

To mitigate real-world security threats, organizations should adopt the following best practices:

- **Zero Trust Architecture:** Implement Zero Trust principles by verifying every request, and enforcing least privilege access.
- **Compliance Automation:** Use OpenShift Compliance Operator to continuously assess security compliance against frameworks such as NIST, CIS, and PCI-DSS.
- **Audit Logging and Threat Detection:** Enable OpenShift Audit Logs, and integrate with SIEM solutions (for example, Splunk, Elastic Security) for real-time threat detection.
- **Security Patch Management:** Automate patching of KubeVirt, OpenShift, and underlying Linux systems to minimize exposure to known vulnerabilities.
- **Red Teaming and Penetration Testing:** Conduct periodic security assessments to identify gaps, and harden defenses against evolving threats.

Conclusion

Security and compliance are critical aspects of any cloud-native infrastructure, particularly in environments like Kubernetes. This chapter emphasized the importance of implementing robust security frameworks, ensuring compliance with industry standards, and leveraging automated tools to monitor vulnerabilities. By adopting the best practices such as Role-Based Access Control (RBAC), network policies, and regular audits, organizations can enhance their security posture, while maintaining compliance with the evolving regulations.

Ultimately, a proactive approach to security and compliance is essential for minimizing risks, and ensuring the resilience of cloud environments. As threats continue to evolve, businesses must remain vigilant, continuously updating their security strategies and leveraging innovations like zero-trust architectures and AI-driven threat detection. By embedding security into every layer of their cloud-native infrastructure, organizations can achieve both operational efficiency and regulatory adherence. Building on this foundation, the next chapter explores how GitOps principles can be applied to OpenShift Virtualization with KubeVirt—demonstrating how automation not only streamlines VM lifecycle management, but also reinforces consistent security and compliance across hybrid and multi-cloud environments.

The next chapter explores how GitOps revolutionizes VM lifecycle management in OpenShift Virtualization by applying declarative, automated, and version-controlled workflows, using tools such as Argo CD and Flux, enhancing consistency, scalability, and operational efficiency.

CHAPTER 8
Automating Virtualization with GitOps

Introduction

Automating Virtualization with GitOps represents a transformative approach in modern infrastructure management, particularly within the context of OpenShift Virtualization powered by KubeVirt. As the complexity of Virtual Machine (VM) lifecycles grows in hybrid and multi-cloud environments, GitOps principles provide a declarative, version-controlled, and automated methodology for provisioning, configuring, and managing VMs. Leveraging Git as the single source of truth enables infrastructure changes to be auditable, reproducible, and consistent across environments. This paradigm shift not only aligns virtualization workflows with the broader DevOps ecosystem, but also enforces a disciplined, code-centric model for managing stateful workloads that traditionally relied on manual operations.

In this chapter, we delve into how GitOps principles can be systematically applied to VM lifecycle management, using tools such as Argo CD and Flux, tightly integrated with OpenShift Pipelines and CI/CD systems. We explore managing VM configurations as declarative code, automating deployments and updates through pipelines, maintaining cluster consistency, and ensuring reliable promotion of virtualized workloads across staging and production. Additionally, we address operational challenges such as drift detection, rollback strategies, and troubleshooting GitOps workflows, specific to KubeVirt resources. Real-world use cases and architectural patterns are presented to illustrate how automation can reduce operational overhead, while increasing agility, security, and scalability in virtualized Kubernetes environments.

Structure

In this chapter, we will cover the following topics:

- Introduction to GitOps for Virtualization
- Managing VM Configurations with GitOps Tools
- Automating Deployment and Updates Using Pipelines
- Maintaining Consistency across Clusters
- CI/CD Integration for Virtualized Workloads
- Troubleshooting GitOps Automation Issues

Introduction to GitOps for Virtualization

In the evolution of cloud-native infrastructure management, GitOps has emerged as a paradigm shift—redefining how we approach application delivery, infrastructure operations, and environment consistency. For virtualized workloads, especially within OpenShift clusters leveraging KubeVirt, GitOps presents a significant opportunity to manage virtual machines with the same rigor and automation as Kubernetes-native workloads. In this section, we will explore GitOps in the context of virtualization, the specific benefits and architectural patterns it introduces, and how it aligns with enterprise-grade requirements such as compliance, auditability, and multi-tenancy.

Defining GitOps in the Context of KubeVirt and OpenShift

GitOps, at its core, is an operational model where Git acts as the single source of truth for declarative infrastructure and application definitions. Changes to the system are made by pull requests to Git repositories which are then reconciled by a GitOps controller—typically Argo CD or Flux—running within the Kubernetes control plane.

When applying GitOps to virtualization via KubeVirt, the model extends beyond Pods, Deployments, and Services to include **`VirtualMachine`** (VM), **`VirtualMachineInstance`** (VMI), DataVolume, and related Custom Resource Definitions (CRDs). Each of these artifacts can be stored as YAML manifests within a Git repository, version-controlled, and promoted across environments using GitOps principles.

Through GitOps, provisioning this VM in a test, staging, or production OpenShift cluster becomes a matter of merging a pull request. The desired state is automatically reconciled with the cluster state by a GitOps controller.

Advantages of GitOps for Virtualization Workloads

GitOps streamlines virtualization management by enabling declarative VM configurations and automated deployments through Git, ensuring consistency and traceability. It also simplifies rollback and recovery, reducing downtime during infrastructure changes.

- **Declarative Infrastructure for Virtual Machines:** By treating VM specifications as code, GitOps enables full lifecycle management through declarative configuration. This significantly reduces the chances of configuration drift—a problem historically prevalent in virtual machine management through imperative methods such as CLI or GUI tools.
- **Auditable, Version-Controlled VM Changes:** Git history provides an immutable audit trail of every VM creation, modification, or deletion. When dealing with regulated industries such as finance, healthcare, or government, GitOps brings clarity and traceability to virtualization workflows, making compliance easier to enforce.
- **Environment Parity and Promotion Pipelines:** Using Git branches to model environments (for example, `dev`, `staging`, `prod`), GitOps enables safe and consistent promotion of VM definitions across clusters. For instance, a test VM can be modified in the `dev` branch, validated by automated CI tests, and later promoted to production by merging into the `prod` branch.
- **Drift Detection and Auto-Reconciliation:** GitOps operators constantly compare the live state of the OpenShift cluster with the declared state in Git. If any unauthorized or manual change is detected—such as a VM being manually powered off—it is automatically reconciled to match the Git state, enhancing reliability and compliance.

GitOps Architecture for KubeVirt on OpenShift

A typical GitOps architecture for OpenShift Virtualization includes:

- **Git Repository:** Stores VM definitions, DataVolume templates, `NetworkAttachmentDefinitions`, and associated Kubernetes manifests.
- **Argo CD:** The preferred GitOps operator for OpenShift, responsible for syncing the declared state in Git with the actual state in the cluster.
- **KubeVirt CRDs:** Extended Kubernetes resources that define and manage VMs, VMIs, and associated storage and networking.
- **CI Pipeline (Optional):** Validates VM YAML syntax, security rules, and policies, before merging into main branches.

The GitOps pipeline can be visualized as:

- **Developer** modifies VM configuration in Git (for example, updates memory from 4Gi to 8Gi).
- **Pull Request** is submitted and reviewed.
- **CI Workflow** validates YAML, and applies policies (for example, limit max CPU/memory).
- **Merge** triggers Argo CD to apply changes.
- **Argo CD Syncs** the OpenShift cluster to the desired state.

Real-World Use Case: DevSecOps for VMs in a Financial Institution

Consider a financial institution using KubeVirt to host legacy middleware services as virtual machines within an OpenShift cluster. Each VM hosts proprietary applications with strict security, and change control requirements.

By adopting GitOps:

- VM configurations are defined in Git, and each update undergoes mandatory code review and validation.
- Environments are modeled as separate branches (`Sandbox`, `qa`, `uat`, `prod`), ensuring controlled promotion.
- A security policy enforces that no VM can request more than 8 vCPUs or run with privileged access–validated during CI linting.
- Argo CD ensures no manual tampering with the VM state, restoring VMs to the desired configuration automatically, if drift is detected.

This model dramatically reduces Mean Time to Recover (MTTR), enforces consistency, and passes security audits more easily than traditional VM management.

Integrating Persistent Volumes and DataVolumes into GitOps

Unlike stateless workloads, virtual machines often require persistent storage. KubeVirt uses DataVolume and `PersistentVolumeClaim` (PVC) resources–typically integrated with Container Storage Interface (CSI) drivers on OpenShift.

The GitOps controller ensures that the appropriate image is pulled, the volume is created, and the VM is ready to boot, without any manual steps.

Best Practices for GitOps-Based Virtualization:

- **Template Reusability:** Parameterize VM definitions using tools such as Kustomize or Helm to manage variations (for example, memory sizes and OS types) across environments.
- **Git Repository Hygiene:** Use directory structures such as `clusters/<env>/vm/<vm-name>.yaml` to separate concerns, and maintain clarity.
- **Policy-as-Code:** Integrate Open Policy Agent (OPA) or Kyverno for security and compliance validation.
- **Change Windows:** Use sync windows in Argo CD to restrict automatic reconciliation during sensitive business hours.
- **Alerting and Monitoring:** Configure alerts for out-of-sync states or failed VM reconciliations to respond quickly to drift or deployment issues.

Extending GitOps to Multi-Cloud and vCluster Deployments

As organizations need to adopt multi-cluster strategies using technologies such as vCluster, vNode or Advanced Cluster Management (ACM), the role of GitOps will expand to support multi-tenant and hybrid workloads. For instance, virtual machines running on edge clusters can be centrally managed via Git repositories, and promoted through policy gates.

Combining GitOps with KubeVirt positions OpenShift as a unified control plane for containerized and virtualized workloads–bridging the gap between traditional IT operations and modern cloud-native principles.

Managing VM Configurations with GitOps Tools

In a production-grade virtualization strategy using OpenShift and KubeVirt, managing virtual machine configurations efficiently is paramount. The shift toward declarative infrastructure and operations has made GitOps not just viable but essential for consistent, repeatable, and auditable VM deployments. In this section, we will explore how GitOps tools can be leveraged to manage VM configurations in an OpenShift Virtualization environment, aligning with the overarching theme of automation, compliance, and scalability in modern hybrid cloud platforms.

Declarative VM Management with KubeVirt

KubeVirt allows the creation of VirtualMachine (VM) and **`VirtualMachineInstance`** (VMI) custom resources in a declarative manner. Unlike traditional hypervisor-based environments, where VM state and configuration are often modified through imperative interfaces (GUI or CLI), KubeVirt enables defining a VM as a Kubernetes YAML object.

GitOps Principles Applied to VM Lifecycle Management

The core GitOps principles–declarative configuration, version control, automated reconciliation, and observability–are directly applicable to VM lifecycle management. Tools such as Argo CD and FluxCD act as GitOps agents that continuously reconcile the state defined in Git with the actual state in the OpenShift cluster.

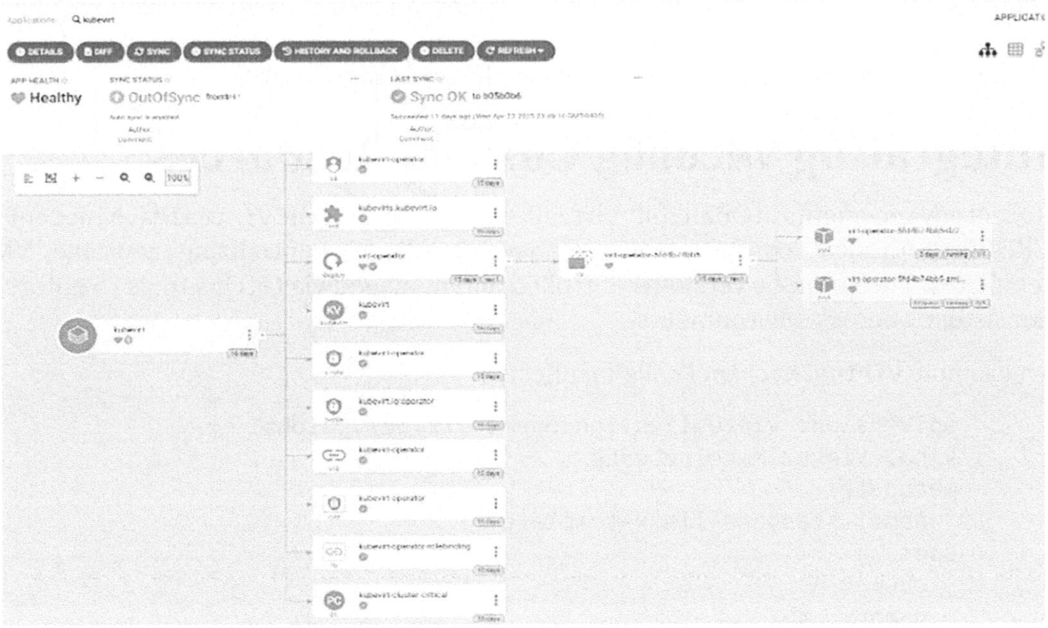

Figure 8.1: *KubeVirt Deployment Using Argocd*

- **Git as the Source of Truth:** By maintaining VM YAML definitions in a Git repository, infrastructure teams can review, audit, and approve changes through pull requests. This ensures that configuration drift is minimized, and compliance policies can be enforced at the code level.
- **Automated Reconciliation:** Argo CD, for instance, watches for changes in the Git repository, and applies them to the cluster. If a manual change occurs

outside Git, Argo CD flags the drift and, depending on the policy, reverts the change or raises an alert.

Real-World Example

Consider a scenario where an enterprise manages hundreds of VMs for multiple development teams. Each team maintains its VM manifested in a dedicated GitOps folder structure:

```
vm-configs/
├── team-a/
│   └── centos-vm.yaml
├── team-b/
│   └── ubuntu-vm.yaml
└── team-c/
    └── windows-vm.yaml
```

Argo CD applications are configured per team, pointing to their respective paths. This allows scoped access, independent release cycles, and RBAC-aligned isolation. When a team updates the VM specification (example, memory size or base image), the Git change triggers a rollout, without requiring cluster-admin intervention.

Integrating `VMConfig` Custom Resources

Recent advancements in OpenShift Virtualization introduce the **`VirtualMachineConfig`** CRD (hypothetical or future-planned) which allows centralizing reusable VM templates. These can be version-controlled and managed via GitOps tools to enforce consistency across environments.

An example **`VirtualMachineConfig`** manifest:

```
apiVersion: virtualization.openshift.io/v1alpha1
kind: VirtualMachineConfig
metadata:
  name: standard-linux-template
spec:
  cpu: 2
  memory: 4Gi
  diskImage: quay.io/containerdisks/ubuntu
  cloudInit:
    userData: |
      #cloud-config
      password: passw0rd
      chpasswd: {expire: False }
```

Teams can reference this config in their VM definitions, enabling the separation of configuration concerns. Updates to the base template propagate via GitOps pipelines, enhancing reusability and governance.

GitOps Pipelines for VM Deployments

While GitOps tools such as Argo CD ensure state reconciliation, incorporating CI/CD pipelines (for example, Tekton, Jenkins, and GitHub Actions) enables validation, security scanning, and templating logic before committing to Git. A sample pipeline may include the following stages:

1. **Validation:** Use **`kubeval`** or **`kubectl apply --dry-run=client`** to validate VM manifests.
2. **Security Checks:** Integrate tools such as **`Trivy`** or **`kube-bench`** to scan images and configurations.
3. **Parameter Substitution:** Need to use tools such as **`Kustomize`** or **`Helm`** to templatize configurations for different environments (**`dev/test/prod`**).
4. **Commit and Push:** Approved and validated manifests are committed to the GitOps repo, including considering the **`master/main`** branch.

This automation pipeline ensures that only compliant, secure, and tested configurations are deployed.

Secrets and SSH Keys Management

Managing secrets such as cloud-init passwords, SSH public keys, or license tokens within Git repositories is a security risk. GitOps platforms can be integrated with secret management solutions such as:

- **External Secrets Operator:** Syncs secrets from external stores (for example, AWS Secrets Manager, HashiCorp Vault) into Kubernetes.
- **Sealed Secrets (Bitnami):** Encrypts secrets before committing to Git, decrypting only inside the cluster with a private key.

This ensures that VM credentials and sensitive configurations are handled securely, without breaking GitOps workflows.

Observability and Auditing

One of the often-overlooked aspects of GitOps-based VM configuration is observability. Integrating Prometheus, Grafana, and Elasticsearch-Fluentd-Kibana (EFK) stacks provides visibility into VM events, resource usage, and reconciliation loops. Argo CD itself exposes rich metrics on sync status, drift detection, and deployment history.

Moreover, Git histories act as an immutable audit trail. Every change to a VM configuration is attributable, timestamped, and reversible–critical for regulated environments such as finance, healthcare, or government.

Challenges and Best Practices

While GitOps offers a robust approach to VM configuration management, it introduces several challenges such as:

- **Template Sprawl:** Excessive use of YAML manifests can become hard to manage. We can use abstraction tools such as Kustomize or Helm.
- **State Management:** VM states (for example, running versus stopped) can be difficult to manage declaratively. Consider separating the config state from the operational state.
- **Coordination with Other Resources:** VM configurations often depend on network policies, storage classes, or node selectors. These must be managed alongside VM manifests.

Best Practices:

- Enforce code reviews for all Git changes.
- Use labels and annotations for searchability and automation hooks.
- Tag Git commits with release identifiers.
- Regularly test drift detection and reconciliation policies.

Automating Deployment and Updates Using Pipelines

In any modern infrastructure paradigm that embraces GitOps, pipelines serve as the essential engine for automating deployment workflows and software delivery processes. With OpenShift Virtualization and KubeVirt, the scope of pipelines extends beyond containerized workloads to include virtual machine images, manifests, lifecycle updates, and integration testing. This section will focus on how to design, implement, and optimize automated pipelines for managing virtualized workloads within an OpenShift GitOps environment, using real-world scenarios and best practices grounded in enterprise architecture.

Understanding the Pipeline Philosophy in GitOps-Driven Virtualization

At the heart of the GitOps methodology is the concept of declarative state. All infrastructure, including VMs, storage, and networking, is codified in Git repositories, and treated as immutable source-of-truth artifacts. Pipelines are the agents that interpret, validate, and apply this declarative state to the cluster. They monitor changes, enforce policy gates, and ensure continuous reconciliation of infrastructure with its desired configuration.

In OpenShift, Tekton Pipelines is the de facto pipeline engine for orchestrating CI/CD tasks. It is fully Kubernetes-native, and integrates seamlessly with Red Hat OpenShift Pipelines, GitOps (Argo CD), and other OpenShift components. When paired with KubeVirt, pipelines enable complete automation of VM builds, image distribution, configuration injection, testing, and rollout–all without manual intervention.

Architectural Design of Virtualization Pipelines

To manage virtual machines in a GitOps-centric environment, pipelines must be architected with the following stages:

1. **Source Control Integration**
    a. Connect to Git repositories containing the KubeVirt VM manifests, **`cloud-init`** configurations, and associated resources.
    b. Monitor changes through Git webhooks or polling mechanisms.
2. **Validation and Policy Enforcement**
    a. Lint and validate the manifest structure, using tools such as **`kubeval`**, **`kustomize build`**, or **`oc apply --dry-run`**.
    b. Integrate Open Policy Agent (OPA) or Kyverno to validate resource-level policies (for example, disallow privileged VM workloads).
3. **Image Build and Distribution**
    a. For container-based VM images (for example, **`ContainerDisk`**), build using Kaniko or **`Buildah`** inside the pipeline.
    b. Push images to a trusted internal registry.
4. **Configuration Management**
    a. Dynamically generate cloud-init YAML, based on environment or Git branches.
    b. Encrypt secrets using **`SealedSecrets`** or SOPS, before injecting them.

5. **Deployment to OpenShift with KubeVirt**
    a. Use `oc apply`, `kubectl`, or Argo CD to deploy VM resources.
    b. Tag environments with labels to control where VMs are scheduled (for example, `nodeSelector: kubernetes.io/hostname=infra-node-1`).
6. **Testing and Verification**
    a. Run post-deployment health checks on the VMs (for example, via SSH or serial console access).
    b. Confirm readiness probes, guest agent availability, and `cloud-init` completion.
7. **Promotion and Rollback**
    a. Use Git branches to promote VMs from `dev` → `staging` → `prod`.
    b. Allow rollback through Git revert, and re-triggered pipeline execution.

Real-World Example: Automating a Windows VM Rollout

Consider an enterprise banking application that relies on a legacy Windows-based workload. A pipeline designed to manage its lifecycle might look as follows:

1. **Git Push Trigger:** Developer updates the Windows VM manifest in the `windows-vms` Git repository.
2. **Tekton Trigger:** The webhook triggers a Tekton pipeline that runs:
    a. YAML schema validation with `kubeval`.
    b. Checks for licensing compliance annotations.
3. **Image Verification:** The pipeline verifies the integrity of the Windows container disk image from Quay.io or the internal registry.
4. **Deployment:** Applies the updated `VirtualMachine` object to the OpenShift Virtualization namespace.
5. **Testing:**
    a. Verifies if the VM boots using guest-agent health checks.
    b. Tests application port availability using `nmap` or a test container pod.
6. **Notification:** Sends status to Slack, and updates Git commit status via GitHub API.

This declarative, event-driven pipeline architecture replaces manual provisioning with a repeatable and auditable automation layer.

Leveraging Tekton and Argo CD for Full Lifecycle Automation

OpenShift Pipelines (Tekton) and Argo CD form a powerful GitOps control loop. Tekton handles the operational orchestration–building, transforming, and validating manifests–while Argo CD performs continuous reconciliation.

The following pattern enables the separation of responsibilities:

- **Tekton Pipelines:** Triggered by Git changes, Tekton updates the appropriate GitOps repository (for example, **`vm-deployments/overlays/prod`**) with new manifests or configurations.
- **Argo CD:** Watches the GitOps repository, and applies the changes to the OpenShift cluster. It ensures drift correction, and enforces idempotency.

By decoupling the transformation and deployment responsibilities, teams can modularize their workflows. This pattern enables security and operations teams to control deployment gates, while developers focus on workload definition.

Version Control and Environment Promotion

The promotion of virtualized workloads across environments must be as disciplined as containerized deployments. This is especially critical for regulatory compliance, disaster recovery, and release traceability.

Git branching strategies such as GitFlow or trunk-based development can be adapted for VM pipelines. Each branch maps to a target environment:

- `main: production`
- `develop: staging`
- `feature/*: developer sandbox`

Promotions occur through Git merges, not direct **`kubectl`** commands. For example:

```
git checkout develop
git merge feature/win10-fix
git push
```

This triggers the pipeline to build and validate, and then updates the manifests in the **`develop`** environment overlay. Argo CD reconciles the state, and the VM is automatically provisioned in the staging cluster segment.

Rollback is as simple as reverting the merge commit:

```
git revert -m 1 <merge-commit-sha>
```

Such traceable automation enhances change control, auditability, and system integrity.

Secure Handling of Secrets and VM Configuration

Many virtualization pipelines must inject configuration data such as administrator passwords, license keys, or `cloud-init` SSH keys. Managing these secrets securely is paramount.

Best Practices for Secret Injection in Pipelines:

- **Use Encrypted Secrets in Git:** Tools such as Mozilla SOPS or `Bitnami SealedSecrets` enable storing encrypted secrets in Git, while keeping the pipeline declarative.
- **Avoid Plaintext in Pipelines:** Inject secrets as Kubernetes environment variables or mounted secrets from HashiCorp Vault via External Secrets Operator.
- **Dynamic Configuration for VMs:** `Cloud-init` allows the injection of metadata and scripts at runtime. Store `user-data` and `meta-data` in Git, and dynamically render them using templates such as `kustomize configMapGenerator`.

Example: Injecting a Cloud-Init SSH Key

1. Encrypt the SSH public key using SOPS.
2. Commit the encrypted `user-data.yaml` to the GitOps repo.
3. Tekton pipeline decrypts the file, and stores it in a ConfigMap.
4. The `VirtualMachine` manifest references this ConfigMap.

```
spec:
  template:
    spec:
      volumes:
        - name: cloudinitdisk
          cloudInitNoCloud:
            userDataSecretRef:
              name: win10-userdata
```

This approach avoids embedding sensitive values in pipeline definitions, while enabling per-environment configuration.

Monitoring, Observability, and Pipeline Resilience

As the automation fabric becomes more complex, visibility into pipeline execution and reconciliation becomes critical. OpenShift provides out-of-the-box observability tools that integrate with pipeline workflows:

- **Tekton Dashboard:** Visual interface to monitor step-level status, logs, and artifacts.
- **Prometheus + Grafana:** Capture custom metrics such as pipeline latency, failure rate, and stage durations.
- **Alertmanager:** Notify teams on failed deployments or stuck VMs.
- **Argo CD App Health:** Monitor the **sync** status of virtual machines as Kubernetes resources.

Pipeline definitions should include retry strategies, timeouts, and circuit breakers to handle transient errors. For example:

```
retries: 3
timeout: "10m"
```

This ensures that pipelines remain resilient under network interruptions or API server load.

Maintaining Consistency across Clusters

As organizations adopt hybrid and multi-cloud strategies, the need to maintain consistency across multiple Kubernetes and OpenShift clusters becomes critical. This requirement intensifies when managing virtualization workloads using KubeVirt, where the implications of misalignment in infrastructure, configuration, or policy can result in severe operational inefficiencies, increased costs, or even system outages. In this section, we will explore how consistency can be maintained across clusters using GitOps principles and tooling, with a focus on KubeVirt workloads deployed on OpenShift.

The Challenge of Multi-Cluster Consistency

In traditional IT operations, maintaining consistency across environments often relies on manual processes, configuration scripts, and periodic audits. However, in a modern, declarative, and container-native world, these approaches no longer scale. Consider the following practical challenges:

- **Configuration Drift:** Differences in manifests or CRDs across clusters can lead to unpredictable behavior.

- **Policy Divergence:** RBAC policies, network configurations, and security contexts can vary.
- **Image and Resource Disparity:** Inconsistent container images, virtual machine templates, or resource quotas can break deployments.
- **Operational Complexity:** Managing many clusters manually introduces human errors, and increases Mean Time to Recovery (MTTR).

To address these challenges, a GitOps-driven approach offers a scalable and auditable way to manage infrastructure and workloads across clusters.

GitOps as the Foundation for Consistency

GitOps applies DevOps practices to infrastructure and cluster management by using Git as the single source of truth. It uses declarative configuration files stored in Git repositories to define the desired state of a system. Continuous reconciliation is achieved through GitOps operators such as ArgoCD or Flux, which compare the live state of a cluster with the desired state in Git, and reconcile any differences.

For multi-cluster consistency, GitOps provides the following benefits:

- **Version Control and Auditability:** All changes are tracked via Git history.
- **Repeatability:** Identical configurations can be applied across clusters.
- **Rollback and Recovery:** Easy to revert to a known good state.
- **Automation:** GitOps operators ensure that the actual state continuously aligns with the desired state.

Architecture for Multi-Cluster Consistency with KubeVirt

When integrating KubeVirt into a GitOps architecture across multiple OpenShift clusters, the architecture should typically include:

- A **centralized Git repository** containing declarative definitions for KubeVirt CRDs, VMs, templates, network configurations, and RBAC policies.
- **ArgoCD `ApplicationSets`** or Flux multi-cluster agents that deploy and reconcile configuration across clusters.
- **Cluster-specific overlays** using tools such as Kustomize or Helm to manage environment-specific values.
- **Secrets management** integrated with GitOps pipelines using tools such as Sealed Secrets, External Secrets Operator, or Vault.

For example, a Git repository might be structured as follows:

```
├── clusters/
│   ├── us-east-1/
│   │   ├── kubevirt/
│   │   └── virtualmachines/
│   ├── us-east-2/
│   │   ├── kubevirt/
│   │   └── virtualmachines/
├── base/
│   ├── kubevirt/
│   └── virtualmachines/
├── overlays/
│   ├── dev/
│   └── prod/
```

Using this structure, ArgoCD **`ApplicationSets`** can instantiate the appropriate overlays per cluster, ensuring consistent but environment-aware deployments.

Managing KubeVirt-Specific Resources

Maintaining consistency is particularly critical for KubeVirt resources which include Custom Resource Definitions (CRDs) such as **`VirtualMachine`**, **`VirtualMachineInstance`**, **`VirtualMachinePreset`**, and **`VirtualMachineTemplate`**. Misalignments in these definitions across clusters can cause workloads to fail or behave differently. To address this:

- **Store CRDs and Templates in Git:** Ensure all VM templates, presets, and other KubeVirt resources are version-controlled.
- **Define Base and Overlay Layers:** Use base manifests for common configuration and overlays to inject cluster-specific settings (for example, storage class, node selectors).
- **Standardize Labels and Annotations:** Consistent use of labels helps with observability, automation, and troubleshooting.
- **Align `ResourceQuotas` and `LimitRanges`:** Virtualization workloads are resource-intensive. Enforce consistent resource policies to avoid over- or under-provisioning.

Real-World Example: Deploying a Windows VM across Two Clusters

Suppose, we want to deploy the same Windows virtual machine on both **`cluster-east`** and **`cluster-west`** using GitOps. We would define a base VM template in the repository under **base/virtualmachines/windows-vm.yaml**, and apply overlays for each cluster with environment-specific settings:

```
apiVersion: kubevirt.io/v1
kind: VirtualMachine
metadata:
  name: windows-vm
spec:
  running: false
  template:
    metadata:
      labels:
        kubevirt.io/domain: windows-vm
    spec:
      domain:
        devices:
          disks:
          - name: rootdisk
            disk:
              bus: virtio
        resources:
          requests:
            memory: 8Gi
            cpu: "4"
      volumes:
      - name: rootdisk
        containerDisk:
          image: quay.io/containerdisks/windows10:latest
```

Each cluster's overlay might define the storage class and node selectors:

```
# overlays/cluster-east/virtualmachines/kustomization.yaml
resources:
  - ../../base/virtualmachines/windows-vm.yaml
patchesStrategicMerge:
  - patch-storage.yaml

# overlays/cluster-east/virtualmachines/patch-storage.yaml
apiVersion: kubevirt.io/v1
kind: VirtualMachine
metadata:
  name: windows-vm
spec:
  template:
    spec:
      nodeSelector:
        region: east
      volumes:
```

```
          - name: rootdisk
            persistentVolumeClaim:
              claimName: windows-rootdisk-east
```

Using ArgoCD ApplicationSets, these overlays can be continuously synchronized with the target clusters.

Synchronizing RBAC and Cluster Policies

RBAC roles and security policies often drift in multi-cluster environments, particularly when clusters are owned by different teams or span different regions or clouds. To maintain alignment:

- Define RBAC policies in Git, segmented by function (for example, admins, devs, ops).
- Use Kubernetes **ClusterRoleBindings** and **RoleBindings** to enforce access control.
- Reconcile policies via GitOps operators to avoid manual changes.
- Integrate with identity providers using SSO for consistency in authentication.

A typical RBAC manifest might look like:

```
apiVersion: rbac.authorization.k8s.io/v1
kind: ClusterRole
metadata:
  name: kubevirt-vm-admin
rules:
  - apiGroups: ["kubevirt.io"]
        resources: ["virtualmachines"]
        verbs: ["create", "delete", "get", "list", "watch",
"update"]
```

Ensure that such roles are identically defined and bound in each cluster by syncing them from Git.

CI/CD Integration for Virtualized Workloads

As organizations increasingly adopt containerized infrastructure on Kubernetes platforms such as OpenShift, the need to seamlessly integrate virtualized workloads into their CI/CD pipelines becomes paramount. This section delves into the architecture, tooling, and implementation patterns required to enable Continuous Integration and Continuous Deployment (CI/CD) for virtual machines managed via KubeVirt within OpenShift. By extending GitOps principles to VMs, platform teams can standardize and automate the entire lifecycle of hybrid workloads, ensuring consistency, reproducibility, and operational efficiency.

Architectural Considerations

CI/CD pipelines for virtualized workloads must accommodate both stateless container images and stateful VM artifacts. Unlike container images that can be easily pushed to, and pulled from registries, virtual machine disk images (PVC-backed or `containerDisk`) involve more stateful infrastructure, and require careful handling.

An effective CI/CD design for KubeVirt-based virtualization includes the following components:

- **Version-Controlled Infrastructure Definitions:** VM definitions (example, `VirtualMachine`, `DataVolume`, and `VirtualMachineInstance`) stored in Git repositories.
- **Pipeline Orchestrator:** Tekton or Jenkins X integrated with OpenShift Pipelines to trigger build and deployment jobs.
- **Image Build and Storage:** Use of tools such as `virt-builder`, `packer`, or `qemu-img` to build VM disk images, stored in container registries or ObjectStorage-backed PVCs.
- **GitOps Controllers:** Argo CD or Flux continuously monitors the Git repository, and syncs VM workloads to the OpenShift cluster.
- **Artifact Repositories:** Persistent artifact stores (for example, S3, Nexus, or Quay) for storing VM images and cloud-init scripts.

Pipeline Design Patterns

Image-Building Pipelines: Image-building pipelines are designed to generate VM disk images from base OS templates, apply configuration through `cloud-init`, and publish the result as a container image or `DataVolumeTemplate`.

Example: A Tekton pipeline triggered on changes to a Git branch containing VM image configurations might perform the following steps:

1. Clone the Git repo containing OS and cloud-init specs.
2. Build the VM image using `packer`, and output it to a raw disk image.
3. Can be converted, and containerize the image using `qemu-img`.
4. Push the `containerDisk` image to an internal registry.
5. Update the `VirtualMachine` manifest in Git with the new image reference.

This process ensures repeatable and versioned VM images that are a part of the CI process.

VM Deployment Pipelines: VM deployment pipelines handle the instantiation and lifecycle management of virtual machines, based on GitOps changes.

Example: Upon merging a pull request modifying a **`VirtualMachine`** manifest, the GitOps controller (example, Argo CD) picks up the change and applies it to the OpenShift cluster. Tekton tasks can be configured to validate the manifest using **`kubeval`**, and enforce policy compliance using **`OPA Gatekeeper`**, before the deployment proceeds.

This setup ensures that all deployments are pre-validated, and conform to organizational standards.

Operations Pipelines: Operations such as VM snapshots, scaling, patching, or migration can also be automated through CI/CD workflows.

Example: A scheduled pipeline job can:

- Take a VM snapshot, using the **`VirtualMachineSnapshot`** API.
- Perform live migration of VMs, using KubeVirt's **`VirtualMachineInstanceMigration`** resource.
- Apply OS patches via SSH or Ansible playbooks.

By integrating these workflows into GitOps pipelines, teams can handle VM lifecycle tasks declaratively.

Real-World Example: GitOps for Ubuntu-based Development Environments

Consider an enterprise offering Ubuntu-based virtual environments for development. Each environment is a KubeVirt VM with specific toolchains installed via cloud-init.

- **Git Repository:** Stores VM manifests, **`cloud-init`** scripts, and Tekton pipeline definitions.
- **Pipeline Trigger:** A developer updates a YAML to include a new tool (for example, **`golang`**) in the cloud-init script.
- **Pipeline Action:**
    - The VM image is rebuilt with the updated tool.
    - The new **`containerDisk`** image is pushed to the internal registry.
    - The **`VirtualMachine`** manifest is updated with the new image hash.
    - Argo CD syncs the cluster state to deploy the updated VM.

This allows developers to self-serve fresh environments with minimal Ops involvement.

Toolchain Recommendations

A production-grade CI/CD pipeline for KubeVirt VMs typically includes:

Tool	**Purpose**
Tekton	Pipeline orchestration for building and deploying workloads
ArgoCD	Gitops synchronization and deployment control
`virt-` builder/packer	VM image generation
`qemu-img`	Disk image conversion and manipulation
Quay/Nexus/S3	Image and artifact storage
kubeval/OPA Gatekeeper	Manifest validation and policy enforcement
Ansible/SSH	Configuration and post-deployment operations

Table 8.1: *CI/CD Process*

Security and Compliance Considerations

CI/CD pipelines for virtualized workloads must incorporate stringent security measures such as:

- **Access Control:** RBAC policies for pipeline triggers, image repositories, and VM resources.
- **Image Signing:** Use of **`cosign`** or **`sigstore`** to sign and verify VM disk images.
- **Secrets Management:** Integration with OpenShift Vault or sealed-secrets for handling credentials.
- **Auditability:** All changes must be logged and traceable to Git commits or pipeline executions.

Troubleshooting GitOps Automation Issues

As we progress deeper into automating virtualization using GitOps workflows in OpenShift with KubeVirt, understanding how to effectively troubleshoot automation issues becomes crucial for maintaining the reliability and velocity of your continuous deployment pipeline. In a declarative infrastructure model, drift detection, convergence behavior, and automated reconciliation are core advantages; however, these benefits can be undermined, if failures in the automation stack are not correctly diagnosed and addressed.

This section explores the common failure scenarios, diagnostic methods, and structured remediation steps for troubleshooting GitOps automation issues, specific to the OpenShift + KubeVirt context.

Understanding the GitOps Execution Path

Before diving into troubleshooting, it is important to have a clear mental model of the GitOps execution pipeline. At a high level, the following components orchestrate the end-to-end lifecycle:

- **Git Repository:** The single source of truth containing Kustomize or Helm manifests, KubeVirt YAMLs, and other declarative artifacts.
- **GitOps Operator (for example, Argo CD):** Watches the Git repository, and reconciles the desired state to the actual state of the cluster.
- **OpenShift/KubeVirt API Servers:** The targets of reconciliation where the declarative resources are applied.
- **Workload Controllers:** Kubernetes and KubeVirt controllers ensure the ongoing health and availability of Pods, VMs, PVCs, and so on.

An issue in any of these layers—from Git commit to CRD application—can cause automation to fail silently or visibly. Thus, it is vital to isolate which part of the system has deviated.

Common Categories of Automation Failures

Git Repository Misconfigurations: Issues at the Git layer often stem from structural or syntax errors in the declarative configuration.

Examples include:

- Invalid or missing **`apiVersion`** or **`kind`** fields
- Improper indentation in YAML files
- Broken symbolic links or submodules
- Invalid references in Helm charts or Kustomize overlays

Example: A virtual machine defined in a Kustomize base references a non-existent data volume template. The Argo CD UI shows the application in a degraded state.

Remediation:

- Use **`kubeval`** or **`kubeconform`** locally to validate manifests, before pushing them to Git.
- Employ pre-commit hooks to lint Helm/Kustomize artifacts.
- Run **`argocd app diff`** to compare live vs. desired state, before promotion.

Reconciliation Errors from Argo CD: The GitOps engine may fail to reconcile resources due to authentication issues, RBAC problems, or network segmentation.

Example: Argo CD fails to apply a `VirtualMachine` CRD due to missing permissions in the service account.

Remediation:

- Review logs in the `argocd-repo-server` and `argocd-application-controller` pods.
- Verify that the Argo CD instance has appropriate `ClusterRoleBindings`.
- Confirm that any image pull secrets are available in the target namespace.

KubeVirt Controller Failures: Once resources are applied, the KubeVirt controllers take over to instantiate virtual machines. Failures in this layer often involve:

- `PodNetworking` errors
- Storage provisioning delays
- Resource quota exhaustion

Example: A `VirtualMachineInstance` (VMI) is stuck in the `Scheduling` phase due to insufficient CPU/memory on the node pool.

Remediation:

- Use `kubectl describe vmi <name>` to examine scheduling constraints.
- Check `virt-controller`, `virt-handler`, and `virt-launcher` logs for anomalies.
- Ensure that node selectors, tolerations, and affinity rules are correctly specified.

Drift and Incomplete Reconciliation: Sometimes, resources may be only partially applied, leading to drift between the desired and live state.

Example: A `ServiceAccount` referenced by a KubeVirt VM is not created due to a Helm template logic bug, causing the VM to fail at runtime.

Remediation:

- Enable Argo CD diffing and drift detection with `argocd app diff` or auto-sync features.
- Use Argo CD's health checks to define custom health statuses for CRDs such as `VirtualMachine`.
- Integrate policy-as-code tools such as Open Policy Agent (OPA) to validate manifest integrity.

Diagnostic Tooling and Observability

Troubleshooting is most effective, when supported by observability. The following tools aid in diagnosing issues in GitOps workflows:

- **Argo CD Dashboard:** Visualizes sync status, health states, and diff results.
- **OpenShift Console:** Useful for correlating Pod, PVC, and Node events with VM behavior.
- **KubeVirt UI Plugin:** Adds a virtualization lens to OpenShift Console.
- **Prometheus and Grafana:** Telemetry from Argo CD and KubeVirt controllers can highlight performance bottlenecks.
- **Jaeger Tracing:** Helps trace request paths across controllers and webhook interactions.

Example Workflow:

1. Detect sync failure in the Argo CD dashboard.
2. Jump to the OpenShift console logs for relevant VM or Pod controllers.
3. Cross-reference Prometheus alerts for node capacity or network timeouts.

Best Practices for Resilient GitOps Pipelines

Preventing automation issues is preferable to reactive troubleshooting. Here are some key architectural practices:

- **Immutable and Testable Git Commits:** Use PR-based workflows with automatic validation pipelines.
- **Declarative Resource Ordering:** Structure Helm/Kustomize to ensure dependencies (for example, PVCs before VMs) are created in the correct order.
- **Progressive Delivery:** Employ canary or blue-green deployment strategies for VM upgrades.
- **Event-Driven Pipelines:** Integrate external triggers using Tekton or OpenShift Pipelines for customized automation.
- **Namespace Isolation:** Use tenant-specific namespaces to limit blast radius during failures.

Real-World Troubleshooting Scenario

Scenario: A GitOps deployment for a Windows-based KubeVirt VM fails to boot. Argo CD reports sync success, but the VMI does not transition to `Running`.

Investigation Path:

- Validate that the Windows disk image URL is reachable from the cluster network.
- Inspect `virt-launcher` pod logs for QEMU errors.
- Confirm that the required feature gates (example, `HyperV`) are enabled in the KubeVirt configuration.
- Review Security Context Constraints (SCC) applied to the namespace to ensure VM pods are not blocked.

Outcome: The image pulls failed due to an expired certificate in the hosting repository. This was not captured by Argo CD since the resource spec was technically correct. The issue was detected through runtime logs, and resolved by updating the disk import source.

Conclusion

The application of GitOps principles to virtualized infrastructure within OpenShift–particularly when managing KubeVirt workloads–enables a declarative, scalable, and auditable automation strategy for VM lifecycle operations. By leveraging tools such as Argo CD and Tekton pipelines, organizations can transform manual VM configuration and deployment into repeatable processes governed by version control. This not only ensures configuration drift is minimized across multiple clusters, but also promotes compliance and operational resilience. For instance, using Git repositories to store VM manifests and pipeline definitions enables automated deployment of Windows and Linux VMs in dev, staging, and production environments with environment-specific overlays managed via Kustomize or Helm.

Furthermore, integrating CI/CD pipelines for VM image builds and orchestrated rollouts allows teams to respond swiftly to updates or security patches, without disrupting platform stability. Real-world implementations, such as applying GitOps to maintain consistent VM definitions for legacy application support across hybrid clusters, and demonstrate how OpenShift Virtualization becomes production-ready at scale. As a cloud architect, adopting these methodologies not only bridges the gap between VM-based and container-native operations, but also aligns virtualized workloads with the same modern delivery practices expected in cloud-native ecosystems.

The next chapter explores advanced monitoring and performance optimization for KubeVirt workloads, using Prometheus and Grafana, focusing on deep observability, intelligent alerting, and fine-tuning techniques to ensure scalable and efficient virtualized infrastructure.

CHAPTER 9
Monitoring and Performance Optimization

Introduction

In modern hybrid infrastructure environments, especially those integrating virtual machines within container-native platforms such as OpenShift, monitoring and performance optimization are not just operational luxuries—they are architectural imperatives. KubeVirt introduces a new dimension to observability by extending Kubernetes-native monitoring principles to virtualized workloads. This chapter presents a structured approach to monitoring KubeVirt workloads by leveraging the powerful telemetry stack of Prometheus and Grafana. By integrating custom exporters, collecting VM-specific metrics, and visualizing trends through Grafana dashboards, platform engineers can gain deep visibility into both system-level and workload-level performance indicators.

Beyond passive monitoring, this chapter focuses on configuring intelligent alerting strategies for proactive incident response, diagnosing performance anomalies, and fine-tuning virtual machine configurations to achieve optimal resource efficiency. Techniques such as CPU pinning, hugepages, I/O tuning, and memory ballooning will be examined in real-world scenarios to highlight performance trade-offs and gains. Furthermore, we will address how to identify and mitigate bottlenecks that commonly arise in KubeVirt environments—ranging from misconfigured quotas to suboptimal storage or network provisioning. With an emphasis on observability, resilience, and cost-aware optimization, this chapter equips readers with the technical strategies necessary to operate KubeVirt-based virtualized infrastructure at scale, with confidence and control.

Structure

In this chapter, we will cover the following topics:

- Setting Up Monitoring for KubeVirt Workloads
- Using Prometheus and Grafana for Visualization
- Configuring Alerts for Proactive Monitoring
- Analyzing Performance Metrics for Optimization
- Troubleshooting Performance Bottlenecks
- Resource Optimization Techniques for Virtual Machines

Setting Up Monitoring for KubeVirt Workloads

As virtual machine workloads become first-class citizens within Kubernetes through KubeVirt, ensuring observability becomes essential. Unlike traditional hypervisors, where monitoring is tightly coupled with infrastructure management tools, KubeVirt workloads must integrate with Kubernetes-native observability platforms. This chapter explores the systematic approach to setting up monitoring for KubeVirt VMs in an OpenShift environment, leveraging Prometheus, Grafana, and OpenShift Monitoring stack, while offering deep insights into real-world configuration, metrics collection, and operational considerations.

The Need for VM Observability in Kubernetes

Virtual Machine workloads differ from containerized applications in several ways:

- They have a different lifecycle managed by the `virt-launcher` pod.
- They consume system resources differently, often involving disk-intensive operations.
- They require monitoring not only at the container or pod level, but also at the virtualization level (vCPU, vNIC, and vDisk).
- Their troubleshooting signals such as kernel logs or QEMU metrics, are exposed differently than traditional container logs.

Enabling KubeVirt Monitoring on OpenShift

OpenShift simplifies KubeVirt observability by exposing metrics via Prometheus endpoints, once the KubeVirt Operator and its monitoring components are installed.

KubeVirt Metrics Overview

KubeVirt exports metrics through its control plane components, especially:

- **`virt-handler`**: Per-node daemon exposing VM lifecycle and resource usage.
- **`virt-launcher`**: Sidecar pod running the QEMU process for a VM.
- **`virt-controller`**: Control loop responsible for VM state reconciliation.
- **`virt-api`**: Exposes VM API server and authentication metrics.

These components export metrics at :8443/metrics endpoints, formatted in Prometheus exposition style.

Configuring Prometheus to Scrape KubeVirt Metrics

The Prometheus instance managed by OpenShift needs access to scrape KubeVirt metrics securely.

Configuring RBAC for Metrics Scraping

Need to ensure that Prometheus instance can access KubeVirt component metrics, using appropriate **`ServiceAccounts`** and **`ClusterRoleBindings`**:

```
apiVersion: rbac.authorization.k8s.io/v1
kind: ClusterRoleBinding
metadata:
  name: prometheus-kubevirt-access
roleRef:
  apiGroup: rbac.authorization.k8s.io
  kind: ClusterRole
  name: kubevirt.io:metrics
subjects:
  - kind: ServiceAccount
    name: prometheus-k8s
    namespace: openshift-monitoring
```

Example `ServiceMonitor` for `virt-handler`

```
apiVersion: monitoring.coreos.com/v1
kind: ServiceMonitor
metadata:
  name: kubevirt-virt-handler
  namespace: openshift-cnv
spec:
  endpoints:
  - port: metrics
```

```
        interval: 30s
      selector:
        matchLabels:
          kubevirt.io: virt-handler
```

With the above in place, Prometheus will start collecting metrics such as:

- `kubevirt_vmi_phase_count`
- `kubevirt_vmi_memory_used_bytes`
- `kubevirt_vmi_network_traffic_bytes_total`

These metrics offer a granular view of the lifecycle phase and resource consumption of VMIs (**`VirtualMachineInstances`**).

Visualizing Metrics with Grafana Dashboards

KubeVirt Monitoring comes with pre-built Grafana dashboards designed for both operators and developers.

Importing KubeVirt Dashboards

The following dashboards can be imported directly from the KubeVirt Monitoring repository or configured via **`GrafanaConfig`** custom resources:

- VMI Metrics Overview
- VM Lifecycle and Status
- QEMU Metrics
- virt-launcher Network and Disk IO

Example of importing via `ConfigMap`:

```
apiVersion: v1
kind: ConfigMap
metadata:
  name: kubevirt-grafana-dashboards
  namespace: openshift-config
data:
  kubevirt-vmi-overview.json: |
    { ... JSON content of the dashboard ... }
```

Once configured, these dashboards provide insights such as:

- Average memory and CPU usage per VM.
- QEMU I/O performance bottlenecks.
- VM restart count due to migration or failure.
- Network throughput segregated by interface.

Advanced Observability Techniques

- **Integrating Custom Exporters:** For workloads running inside the VM, standard node exporters or application-specific exporters (for example, PostgreSQL and Redis) can be installed. Prometheus scrapes these metrics via NodePort or sidecar patterns.
- **Collecting Logs from virt-launcher and QEMU:** Logs from the virtualization layer, particularly virt-launcher and QEMU process logs, are collected using OpenShift's EFK (Elasticsearch-Fluentd-Kibana) stack.

```
oc logs virt-launcher-xyz -c compute
```

- **Tracing and OpenTelemetry:** For advanced setups, enabling tracing via Jaeger or OpenTelemetry provides distributed traces, when KubeVirt is used in multi-tier applications. VM startup time, disk attachment latency, and live migration duration can be traced across components.

Using Prometheus and Grafana for Visualization

In a production-grade OpenShift environment managing virtualized workloads with KubeVirt, observability is not a luxury–it is a necessity. Given the layered complexity of container orchestration, virtualization, and hybrid deployments, a robust monitoring and visualization strategy ensures both operational excellence and early anomaly detection. In this chapter, we will explore how Prometheus and Grafana–widely adopted open-source observability tools–can be effectively configured and extended to monitor and visualize the health, performance, and behavior of KubeVirt workloads on OpenShift.

Architecture Overview of Monitoring in OpenShift with KubeVirt

OpenShift ships with a built-in monitoring stack, based on Prometheus and Alertmanager which is fully integrated with the Operator Lifecycle Manager (OLM) and Kubernetes-native resource definitions. When KubeVirt is deployed via its Operator, additional metrics endpoints are exposed by the **`virt-controller`**, **`virt-api`**, **`virt-handler`**, and the **`virt-launcher`** components running alongside the Virtual Machine Instances (VMIs).

Core Monitoring Components:

- **Prometheus Operator:** Manages the lifecycle of Prometheus instances, and facilitates easy integration with **`ServiceMonitors`** and **`PodMonitors`**.

- **Prometheus:** Responsible for scraping metrics from KubeVirt services, and storing time-series data.
- **Grafana:** Connects to Prometheus as a data source to visualize these metrics through configurable dashboards.
- **Alertmanager:** Sends notifications, based on rules triggered in Prometheus.

This architecture supports multi-tenant visibility, fine-grained alerting, and flexible integration with external systems such as Slack, PagerDuty, or webhooks.

Configuring Prometheus to Monitor KubeVirt Components

Prometheus in OpenShift uses custom resource definitions such as **`ServiceMonitor`** and **`PodMonitor`** to define scraping targets. KubeVirt services expose Prometheus-compliant metrics on port **`8443`** by default, often secured with TLS.

Example: `ServiceMonitor` for `virt-controller`

```
apiVersion: monitoring.coreos.com/v1
kind: ServiceMonitor
metadata:
  name: virt-controller
  labels:
    release: prometheus-k8s
spec:
  selector:
    matchLabels:
      kubevirt.io: virt-controller
  endpoints:
    - port: metrics
      scheme: https
      interval: 30s
      tlsConfig:
        insecureSkipVerify: true
  namespaceSelector:
    matchNames:
      - kubevirt
```

This configuration ensures that Prometheus scrapes metrics from the **`virt-controller`** in the KubeVirt namespace over HTTPS, every 30 seconds. A similar configuration should be applied for **`virt-api`**, **`virt-handler`**, and **`virt-launcher`** components.

Understanding Key KubeVirt Metrics

Once the metrics pipeline is operational, Prometheus begins collecting a broad range of telemetry. Here are certain critical metrics to understand and watch:

Metric	Description
`Kubevirt_vmi_phase_count`	Count of VMIs per phase (Running, Scheduled, Failed, and so on)
`kubevirt_vmi_memory_resident_bytes`	Resident memory usage per VMI
`kubevirt_vmi_cpu_usage_seconds_total`	Total CPU usage per VMI
`kubevirt_vmi_network_traffic_bytes_total`	Network traffic (Rx/Tx) per VMI
`kubevirt_vmi_storage_iops`	Input/output operations per second on disks

Table 9.1: *KubeVirt VMI Metrics*

These metrics offer both a high-level and granular view of the resource consumption, health, and lifecycle of virtual machines within OpenShift.

Integrating and Customizing Grafana Dashboards

Grafana excels in translating complex metric data into intuitive dashboards. OpenShift exposes a secured Grafana instance, but you may also deploy a separate instance, using the Grafana Operator for extended customization.

Real-World Use Case: SLA Monitoring for Virtualized Workloads

Consider a financial institution using OpenShift and KubeVirt to host a portfolio of regulatory applications in a hybrid cloud setting. Ensuring compliance with a strict SLA (for example, 99.95% uptime) for each virtualized workload is non-negotiable.

By instrumenting:

- `kubevirt_vmi_phase_count{phase="Failed"}` over time
- `up{job="virt-launcher"} and up{job="virt-handler"}` status
- Latency histograms for storage and network access

They can construct a comprehensive SLA monitoring dashboard with automated alerts configured in Prometheus:

```
groups:
- name: kubevirt-alerts
  rules:
  - alert: VMIFailureRate
    expr: increase(kubevirt_vmi_phase_count{phase="Failed"}[5m])
> 5
    for: 1m
    labels:
      severity: critical
    annotations:
      summary: "High VMI failure rate detected"
      description: "More than 5 VMIs failed in the last 5
minutes."
```

This ensures that incidents are detected early and escalated via `Alertmanager` integrations (email, OpsGenie, and so on) for immediate remediation.

Best Practices for Observability in KubeVirt-Enhanced OpenShift Clusters

To operationalize monitoring and visualization effectively in a KubeVirt-enabled OpenShift environment, adhere to the following best practices:

Namespace Segmentation: Deploy dashboards and alerts on a per-namespace basis for multi-tenancy and RBAC control.

- **Label-Based Filtering:** Leverage consistent labels on VMIs for precise metric queries (for example, `app=postgres-vm, environment=prod`).
- **Retention and Storage Management:** Configure Prometheus TSDB retention policies carefully to avoid out-of-disk issues on long-running clusters.
- **Exporters for Guest OS Monitoring:** Need to use node-exporter or custom VM agents to expose metrics from within guest VMs, when deeper introspection is required.
- **Automated Dashboard Provisioning:** Store dashboard definitions in Git, and apply them via GitOps pipelines (for example, ArgoCD) to maintain consistency across clusters.

Configuring Alerts for Proactive Monitoring

Proactive monitoring is a cornerstone of modern infrastructure operations, especially in virtualized environments orchestrated through Kubernetes and extended by KubeVirt. While metrics and dashboards provide visibility into system behavior, it is the configuration of meaningful and context-aware alerts that transforms observability into actionable operations. In this section, we will explore how to define, deploy, and fine-tune alerts for KubeVirt workloads running on OpenShift, enabling infrastructure and platform teams to detect anomalies, and respond to issues before they impact availability or performance.

We will leverage **Prometheus Alertmanager**, which is integrated into the OpenShift Monitoring stack, and extend it to cover KubeVirt-specific use cases, including virtual machine lifecycle, resource saturation, disk I/O contention, and network throughput anomalies.

Alerting Architecture in OpenShift-KubeVirt Environments

OpenShift comes with an integrated monitoring stack that includes Prometheus, Alertmanager, Thanos, and Grafana. KubeVirt exports additional metrics through the **`virt-handler`**, **`virt-controller`**, and **`virt-launcher`** components, which are scraped by Prometheus.

Defining Effective Alerting Rules

An alert rule must be **precise**, **actionable**, and **resistant to noise**. In a KubeVirt-integrated cluster, alerting rules can be crafted around various domains:

Virtual Machine (VM) Status

Monitoring the health and availability of virtual machines is critical. A VM stuck in a pending or failed state often signals a problem in the underlying infrastructure, such as insufficient compute resources or storage errors.

```
apiVersion: monitoring.coreos.com/v1
kind: PrometheusRule
metadata:
  name: vm-health-rules
  namespace: openshift-monitoring
spec:
  groups:
  - name: virt-vm.rules
    rules:
    - alert: VMStuckInPending
      expr: kubevirt_vmi_phase_count{phase="Pending"} > 3
      for: 5m
```

```
      labels:
        severity: warning
      annotations:
        summary: "Multiple Virtual Machines are stuck in Pending 
state."
        description: "There are more than 3 VMIs in 'Pending' 
state for over 5 minutes. Check if nodes have enough CPU/memory 
and if required volumes are available."
```

Resource Saturation

Virtual machines tend to consume predictable but high levels of compute and memory. Alerts based on sustained CPU saturation or memory pressure can prevent node-level outages.

```
- alert: VMHighCPUUsage
  expr: avg by (namespace, name) (rate(container_cpu_usage_
seconds_total{container="virt-launcher"}[5m])) > 0.8
  for: 2m
  labels:
    severity: critical
  annotations:
    summary: "High CPU usage detected for virtual machines"
    description: "One or more VMs are using more than 80% CPU 
consistently for over 2 minutes."
```

Disk I/O Bottlenecks

PersistentVolume-based VM disks can experience latency under high IOPS demand. Prometheus can be configured to scrape **kubevirt_vmi_storage_*** metrics for thresholds on read/write delays.

```
- alert: VMDiskHighLatency
  expr: rate(kubevirt_vmi_storage_read_latency_seconds_sum[5m]) / 
rate(kubevirt_vmi_storage_read_latency_seconds_count[5m]) > 0.05
  for: 5m
  labels:
    severity: warning
  annotations:
    summary: "VM disk read latency exceeds 50ms"
    description: "Check PVC performance or node storage I/O 
saturation."
```

Integrating with `Alertmanager` for Notification Routing

`Alertmanager` allows flexible routing and escalation policies. A production-grade setup should define receivers for:

- Slack channels (DevOps, Platform Ops)
- Email notifications for low-priority warnings
- PagerDuty for critical production alerts

```
route:
  receiver: default
  group_by: ['alertname', 'namespace']
  routes:
    - match:
        severity: critical
      receiver: pagerduty
    - match:
        severity: warning
      receiver: email
receivers:
- name: pagerduty
  pagerduty_configs:
    - service_key: '<pd_service_key>'
- name: email
  email_configs:
    - to: 'admin@example.com'
      from: 'alerts@cluster.local'
      smarthost: 'smtp.example.com:587'
      auth_username: 'alerts'
```

Tuning Alert Sensitivity and Preventing Alert Fatigue

Alert fatigue is a real risk in VM-intensive environments. The following strategies help mitigate it:

- **Rate-limiting alerts:** Ensure that the same alert does not fire repeatedly within a short interval.
- **Multi-window thresholds:** Use both short and long-term average metrics to confirm anomalies.
- **Silencing during maintenance:** Integrate with OpenShift maintenance windows or annotate resources with **`alerts.kubernetes.io/silence=true`**.

Example of tuning using a composite rule:

```
- alert: VMHighMemoryUsage
  expr: (
    avg_over_time(container_memory_usage_bytes
{container="virt-launcher"}[5m])
    / container_spec_memory_limit_bytes{container="virt-
launcher"}
  ) > 0.85
  for: 10m
  labels:
    severity: critical
```

Best Practices for Alert Lifecycle Management

- **Version control alert rules** using GitOps practices. Keep alert definitions in sync with cluster Git repositories.
- **Test alerts** in a staging environment with mock metrics or synthetic workloads.
- **Document each alert**—severity, trigger conditions, troubleshooting steps—in an internal runbook.
- **Review alert impact** during post-incident analysis, and update thresholds or durations accordingly.

Analyzing Performance Metrics for Optimization

In high-performance virtualized environments such as those powered by KubeVirt on OpenShift, performance optimization is not a one-time activity—it is a continuous, iterative process. Effective optimization depends on data-driven decisions, and this necessitates the collection, analysis, and interpretation of meaningful performance metrics. This chapter outlines a structured approach to analyzing performance metrics for optimization within KubeVirt workloads on OpenShift, supported by practical examples and production-ready insights.

We will delve into the layers of observability, highlight which metrics matter, show how to gather and interpret them, and illustrate how to optimize compute, storage, and network resources, based on analytical evidence.

Observability Architecture for KubeVirt in OpenShift

Observability for virtual machine workloads managed via KubeVirt extends across multiple layers:

- **Kubernetes Layer:** Includes pod lifecycle, node resource consumption, and control plane metrics.
- **OpenShift Platform Layer:** Involves cluster operators, scheduling behavior, and storage/ingress controller metrics.
- **KubeVirt Layer:** Specific to `VirtualMachineInstances` (VMIs), covering metrics such as CPU throttling, memory usage, disk I/O, and vCPU steal time.
- **Guest OS Layer:** Internal metrics obtained via agents such as `qemu-guest-agent` or through application-level instrumentation.

KubeVirt integrates well with Prometheus and Grafana, enabling custom dashboards and alerting rules. It also provides a dedicated Prometheus exporter through the `virt-handler` and `virt-controller` components that expose metrics for VM lifecycle and runtime behavior.

Key Performance Metrics for Optimization

CPU Metrics:

- `kubevirt_vmi_cpu_usage_seconds_total`
- `node_cpu_seconds_total (for host-level CPU insights)`
- `kubevirt_vmi_vcpu_wait_seconds_total`

Interpretation:

- **CPU Throttling**: If the CPU usage is close to or exceeds the allocated limits, VMs may experience throttling. Use `cpu.cfs_throttled_periods` to measure this.
- **vCPU Wait Time**: High values indicate contention on the host's physical CPUs. Pinning vCPUs or adjusting VM placement may be required.

Optimization Example

In a real-world scenario, a workload running in a 2 vCPU VM on an overcommitted node showed consistent latency spikes. On analyzing `kubevirt_vmi_vcpu_wait_seconds_total`, it was found that vCPUs waited excessively due to contention. By adjusting the VM placement, using node selectors and increasing `cpuRequest`, while maintaining `cpuLimit`, the problem was mitigated.

Memory Metrics:

- `kubevirt_vmi_memory_used_bytes`
- `kubevirt_vmi_memory_available_bytes`
- `container_memory_working_set_bytes (for pod container-level insights)`

Interpretation:

- A high memory usage with low available memory indicates the VM is near capacity.
- If the working set memory approaches the limit set in the resource quota, eviction risks and swap activity (if configured) increase.

Optimization Strategy: Use HugePages for performance-critical VMs such as those running in-memory databases. Ensure that VMs are placed on nodes with hugepages-2Mi or hugepages-1Gi availability.

Disk I/O Metrics

- `kubevirt_vmi_storage_read_traffic_bytes_total`
- `kubevirt_vmi_storage_write_traffic_bytes_total`
- `kubevirt_vmi_storage_iops_read_total`
- `kubevirt_vmi_storage_latency_seconds`

Interpretation:

- IOPS spikes with high latency suggest either an under-provisioned storage backend or improper storage class usage.
- **`PersistentVolumeClaims`** (PVCs) should match the performance profile of the workload (for example, use gp3 for burst performance on AWS).

Optimization Strategy: Use ephemeral storage (**`emptyDir`**) for cache-intensive VMs, and dedicate storage classes with SSD backing for latency-sensitive workloads.

Network Metrics:

- `kubevirt_vmi_network_receive_bytes_total`
- `kubevirt_vmi_network_transmit_bytes_total`
- `kubevirt_vmi_network_receive_drop_total`

Interpretation:

- High packet drops or transmit latency typically stem from poor pod placement, excessive VMI migrations, or node-to-node cross-talk.
- The use of Multus networks and SR-IOV interfaces can dramatically enhance network performance.

Optimization Strategy: For high-throughput VMs, isolate network traffic using SR-IOV and offload the `virtio` stack. Bind these VMs to dedicated worker nodes via taints and tolerations to avoid noisy neighbor problems.

Setting Performance Baselines

Optimization requires a reference point. Baselines can be established using benchmarking tools such as:

- **`sysbench`:** CPU, memory, I/O benchmarks within the guest OS.
- **fio:** For detailed disk I/O patterns.
- **`iperf3`:** For network throughput and latency.

A baseline should capture average and peak utilization across a full business cycle (daily, weekly, or monthly). This informs scaling decisions, and helps detect regressions during updates.

Detecting Performance Bottlenecks

Grafana's multi-panel views and heatmaps help correlate system metrics and highlight outliers, while Prometheus recording rules optimize performance by pre-aggregating data for faster queries and alerts. Together, they streamline bottleneck detection across dynamic VM environments.

- **Correlation Analysis:** Use Grafana's multi-panel views to correlate CPU spikes with disk latency or network drops.
- **Heatmaps and Histograms:** Ideal for identifying outlier behavior in VM groups (for example, web servers under autoscaling).
- **Prometheus Recording Rules:** Pre-aggregate heavy metrics to speed up dashboard rendering and alerting.

Example: A cluster-wide latency degradation was initially suspected to be network-related. However, time-series heatmaps showed consistent correlation with storage IOPS peaks. This led to identifying a misconfigured backup job causing disk saturation.

Alerts and Automation for Performance Degradation

Recommended Alert Rules:

- VM CPU usage > 90% for 5 minutes
- Memory available < 10%

- Disk latency > 20 ms for 1 minute
- vCPU wait time > threshold

Integrate alerts with OpenShift's **`alertmanager`** or external systems (for example, PagerDuty). Use GitOps practices to version, and deploy alert rules declaratively.

Troubleshooting Performance Bottlenecks

Performance bottlenecks in a virtualized environment such as OpenShift Virtualization (backed by KubeVirt) can manifest in multiple layers – from the host node, through the hypervisor layer, to the guest VM, and the application stack running inside it. As a cloud architect operating in high-performance and multi-tenant Kubernetes environments, understanding where these bottlenecks arise, and how to systematically isolate them is crucial for maintaining workload SLAs, optimizing infrastructure cost, and ensuring user satisfaction.

This chapter presents a structured approach to identifying and resolving performance bottlenecks in OpenShift Virtualization environments, with real-world scenarios, command-line diagnostics, and telemetry tooling integration.

Understanding the Anatomy of a Bottleneck

A bottleneck occurs when a particular subsystem reaches its limit, and degrades the performance of the entire virtualized workload. In OpenShift Virtualization, the stack spans across:

- **Physical host (Node):** CPU, Memory, Disk, and Network interfaces.
- **KubeVirt layer:** KVM hypervisor, libvirt process, and **`virt-launcher`** pod.
- **Guest virtual machine:** vCPU, memory ballooning, I/O wait, and kernel scheduling.
- **Application workloads:** Java JVM tuning, database indexes, and thread pools.

Each of these must be examined in isolation and in correlation. A CPU-starved VM could be the result of CPU overcommit on the host or a container-level **`cgroup`** misconfiguration.

Symptom-Based Troubleshooting Framework

To facilitate rapid resolution, categorize symptoms before diving into diagnostics:

Symptom	Possible Source	Diagnostic Focus
High CPU usage	Host, libvirt, VM application	Node-level CPU saturation, overcommit

I/O latency or slow disk	PVC, host block device, VM disk I/O	PersistentVolume performance, IOPS
Network throughput drops	SR-IOV, virtio driver, CNI plugin	VM NIC binding, MTU, latency tracing
VM boot is slow	Image pull, virt-launcher, CPU throttle	Init overhead, cold start, throttling

Table 9.2: *Troubleshooting Virtualization Performance*

Tools and Techniques

We can use the following tooling matrix:

Layer	**Tools**	**Purpose**
Node (physical)	`top`, `htop`, `iostat`, `nmon`, `vmstat`	OS-Level resource monitoring
kubevirt	`kubectl`, `virtctl`, `oc adm top node`	Resource usage , pod analysis, eviction
Vm internal	`dstat`, `perf`, `iotop`, `netstat`	In-guest diagnostics
Cluster Observability	`Prometheus, Grafana, Kiali, Jaeger`	Historical trends, Correlation, tracing

Table 9.3: *Tooling Matrix Provider*

Bottleneck Scenario 1: CPU Saturation in KubeVirt Nodes

Symptoms:

- VMs running slower than expected.
- Periodic pod evictions due to CPU pressure.
- Node reports high CPU utilization, despite low pod count.

Diagnostics:

1. Need to Inspect Node Metrics.

   ```
   oc adm top node
   oc describe node <node-name>
   ```

   Look for **`Allocatable`** vs **`Capacity`**, and whether **`kubelet`** is throttling pods.

2. **Check CPU Pinning (if used):** Use **`CPUManager`** and NUMA alignment to avoid cross-socket penalties. A misaligned pinned VM can experience higher context switching.

3. **`virt-launcher` Container Analysis:** Each VM runs inside a **`virt-launcher`** pod. Run:

   ```
   oc exec <virt-launcher-pod> -c compute -- ps -aux
   ```

   Need to look for high CPU usage by **`qemu`** process. If **`qemu`** is CPU-bound, it may be due to under-allocated vCPUs or noisy neighbors.

4. **Guest OS Checks:** Inside the VM:

   ```
   top - 15:03:04 up 3 days,  1:22,  1 user,  load average: 5.92,
   6.10, 5.87
   Look at wa (I/O wait), us (user CPU), and st (steal time).
   ```

Resolution:

```
Right-size vCPUs in VM spec:
domain:
  cpu:
    cores: 4
    sockets: 1
    threads: 2
```

Need to avoid overcommitting beyond the node's CPU ratio. Use node selectors or affinity rules for critical VMs.

Bottleneck Scenario 2: Memory Pressure and Ballooning

Symptoms:

- VMs are **`OOMKilled`** or swap extensively.
- Host shows memory pressure, despite ample total memory.

Diagnostics:

- **Node-level Analysis**:

  ```
  oc adm top node
  free -m
  ```

  Need to pay attention to swap usage and the value of the **`available`**.

- **`cgroup` Memory Throttle:** Need to use **`crictl stats`** to see per-container memory limit and usage.
- **VM Memory Configuration:** Need to verify that **`requests`** and **`limits`** are set properly in the VM spec. KubeVirt supports memory overcommit, but incorrect settings can backfire:

```
resources:
  requests:
    memory: 2Gi
  limits:
    memory: 4Gi
```

- **Inside Guest:** Need to Use **`vmstat`**, **`free`**, **`top`** inside VM to check actual memory load. Need to check for balloon device status:

  ```
  lsmod | grep virtio_balloon
  ```

Resolution:

- Need to avoid aggressive memory overcommit.
- Need to use **`guestMemoryOverhead`** to fine-tune.

  ```
  overhead:
        guestMemoryOverhead: 256Mi
  ```

- Pre-allocate memory using **`hugepages`** for latency-sensitive workloads.

Bottleneck Scenario 3: Disk and I/O Performance

Symptoms:

- Long file copy or database latency.
- VM workloads with high IOPS are throttled.
- Slow VM startup or migration.

Diagnostics:

1. **PVC Backend Check:** Need to ensure that the PVCs used by VMs are on the right storage class. For instance, using **`ceph-rbd`** vs **`hostPath`** has performance implications.
2. **Check Disk Stats from Host:**

   ```
   iostat -x 1
   ```

   Need to observe **`%util`**, **`await`**, and **`svctm`**. High **`await`** may indicate disk queue saturation.
3. **In-VM Tools:**

   ```
   fio --name=randwrite --ioengine=libaio --rw=randwrite --bs=4k
   --size=1G --numjobs=4 --runtime=60 --group_reporting
   ```

4. **`PersistentVolume` Mount Options:** Some storage systems are mounted with **`noatime`** or **`nobarrier`** options that impact performance.

Resolution: For transactional workloads, use storage classes with low latency and support for block mode access.

Tune **virtio** disk parameters:

```
disks:
- name: containerdisk
  disk:
    bus: virtio
```

Bottleneck Scenario 4: Network Latency and Throughput

Symptoms:

- Packet drops or high ping latency from VM.
- Applications report socket timeout.
- Network saturation on host with multiple VMs.

Diagnostics:

1. **CNI Configuration:** Need to validate that the default CNI plugin (OpenShift SDN and OVN-Kubernetes) supports your performance needs.
2. **Inspect Interface Statistics:**

   ```
   ip -s link
   ethtool -S eth0
   ```

3. **SR-IOV and Multus:** If using SR-IOV for performance, ensure VF assignment is stable:

   ```
   oc describe network-attachment-definitions
   ```

4. **Packet Tracing:** Need to use **tcpdump** on **virt-launcher** and guest interfaces to isolate slow connections.

Resolution:

- For high-throughput, configure passthrough interfaces or use SR-IOV.
- Need to tune MTU to avoid fragmentation if jumbo frames are in use.
- Need to use dedicated physical NICs per class of workload for isolation.

Resource Optimization Techniques for Virtual Machines

In virtualized environments, resource optimization plays a pivotal role in ensuring performance, scalability, and cost-efficiency. When deploying Virtual Machines (VMs) on OpenShift using KubeVirt, it becomes even more critical to manage CPU, memory, disk I/O, and network resources effectively. This chapter delves into resource optimization strategies tailored for KubeVirt-based VMs, offering both foundational concepts and advanced techniques backed by real-world deployment scenarios.

Understanding Resource Allocation Models in KubeVirt

KubeVirt abstracts VM management into the Kubernetes ecosystem, integrating traditional virtualization with container-native workflows. However, unlike containers, VMs often have more rigid resource requirements. Misallocation—either overcommitting or under-provisioning—can lead to severe degradation in application performance or unnecessary waste of infrastructure capacity.

KubeVirt supports resource requests and limits for CPU and memory at the VM level, akin to Kubernetes pods. These configurations guide the KubeVirt scheduler on how to place workloads across nodes, while enforcing the QoS (Quality of Service) classes: Guaranteed, Burstable, or BestEffort.

Example: CPU and Memory Request Configuration

```
apiVersion: kubevirt.io/v1
kind: VirtualMachine
metadata:
  name: optimized-vm
spec:
  template:
    spec:
      domain:
        resources:
          requests:
            memory: 2Gi
            cpu: "2"
          limits:
            memory: 4Gi
            cpu: "4"
```

In this example, the VM will be guaranteed 2 CPUs and 2GiB RAM, but can burst up to 4 CPUs and 4GiB RAM, when available. This is suitable for variable-load applications like development databases or CI runners.

Right-Sizing Virtual Machines

Right-sizing involves allocating just enough resources to a VM to meet application requirements, while avoiding overprovisioning. This is often overlooked in lift-and-shift migrations, where legacy VMs are moved into OpenShift with legacy sizing, leading to underutilization.

Techniques:

- **Utilization Metrics Collection:** Integrate with Prometheus and use **`kubevirt_vmi_memory_used_bytes`** and **`kubevirt_vmi_cpu_usage_seconds_total`** to assess actual consumption.
- **Time-Series Analysis:** Use Grafana dashboards to visualize usage patterns over time, identifying idle VMs or resources allocated, but never used.
- **Scheduled Right-Sizing:** Use automation scripts or Ansible playbooks to periodically adjust VM specs, based on observed trends.

Real-World Example: A financial services firm reduced its average VM memory footprint by 35% after analyzing 60 days of Prometheus metrics, freeing up resources for batch workloads during end-of-month reconciliation windows.

Leveraging HugePages for Memory Optimization

For high-performance workloads, memory access latency is a critical factor. KubeVirt allows VM memory backing with HugePages which reduces TLB (Translation Lookaside Buffer) misses, and improves throughput for applications such as in-memory databases or network functions.

Configuration Example:

```
spec:
  domain:
    memory:
      hugepages:
        pageSize: "1Gi"
```

HugePages must be pre-allocated on the node which requires updates to the node's **`kubelet`** configuration and kernel parameters. This technique is especially useful for real-time video processing, low-latency trading applications, and telecom workloads.

CPU Pinning and NUMA-Aware Scheduling

VMs with latency-sensitive applications can benefit significantly from CPU pinning and NUMA (Non-Uniform Memory Access) affinity. These configurations ensure deterministic performance by avoiding context switching and cross-socket memory access.

CPU Pinning Example:

```
spec:
  domain:
    cpu:
      cores: 4
      dedicatedCpuPlacement: true
      numa:
        guestMappingPassthrough: {}
```

When combined with the CPUManager policy set to **`static`** on the OpenShift node, this allows exclusive CPU assignment to the VM, enhancing performance for real-time systems and High-Performance Computing (HPC) workloads.

Disk I/O Optimization

VM disk I/O can become a bottleneck, especially in storage-intensive applications such as OLTP databases or large-scale logging systems.

Strategies:

- **Use of `virtio` Disk Bus:** Provides paravirtualized performance.
- **Enable I/O Threads:** Distribute disk I/O load across CPU threads.
- **SSD-backed Persistent Volumes:** Deploy PVCs on SSD-backed storage classes for low-latency IOPS.
- **Block Mode Access:** Where possible, use raw block devices instead of filesystem-based volumes to eliminate overhead.

Example of Virtio Disk and IOThreads:

```
spec:
  domain:
    devices:
      disks:
      - name: datadisk
        disk:
          bus: virtio
      ioThreadsPolicy: auto
```

Real-World Outcome: An analytics team observed a 2x increase in ETL job throughput after switching to block-mode PVCs with dedicated I/O threads for their data-processing VMs.

Network Optimization for Virtual Machines

Networking plays a crucial role in multi-tenant, distributed architectures. KubeVirt supports both bridged (L2) and masquerade (NAT) networking modes, with advanced configurations such as SR-IOV for ultra-low latency.

Techniques:

- **SR-IOV Integration:** Bypass the software network stack for near-native performance.
- **Multi-NIC VMs:** Attach multiple interfaces for separating management and data planes.
- **Custom Network Policies:** Define Kubernetes NetworkPolicies for fine-grained traffic control.
- **Network QoS Classes:** Limit bandwidth per interface to ensure fairness in multi-tenant setups.

SR-IOV Example:

```
spec:
  domain:
    devices:
      interfaces:
      - name: sriov-net
        sriov: {}
```

Need to ensure that the node is configured with SR-IOV Device Plugins, and corresponding `NetworkAttachmentDefinition` objects.

Using Live Migration Strategically

KubeVirt supports live migration of VMs which is valuable for load balancing, hardware maintenance, or power efficiency (for example, node consolidation during off-peak hours). However, migrations consume network and compute resources, so that they should be used judiciously.

Recommendations:

- Schedule during low-traffic windows.
- Avoid frequent migrations of high-memory VMs.
- Monitor migration metrics such as downtime and completion duration.

Real-World Example: A research institution with GPU-intensive VMs used live migration during non-peak hours to consolidate workloads, and shut down idle GPU nodes, saving over $10,000/month in power and cooling.

Automating Optimization with GitOps and Pipelines

To sustain optimization over time, infrastructure-as-code principles must be extended to VM configurations. Use GitOps workflows with Argo CD or OpenShift Pipelines to implement:

- **Declarative Resource Specs:** Track and update VM resource allocations via Git.
- **Policy Enforcement:** Integrate with Open Policy Agent (OPA) or Kyverno to reject overprovisioned VM specs.
- **Observability-Driven Automation:** Trigger resource tuning pipelines, based on Prometheus alert thresholds.

Pipeline Example:

1. Need to Monitor resource usage.
2. Commit updated VM spec with right-sized requests to Git.
3. Apply changes through GitOps sync.

This approach ensures consistency, auditability, and proactive resource management at scale.

Conclusion

In this chapter, we explored the critical aspects of observability and performance optimization within KubeVirt-powered OpenShift environments. Beginning with the setup of robust monitoring for KubeVirt workloads, we laid the groundwork for systematic observability by integrating Prometheus and Grafana—two of the most widely adopted tools in cloud-native ecosystems. By configuring metrics collection through custom ServiceMonitors, and leveraging OpenShift's built-in monitoring stack, we ensured a comprehensive view of VM performance and cluster health. Our deep dive into Grafana dashboards illustrated how curated visualizations can transform raw telemetry data into actionable insights, supporting both operations teams and platform engineers in maintaining workload efficiency and SLA compliance.

Real-world examples such as alerting on high CPU steal time or abnormal disk I/O latency in VM workloads, demonstrated the importance of proactive alerting, using Prometheus rules. We emphasized the need for fine-tuned alert thresholds to reduce noise, and increase the reliability of operational responses.

Furthermore, through detailed performance analysis and troubleshooting of common bottlenecks—such as resource contention at the node level or suboptimal virt-launcher pod placement—we highlighted data-driven approaches to root cause analysis. Finally, we addressed VM-specific resource optimization strategies, including vertical scaling, live migration, and dynamic CPU/memory allocation, ensuring that readers are equipped to run virtualized workloads on OpenShift with resilience and cost-efficiency. This monitoring and optimization blueprint is essential for sustaining high-performance, production-grade KubeVirt deployments.

The next chapter guides developers in automating KubeVirt using the Go client library, covering VM lifecycle management, resource adjustments, and integration with external systems for streamlined virtualization workflows.

CHAPTER 10
Programming KubeVirt Functionality

Introduction

This chapter is designed for developers who want to extend and automate KubeVirt, using the Go client library. It begins with setting up your Go development environment, and familiarizing yourself with the KubeVirt API objects as well as their interactions. The primary focus is using the Go client to interact with KubeVirt's Custom Resource Definitions (CRDs), teaching you how to programmatically create, list, update, and delete VMs.

Advanced operations such as dynamically adjusting VM resources, managing VM snapshots, and interacting with DataVolumes using the Go client, are also covered. Thus, by the end of this chapter, you will be able to write Go programs to automate VM management, integrate KubeVirt with external systems, and create custom tooling to streamline your virtualization workflows.

Structure

In this chapter, the following topics are being covered:

- Setting up your Go Environment and KubeVirt Client
- Interacting with KubeVirt API Objects
- Advanced Operations

Setting Up Your Go Environment and KubeVirt Client

Go applications interacting with KubeVirt must first authenticate to the Kubernetes API server. The **`k8s.io/client-go`** library, which **`kubevirt.io/client-go`** builds upon, provides mechanisms for this authentication, primarily by leveraging **`kubeconfig`** files for out-of-cluster scenarios and **`ServiceAccount`** tokens for in-cluster scenarios.

The Role of `kubeconfig` Files

`kubeconfig` files are YAML documents that store cluster access information, enabling **`kubectl`** and client libraries to connect and authenticate to Kubernetes clusters.

A kubeconfig file typically comprises three main sections:

- **clusters:** These define the Kubernetes clusters. Each cluster entry specifies a name, the API server URL (server), and the certificate authority data (certificate-authority-data or a path to a CA file) used to verify the API server's identity.
- **users:** Defines user identities. Each user entry specifies a name and their credentials, which can be client certificates and keys (client-certificate-data, client-key-data), bearer tokens (token), or configurations for authentication providers (for example, OIDC via auth-provider, or external command execution via exec for credential plugins).
- **contexts:** Links a user to a cluster, and optionally a default namespace. Each context entry has a name, and specifies the cluster name and user name to use. Additionally, a current-context field indicates which context is active by default.

Out-of-Cluster Authentication with `client-go`

When a Go application runs outside a Kubernetes cluster (for example, on a developer's local machine or a CI/CD server), it needs to use a kubeconfig file to authenticate. The **`k8s.io/client-go/tools/clientcmd`** package provides the necessary utilities.

The primary goal is to construct a **`*rest.Config`** object, which encapsulates all connection and authentication information needed by the **`clientset`**. Several functions can achieve this:

- **`clientcmd.BuildConfigFromFlags(masterURL, kubeconfigPath string) (*rest.Config, error)`**

Example:

```
import (
	"flag"
	"path/filepath"
	"k8s.io/client-go/tools/clientcmd"
	"k8s.io/client-go/util/homedir"
	// kubernetes "k8s.io/client-go/kubernetes"
	// kubevirt "kubevirt.io/client-go/generated/kubevirt/
clientset/versioned"
)

func buildConfigOutOfCluster() (*rest.Config, error) {
	var kubeconfig *string
	if home := homedir.HomeDir(); home!= "" {
	kubeconfig = flag.String("kubeconfig", filepath.Join(home,
".kube", "config"), "(optional) absolute path to the kubeconfig
file")
	} else {
	kubeconfig = flag.String("kubeconfig", "", "absolute path to
the kubeconfig file")
	}
	flag.Parse()

	// Use the current context in kubeconfig
	config, err := clientcmd.BuildConfigFromFlags
("", *kubeconfig)
	if err!= nil {
	return nil, err
	}
	return config, nil
}
```

- **`clientcmd.NewClientConfigFromBytes(configBytes []byte) (ClientConfig, error):`** This function is useful, if the **kubeconfig** content is available as a byte slice, for instance, read from a secret or embedded in the application.

In-Cluster Authentication Using `ServiceAccounts`

When a Go application is deployed as a Pod within a Kubernetes cluster (for example, as part of a KubeVirt controller, operator, or any in-cluster tool), it should use in-cluster authentication. This method leverages Kubernetes **`ServiceAccounts`**.

Kubernetes automatically creates and manages **`ServiceAccounts`**. When a Pod is created, it is associated with a **`ServiceAccount`** (by default, the default **`ServiceAccount`** in its namespace, unless specified otherwise). Kubernetes mounts the **`ServiceAccount's`** token, and the cluster's CA certificate into the Pod's filesystem at a well-known location: **`/var/run/secrets/kubernetes.io/serviceaccount/`**

Using `k8s.io/client-go/rest.InClusterConfig()`

The **`client-go`** library provides the **`rest.InClusterConfig()`** function which is designed specifically for this scenario. This function:

- Checks for the presence of Kubernetes service host and port environment variables (**`KUBERNETES_SERVICE_HOST and KUBERNETES_SERVICE_PORT`**).
- Reads the **`ServiceAccount`** token from **`/var/run/secrets/kubernetes.io/serviceaccount/token`**.
- Reads the CA certificate from **`/var/run/secrets/kubernetes.io/serviceaccount/ca.crt`**.
- Constructs and returns a **`*rest.Config`** object configured to communicate with the API server from within the cluster.

Example:

```
import (
	"k8s.io/client-go/rest"
	// kubernetes "k8s.io/client-go/kubernetes"
	// kubevirt "kubevirt.io/client-go/generated/kubevirt/cli-
entset/versioned"
)

func buildConfigInCluster() (*rest.Config, error) {
	config, err:= rest.InClusterConfig()
	if err!= nil {
	return nil, err
	}
	return config, nil
}
```

KubeVirt's Go Client Libraries

`kubevirt.io/client-go` is the official Go client library for KubeVirt. Its primary purpose is to enable Go applications to programmatically manage KubeVirt's Custom Resource Definitions (CRDs) such as VirtualMachine (VM), **`VirtualMachineInstance`** (VMI), DataVolume, and others that define and control virtualized workloads within Kubernetes.

Relationship to `k8s.io/client-go`: `kubevirt.io/client-go` is designed to be consistent with k8s.io/client-go, the standard client library for core Kubernetes resources (such as Pods, Deployments, and Services).

In practice, many KubeVirt applications will import and use both **`k8s.io/client-go`** (for interacting with underlying Kubernetes objects or cluster features) and **`kubevirt.io/client-go`** (for KubeVirt-specific operations). **`kubevirt.io/client-go`** can be thought of as an extension, providing a generated clientset tailored for KubeVirt's API groups and resource types.

Key Features:

- **Typed Clients:** Provides Go types representing KubeVirt CRDs and methods for performing CRUD (Create, Read, Update, and Delete) operations on them.
- **Informers and Listers:** Offers mechanisms for watching KubeVirt resource changes, and maintaining local caches, essential for building controllers.
- **Scheme Registration:** Includes utilities to register KubeVirt API types with the Kubernetes runtime scheme, enabling proper serialization and deserialization.

Comparison of `kubevirt.io/client-go and k8s.io/client-go`

The following table provides a concise comparison between `` `k8s.io/client-go` ``, the standard Go client for core Kubernetes API resources, and `` `kubevirt.io/client-go` ``, its specialized counterpart for managing KubeVirt Custom Resource Definitions (CRDs). It highlights their distinct purposes, managed resources, API groups, and typical usage patterns within KubeVirt projects.

Feature	**`k8s.io/client-go`**	**`kubevirt.io/client-go`**
Primary Purpose	Interact with core Kubernetes API resources.	Interact with KubeVirt Custom Resource Definitions (CRDs).
Managed Resources	Pods, Services, Deployments, ConfigMaps, Secrets, Nodes, and so on.	VirtualMachines (VMs), and **`VirtualMachineInstances`** (VMIs). DataVolumes, **`VirtualMachineInstanceReplicaSets`**, and so on.

API Groups	`core/v1`, `apps/v1`, `batch/v1`, `rbac.authorization.k8s.io/v1`, and so on.	`kubevirt.io/v1`, `cdi.kubevirt.io/v1beta1`, `snapshot.kubevirt.io/v1alpha1`, `export.kubevirt.io/v1beta1`, and so on.
Generation	Generated from core Kubernetes API definitions.	Generated from KubeVirt API definitions (found in **kubevirt.io/api**) using tools like **client-gen**.
Typical Usage in KubeVirt Projects	Used for managing underlying Kubernetes objects (for example, Pods backing VMIs), ServiceAccounts, RBAC, or interacting with core K8s functionalities.	Used for all direct KubeVirt resource management (VM lifecycle, configuration, snapshots, exports).
Relationship	**kubevirt.io/client-go** depends on, and utilizes the patterns and libraries from `k8s.io/client-go` (for example, apimachinery, rest, tools/cache).	Complements **k8s.io/client-go** by providing specialized clients for KubeVirt's domain.

Table 10.1: *Comparison of Kubernetes Client and KubeVirt Client*

Initializing the KubeVirt Clientset

Once the **kubevirt.io/client-go** dependency is added and a ***rest.Config** object has been obtained through either out-of-cluster or in-cluster authentication, a KubeVirt clientset can be initialized. This **clientset** is the primary interface for interacting with KubeVirt resources.

The most common way to create the **clientset** is by using the **NewForConfig** (or **NewForConfigOrDie**) function provided by the generated KubeVirt clientset package.

Example:

```
import (
    "log"

    "k8s.io/client-go/rest"
    // Import the KubeVirt versioned clientset
    kubevirtclientset "kubevirt.io/client-go/generated/kubevirt/
clientset/versioned"
    // For KubeVirt specific API group clients, if needed more
granularly:
    // kubevirtcorev1 "kubevirt.io/client-go/generated/kubevirt/
clientset/versioned/typed/core/v1"
)
```

```
func initializeKubeVirtClient(config *rest.Config) (kubevirtclient-
set.Interface, error) {
    // Create a new KubeVirt clientset for the given config.
    clientset, err := kubevirtclientset.NewForConfig(config)
    if err!= nil {
        log.Printf("Error creating KubeVirt clientset: %v", err)
        return nil, err
    }
    log.Println("KubeVirt clientset initialized successfully.")
    return clientset, nil
}
```

Using Controller-Runtime Client Instead

An alternative to using the typed client-go clientsets is to use the client provided by the controller-runtime library. The client-go clientsets provide statically typed clients, meaning that they are generated with specific Go types and methods for each known Kubernetes API **`GroupVersionKind`** (GVK) like Pods or Deployments. This offers compile-time safety and directness as API paths are essentially pre-defined. In contrast, the controller-runtime client offers a more dynamic and generic interface, typically operating on **`client.Object`** interfaces. It uses a **`runtime.Scheme`** to identify an object's GVK and a **`meta.RESTMapper`** (which often queries the Kubernetes discovery API) to determine the correct REST endpoint and resource scope dynamically. This makes the controller-runtime client highly adaptable for handling a diverse range of resources, including Custom Resource Definitions (CRDs), without requiring pre-generated code for every type.

Let us see the process with an example:

```
import (
        clientgoscheme "k8s.io/client-go/kubernetes/scheme"
        kubevirtcorev1 "kubevirt.io/api/core/v1"
        cdiv1 "kubevirt.io/containerized-data-importer-api/pkg/
apis/core/v1beta1"
"k8s.io/apimachinery/pkg/runtime" "sigs.k8s.io/controller-
runtime/pkg/client" "sigs.k8s.io/controller-runtime/pkg/client/
config"
)

var (
        scheme = runtime.NewScheme()
)

func init() {
   if err := kubevirtcorev1.AddToScheme(scheme); err != nil {
       panic(err)
```

```
    }
    if err := clientgoscheme.AddToScheme(scheme); err != nil {
        log.Fatalf("Failed to add corev1 to scheme: %v", err)
    }
    if err := cdiv1.AddToScheme(scheme); err != nil {
        log.Fatalf("Failed to add cdiv1 to scheme: %v", err)
    }
}

func createControllerRuntimeClientWithScheme() {
        c, err := client.New(config.GetConfigOrDie(), client.
Options{
                Scheme: scheme,
        })
        if err != nil {
                panic(err)
        }
}
```

Interacting with KubeVirt API Objects

With an initialized KubeVirt clientset, applications can perform Create, Read, Update, and Delete (CRUD) operations on KubeVirt resources like VirtualMachines (VMs) and VirtualMachineInstances (VMIs).

The same is also possible with the controller-runtime client as well.

Performing CRUD Operations on KubeVirt Resources

The general pattern for these operations is:

`kubevirtClient.ApiGroupVersionInterface().ResourceTypeInterface(namespace).Action(ctx, nameOrObject, options)`

- **`kubevirtClient`:** The initialized KubeVirt clientset.
- **`ApiGroupVersionInterface()`:** Accesses the client for a specific API group and version, for example, **`KubevirtV1()`** for the **`kubevirt.io/v1`** API group.
- **`ResourceTypeInterface(namespace)`:** Accesses the client for a specific resource type (for example, **`VirtualMachineInstances(namespace)`** or **`VirtualMachines(namespace)`**). For cluster-scoped resources, the namespace argument is omitted.
- **`Action(...)`:** The specific CRUD operation (for example, **`Create`**, **`Get`**, **`List`**, **`Update`**, **`Delete`**).

- **`ctx`**: A **`context.Context`** for managing deadlines, cancellations, and so on. **`context.TODO()`** or **`context.Background()`** are often used for simple cases.
- **`nameOrObject`**: The name of the resource (for **`Get`**, **`Delete`**) or the resource object itself (for **`Create`**, **`Update`**).
- **`options`**: Action-specific options (for example, **`metav1.GetOptions{}`**, **`metav1.CreateOptions{}`**, **`metav1.ListOptions{}`**).

Listing `VirtualMachineInstances` (VMIs) in a Namespace

```
import (
	"context"
	metav1 "k8s.io/apimachinery/pkg/apis/meta/v1"
	kubevirtclientset "kubevirt.io/client-go/generated/
kubevirt/clientset/versioned"
)

func listVMIsInNamespace(kvClient kubevirtclientset.Interface,
namespace string) error {
	vmiList, err := kvClient.KubevirtV1().VirtualMachineIn-
stances(namespace).List(context.TODO(), metav1.ListOptions{})
	if err!= nil {
		return err
	}
	for _, vmi := range vmiList.Items {
		log.Printf("Found VMI: %s, Status: %s", vmi.Name,
vmi.Status.Phase)
	}
	return nil
}
```

Getting a Specific `VirtualMachineInstance`

```
func getVMI(kvClient kubevirtclientset.Interface, namespace,
vmiName string) (*kubevirtapiv1.VirtualMachineInstance, error) {
	vmi, err := kvClient.KubevirtV1().VirtualMachineInstanc-
es(namespace).Get(context.TODO(), vmiName, metav1.GetOptions{})
	if err!= nil {
		return nil, err
	}
	log.Printf("VMI %s details: CPU Cores %d", vmi.Name, vmi.
Spec.Domain.CPU.Cores)
	return vmi, nil
}
```

Creating a VirtualMachine

```
import (
	kubevirtapiv1 "kubevirt.io/api/core/v1"
	//... other imports
)

func createVM(kvClient kubevirtclientset.Interface, namespace
string, vmDef *kubevirtapiv1.VirtualMachine) (*kubevirtapiv1.
VirtualMachine, error) {
	createdVM, err := kvClient.KubevirtV1().VirtualMa-
chines(namespace).Create(context.TODO(), vmDef, metav1.Create
Options{})
	if err!= nil {
		return nil, err
	}
	log.Printf("Created VirtualMachine: %s", createdVM.Name)
	return createdVM, nil
}
```

Updating a VirtualMachine (example, to change its state)

```
func startVM(kvClient kubevirtclientset.Interface, namespace, vm-
Name string) (*kubevirtapiv1.VirtualMachine, error) {
	vm, err := kvClient.KubevirtV1().VirtualMachines(name-
space).Get(context.TODO(), vmName, metav1.GetOptions{})
	if err!= nil {
		return nil, err
	}

	// Modify the spec to start the VM (if not using a run-
Strategy that keeps it running)
	// For VMs managed by a runStrategy, changing 'running'
might not be the direct way.
	// This example assumes direct control over the 'running'
state.
	if vm.Spec.Running!= nil &&!*vm.Spec.Running {
		newVm := vm.DeepCopy()
		newVm.Spec.Running = Ptr(true) // Ptr is a helper to
get a pointer to a bool
		updatedVM, err := kvClient.KubevirtV1().VirtualMa-
chines(namespace).Update(context.TODO(), newVm, metav1.UpdateOp-
tions{})
	if err!= nil {
		return nil, err
```

```
        }
        log.Printf("VirtualMachine %s updated to running state.",
updatedVM.Name)
                return updatedVM, nil
        }
        log.Printf("VirtualMachine %s is already set to run or
managed by a runStrategy.", vm.Name)
        return vm, nil
}
```

CRUD Operations with Controller-Runtime Based Client

This section delves into advanced operations and use cases for KubeVirt, moving beyond basic CRUD functionalities. We will explore how to programmatically scale resources, and demonstrate how to build a comprehensive platform leveraging Kubernetes and KubeVirt, accessible via an HTTP API. This will showcase the power and flexibility of the Go client libraries in real-world scenarios.

Get or list VMs

```
import (
        "fmt"
        "sigs.k8s.io/controller-runtime/pkg/client"
)

func GetVMs(client client.Client) {
        vms := &kubevirtcorev1.VirtualMachineList{}

        err := client.List(c.Request.Context(), vms, &client.List
Options{
                Namespace: mynamespace,
        })
        if err != nil {
                panic(err)
        }

        for _, vm := range vms.Items {
                fmt.Println("VM Name: %s, Namespace: %s", vm.Name,
vm.Namespace)
        }
}
```

Create VM

The following code snippet is focused on creating a new virtual machine for us:

```
vm := &kubevirtcorev1.VirtualMachine{
        ObjectMeta: metav1.ObjectMeta{
          Name:      Name,
          Namespace: project,
          Labels:    map[string]string{},
        },
        Spec: kubevirtcorev1.VirtualMachineSpec{
              Running: pointer.Bool(true),
              Template: &kubevirtcorev1.VirtualMachineInstance
              TemplateSpec{
             Spec: kubevirtcorev1.VirtualMachineInstanceSpec{
                    Domain: kubevirtcorev1.DomainSpec{
                     Devices: kubevirtcorev1.Devices{
                    Disks: []kubevirtcorev1.Disk{
                          {
                                      Name: "emptydisk",
                                      DiskDevice: kubevirtcor-
                                      ev1.DiskDevice{
                                            Disk: &kubevirtcor-
                                            ev1.DiskTarget{
                                            Bus: kubevirtcor-
                                            ev1.DiskBusVirtio,
                                },
                          },
              },
        },
        Interfaces: []kubevirtcorev1.Interface{
              {
              Name: "default",
              InterfaceBindingMethod:
        kubevirtcorev1.InterfaceBindingMethod{
                    Masquerade:
              &kubevirtcorev1.InterfaceMasquerade{},
                    },
              },
        },
    },
    Resources: kubevirtcorev1.ResourceRequirements{
        Requests: corev1.ResourceList{
              corev1.ResourceMemory: resource.MustParse("512m"),
              corev1.ResourceCPU: resource.MustParse("200m"),
              },
    },
```

```
Machine: &kubevirtcorev1.Machine{
            Type: "",
        },
    },
    Networks: []kubevirtcorev1.Network{
            {
                    Name: "default",
                    NetworkSource: kubevirtcorev1.NetworkSource{
                    Pod: &kubevirtcorev1.PodNetwork{},
            },
    },
    Volumes: []kubevirtcorev1.Volume{
        {
            Name: "emptydisk",
            VolumeSource: kubevirtcorev1.VolumeSource{
                        EmptyDisk: &kubevirtcorev1.EmptyDiskSource{
                              Capacity: resource.MustParse("10GB"),
                        },
                        },
                    },
                },
            },
        },
}

err = d.Client.Create(c.Request.Context(), vm)
if err != nil {
        panic(err)
}
```

Delete VM

```
vm := &kubevirtcorev1.VirtualMachine{
        ObjectMeta: metav1.ObjectMeta{
                Name: "my-vm-name",
                Namespace: "my-vm-namespace",
        },
}

err = d.Client.Delete(c.Request.Context(), vm)
if err != nil {
        panic(err)
}
```

Advanced Operations

In this section, let us explore some advanced use cases that we can perform, using the go based API functions that we have already talked about in the previous sections of this chapter.

Programmatically Scaling Resources

To modify the resources (CPU and memory) of an existing VirtualMachine, you can retrieve the VM object, and update its **`Spec.Template.Spec. Domain.Resources. Requests`** fields with the desired values, and then use the client's Update method to persist the changes. This allows for programmatic scaling of VM resources after creation.

```
vm := &kubevirtcorev1.VirtualMachine{}
err = client.Get(c.Request.Context(), types.NamespacedName{
        Name:          "myvm",
        Namespace:     "my-namespace",
}, vm)
if err != nil {
        panic(err)
}

vm.Spec.Template.Spec.Domain.Resources.Requests[corev1.Resource-
CPU] = resource.MustParse("500m")

vm.Spec.Template.Spec.Domain.Resources.Requests[corev1.Resource-
Memory] = resource.MustParse("1Gi")

err = client.Update(c.Request.Context(), vm)
if err != nil {
        panic(err)
}
```

Creating Platforms around KubeVirt

Building a Platform around Kubernetes and KubeVirt with Controller-Runtime and HTTP API

This involves creating a comprehensive system that leverages the power of Kubernetes and KubeVirt, accessible through a well-defined HTTP API. This approach abstracts the complexities of the underlying infrastructure, and provides a user-friendly interface for managing virtual machines as well as related resources.

Key Components

- **Controller-Runtime:** Provides a framework for building controllers that manage Kubernetes and KubeVirt resources. It also simplifies interactions with the Kubernetes API.
- **Kubernetes and KubeVirt Clients:** Used to communicate with the Kubernetes and KubeVirt APIs, enabling the platform to manage resources.
- **HTTP API:** Exposes endpoints for users to interact with the platform. Also, acts as an abstraction layer over Kubernetes and KubeVirt.
- **Business Logic:** Custom logic that implements platform-specific features and workflows, built on top of the client libraries.

While we have already discussed most of these above components in isolation, the use of controller-runtime client allows us to just depend on a single type of client for operations like interacting with the Kubernetes API Server, KubeVirt API server, and even with orchestrating the CDI project CRDs.

Creating the HTTP Server

We can start by simply defining a gin-based HTTP server as follows:

```
type HTTPServer struct {
	Router      *gin.Engine
	dispatcher *handlers.Dispatcher
	client      client.Client
}
```

Initialize the above struct with the relevant objects as follows:

Initializing the Containing Objects

```
func NewHTTPServer(scheme *runtime.Scheme) *HTTPServer {
	r := gin.Default()

	c, err := client.New(config.GetConfigOrDie(), client.Options{
		Scheme: scheme,
	})
	if err != nil {
		panic(err)
	}


	s := &HTTPServer{
		Router: r,
	dispatcher: routes.NewDispatcher(c, r),
		client:     c,
```

```
        }

        return s
}
```

Defining Routes and Attaching Handlers

Now that we have the server itself, we can think about defining routes, and attaching our handler functions into the dispatcher.

```
import (
        "github.com/gin-gonic/gin"
)

func NewDispatcher(k8s client.Client, router *gin.Engine)
*handlers.Dispatcher {
        d := &handlers.Dispatcher{
                Client:  k8s,

        // other clients or useful libraries etc.
        }

        projv1 := router.Group("/api/v1")

        projv1.POST("/orgs/:orgSlug/projects/:projectSlug/vms",
        d.CreateVM)
        projv1.GET("/orgs/:orgSlug/projects/:projectSlug/vms",
        d.GetVMs)

}
```

Defining Handlers

Implement some minimal versions of these above-mentioned handlers:

```
func (d *Dispatcher) GetVMs(c *gin.Context) {
        vms := &kubevirtcorev1.VirtualMachineList{}

        projectSlug := c.Param("project")

        err := d.Client.List(c.Request.Context(), vms, &client.
ListOptions{
                Namespace: project,
        })
        if err != nil {
                c.JSON(http.StatusInternalServerError, gin.H{
                        "error":   err.Error(),
                        "message": "error listing VMs",
```

```
				})
				return
			}

			items := []*models.VMResponse{}

			for _, vm := range vms.Items {
				item := &models.VMResponse{}
				item.FromEntity(context.WithValue(c.Request.
		Context(), models.KubeQueryClientKey{}, d.Client), &vm)
				items = append(items, item)
			}

			c.JSON(http.StatusOK, gin.H{
				"items": items,
			})
		}
```

Launch the Server

Now, we can just start, and run the server.

```
	fmt.Println("starting webserver")
	s := server.NewHTTPServer(scheme)
	err = s.Router.Run("0.0.0.0:3000")
	if err != nil {
		klog.Error(err, "unable to start server")
		panic(err)
	}
```

Advantages

- **Abstraction:** The HTTP API simplifies interaction, hiding Kubernetes and KubeVirt complexity.
- **Automation:** Controller-Runtime enables automated resource management.
- **Customization:** Business logic can be tailored for specific platform needs.
- **Scalability:** Kubernetes and KubeVirt provide underlying scalability.

This approach creates a powerful, user-friendly platform on top of Kubernetes and KubeVirt.

Conclusion

This chapter has equipped developers with the knowledge to extend and automate KubeVirt functionality using the Go client library. By covering environment setup, interaction with KubeVirt API objects, and advanced operations such as programmatic scaling and platform building, it demonstrated how to programmatically manage VMs, integrate KubeVirt with external systems, and streamline virtualization workflows. The comparison of **`k8s.io/client-go`** and **`kubevirt.io/client-go`**, along with the examples for both typed clients and the controller-runtime client, provided a comprehensive guide for developers aiming to build robust KubeVirt solutions. Ultimately, this chapter empowers users to create sophisticated and automated virtualization platforms atop Kubernetes and KubeVirt.

CHAPTER 11
KubeVirt vs. vCluster

Introduction

This chapter compares KubeVirt and vCluster, two methods for running virtual machines with Kubernetes. It also explains how KubeVirt uses KVM for direct host virtualization, while vCluster creates virtual Kubernetes clusters on an existing Kubernetes cluster. You will learn the architectural differences, use cases, and trade-offs between the two. The chapter will help you decide which technology to use for specific virtualization needs, within your Kubernetes environment.

Through real-world scenarios, the chapter explores the strengths and limitations of both technologies. It discusses when to choose KubeVirt for hybrid workloads, and when to opt for vCluster for environment isolation, development, or testing. The trade-offs in scalability, resource overhead, and operational complexity are also highlighted, helping readers make informed decisions, based on their specific use cases.

Structure

In this chapter, we are going to focus on the following topics:

- Architectural Overview
- Provisioning Isolated vCluster
- Comparing Performance and Resource Utilization
- Hybrid Workloads vs. Multi-Tenant Environments
- Decision Framework

A Detailed Architectural Overview

This section serves as a guide for choosing between KubeVirt and vCluster, based on specific use cases and requirements. It breaks down the decision-making process into distinct scenarios, highlighting when each technology is the optimal solution. The section further provides a comprehensive table to aid in this selection by comparing various features and aspects against the strengths of **KubeVirt and vCluster**.

KubeVirt

As organizations increasingly adopt Kubernetes for container orchestration, the need to manage diverse workloads and operational paradigms within this ecosystem has grown. Two significant technologies addressing these needs are KubeVirt and vCluster.

KubeVirt focuses on workload virtualization, enabling the execution and management of VMs as if they were pods. In contrast, vCluster concentrates on control plane virtualization, allowing the creation of multiple Kubernetes environments, within a single physical cluster. These fundamental differences in their core objectives dictate their respective architectures, primary use cases, and operational models. The emergence and maturation of both KubeVirt and vCluster signal a significant trend such as the unification of diverse workload types, and management paradigms under a consistent, Kubernetes-centric operational model. KubeVirt addresses the modernization of legacy applications by bringing them into the Kubernetes ecosystem, while vCluster simplifies scenarios like multi-tenancy or the creation of ephemeral development environments by making Kubernetes clusters themselves more lightweight and manageable. Thus, both technologies expand the utility of Kubernetes, preventing fragmentation and reinforcing its role as a de-facto infrastructure control plane. Understanding their architectures is crucial for leveraging their capabilities effectively.

KubeVirt's core philosophy revolves around extending Kubernetes to treat VMs as first-class citizens, alongside containers, rather than introducing a separate, parallel infrastructure for virtualization, particularly:

- Unifying VM and Container Management
- Leveraging Kubernetes Primitives
- Supporting Legacy Applications
- Workload Coexistence
- **KubeVirt Razor Principle:** If something is useful for Pods, we should not implement it only for VMs. This principle encourages the reuse and integration with the existing Kubernetes features wherever possible, rather than reinventing functionality, specifically for VMs.

KubeVirt's architecture is composed of several key components that work together to provide virtualization capabilities within Kubernetes. These components are typically deployed and managed by the virt-operator.

Component	Primary Role	Key Interactions
`virt-operator`	Installs, manages, and updates KubeVirt components.	Kubernetes API, other KubeVirt components (for deployment)

virt-api-server	Extends Kubernetes API for KubeVirt CRDs, handles validation and admission control for VM-specific operations.	Kubernetes API Server, kubectl/virtctl, KubeVirt CRDs
virt-controller	Watches KubeVirt CRDs (VM, VMI), manages VMI lifecycle (creation, deletion, state sync), orchestrates migrations.	Kubernetes API Server, virt-handler, VM/VMI CRDs
virt-handler	DaemonSet on each node, manages VMI lifecycle on the node, interacts with libvirt and virt-launcher.	Kubelet, libvirtd (in virt-launcher), VMI objects, virt-controller
virt-launcher	Runs in a dedicated pod per VMI, manages the QEMU process for the VM, sets up namespaces and cgroups.	libvirtd, QEMU, virt-handler, Host OS (via libvirt/QEMU)

***Table 11.1:** An Overview of KubeVirt Core Components*

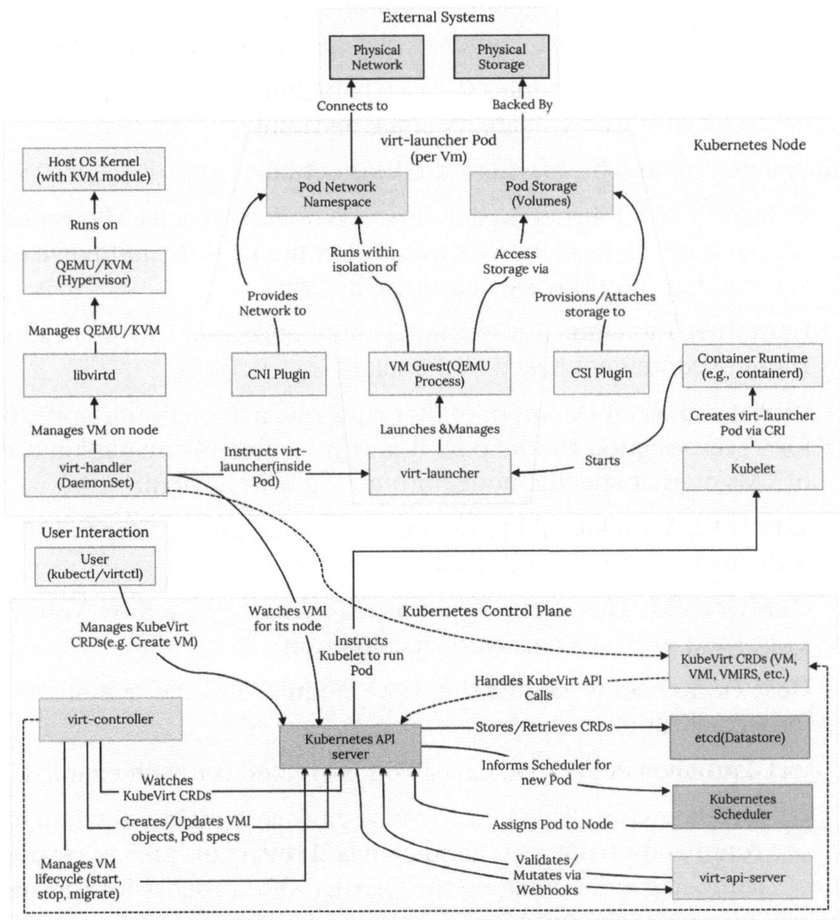

***Figure 11.1:** KubeVirt Architecture Diagram*

Explanation of the Diagram Elements and Flow

- **User Interaction:** The user interacts with the Kubernetes API server using kubectl or the KubeVirt-specific CLI virtctl to manage KubeVirt Custom Resources (CRs) like VirtualMachine (VM) or VirtualMachineInstance (VMI).
- **Kubernetes Control Plane:**
  - **K8s API Server:** This is the central management point. It receives user requests, stores CRD definitions, and objects in etcd.
  - **`etcd`:** The distributed key-value store for all Kubernetes cluster data, including KubeVirt CRs.
  - **virt-api-server:** Extends the Kubernetes API. It handles validation and admission control for KubeVirt-specific API requests.
  - **virt-controller:** Watches for KubeVirt CRs (VM, VMI). It is responsible for the cluster-wide reconciliation of VMs. When a VM is to be started, it typically creates a virt-launcher Pod specification, and a VMI object.
  - **`K8s Scheduler`:** Schedules the virt-launcher Pods onto appropriate nodes, based on resource availability and constraints.
- **Kubernetes Node:** This is where the VMs actually run.
  - **Kubelet:** The Kubernetes agent on each node. It receives Pod specifications from the API server, and ensures that containers (including virt-launcher) are running smoothly as well as are healthy.
  - **Container Runtime:** (for example, containerd, and CRI-O) Responsible for running containers based on Kubelet's instructions.
  - **`virt-handler`:** A DaemonSet that runs on each compute node. It watches for VMIs assigned to its node. It is responsible for managing the lifecycle of VMs on that specific node, interacting with libvirtd.
  - **`libvirtd`:** A toolkit/API to manage virtualization platforms. KubeVirt uses it to interact with QEMU/KVM.
  - **QEMU/KVM:** This is the hypervisor technology used by KubeVirt to run VMs. KVM provides hardware acceleration.
  - **Host OS Kernel:** Provides the KVM module, and the overall environment for virtualization.
  - **virt-launcher Pod:** A dedicated Pod is created for each running VMI.
    - **virt-launcher:** This is the primary process inside this Pod. It receives commands from virt-handler (via **`libvirtd`**), and is responsible for launching and managing the QEMU/KVM process for the specific VM. It provides the necessary cgroups and namespaces for the VM.

    - **VM Guest (QEMU Process):** The actual virtual machine instance running its guest OS.
    - **Pod Network Namespace:** The VM's network interfaces are connected to the Pod's network namespace.
    - **Pod Storage (Volumes):** The VM's disks are backed by Kubernetes volumes (for example, `PersistentVolumeClaims`) attached to the virt-launcher Pod.
  - **CNI Plugin:** Manages the network connectivity for Pods, and thus, for the VMs running inside them.
  - **CSI Plugin:** Manages the lifecycle of storage volumes for Pods.
- **Flow Highlights:**
  - A user defines a VM.
  - virt-controller observes this, and creates a VMI as well as a Pod definition.
  - The K8s scheduler assigns the Pod to a node.
  - Kubelet on the node starts the virt-launcher Pod.
  - `virt-handler` on that node, noticing the VMI, and instructs libvirtd (which is often managed within the virt-launcher pod's context or communicated with by `virt-handler`) to define and start the domain, using QEMU/KVM via the virt-launcher process.
  - The VM runs inside the virt-launcher Pod, utilizing Kubernetes networking (CNI) and storage (CSI).vCluster.

Core Philosophy and Goals

vCluster or VCluster (Virtual Cluster) is a technology designed to create lightweight, isolated Kubernetes control planes that operate as applications within a host Kubernetes cluster. Its core philosophy centers on providing full Kubernetes functionality to users or applications, without the overhead and complexity of provisioning and managing separate physical clusters. The fundamental idea behind vCluster is to offer:

- Lightweight Kubernetes Control Planes
- Control Plane Isolation for Multi-Tenancy
- Resource Efficiency and Reduced Overhead
  - Shared Infrastructure
  - Lightweight Implementation
  - Reduced Host API Load
- No Performance Degradation for Workloads

- Single Namespace Encapsulation (Default)
- Standard Kubernetes Experience
- Flexible and Easy Provisioning

Key Architectural Components

In this section, we are going to discuss some key architectural components and their roles.

Component	Primary Role	Key Interactions
Virtual API Server	Provides Kubernetes API endpoint for the virtual cluster; handles auth, auth admission for virtual resources.	Users (kubectl), Virtual Controller Manager, Virtual Scheduler, Data Store, Syncer [5]
Virtual Controller Manager	Manages controllers for resources (Deployments, Services, etc.) *within* the virtual cluster.	Virtual API Server, Data Store [53]
Virtual Scheduler (Optional)	Schedules pods *within* the virtual cluster if enabled; otherwise, host scheduler is used for synced pods.	Virtual API Server, Data Store [5]
Syncer	Synchronizes selected resources (for example, Pods, Services, PVCs) between the virtual cluster and the host cluster namespace.	Virtual API Server, Host API Server, Data Store [5]
Data Store	Stores the state (API objects) of the virtual cluster.	Virtual API Server, Virtual Controller Manager, Virtual Scheduler

Table 11.2: *vCluster Architectural Components and Their Roles*

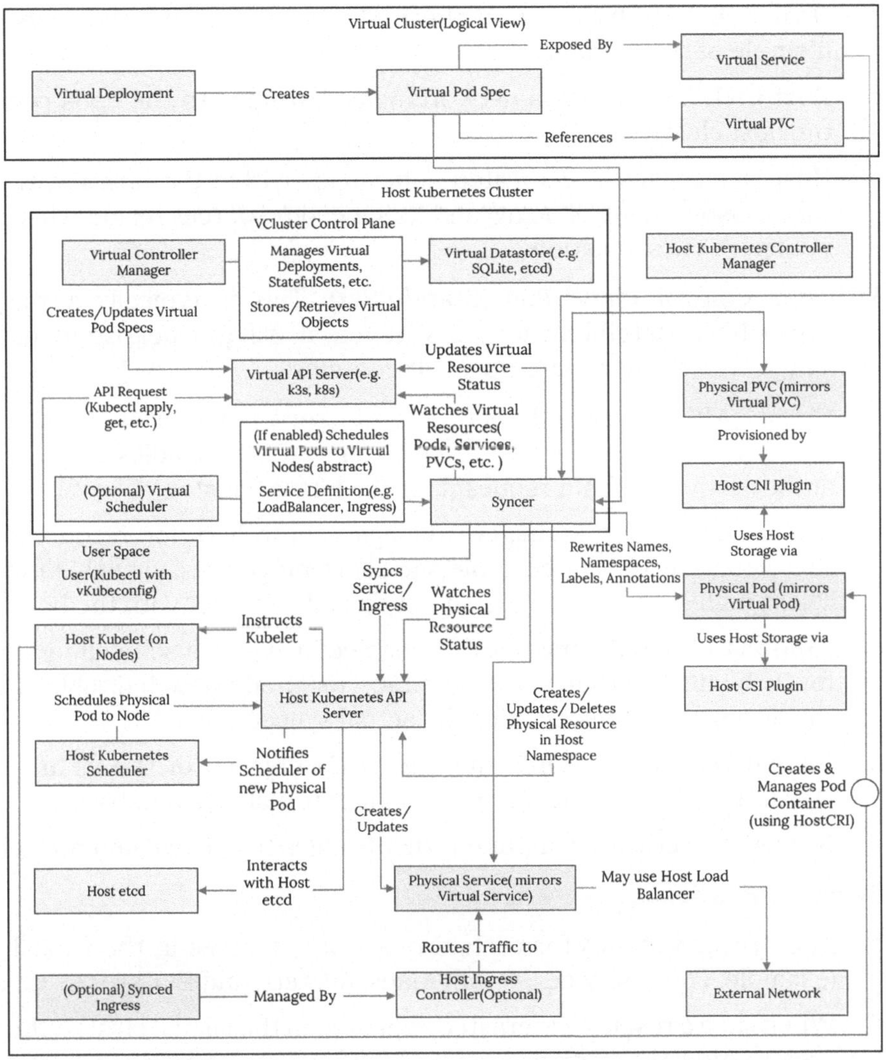

Figure 11.2: *vCluster Architecture Diagram*

Explanation of the Diagram Elements and Flow

1. **User Space:** The user interacts with the vCluster, using kubectl but configured with a Kubeconfig specific to that vCluster (**`vKubeconfig`**). All commands are directed to the **`VirtualAPIServer`**.
2. **Host Kubernetes Cluster:**
    - **Host Control Plane Components (`HostAPIServer`, `HostEtcd`, `HostScheduler`, `HostControllerManager`):** These are the standard components of the underlying "*physical*" Kubernetes cluster.

- **Host Kubelet:** This runs on the host cluster's nodes, and manages the lifecycle of actual Pods.
- **Host CNI/CSI:** Provides networking and storage to the Pods running on the host cluster.
- **Host Namespace:** A dedicated namespace within the host cluster where the vCluster's control plane, and its synced resources reside. This is key to vCluster's encapsulation.

3. **VCluster Control Plane Pod (StatefulSet):** This is typically a single Pod (managed by a StatefulSet for persistence, if using a persistent datastore) running within the host namespace. It contains:
   - **Virtual API Server:** A Kubernetes API server (for example, k3s, vanilla K8s and k0s) that serves the vCluster's API. It handles authentication, authorization, and API requests for the virtual cluster.
   - **Virtual Controller Manager:** Manages controllers for resources within the virtual cluster (for example, virtual Deployments, virtual StatefulSets). These high-level controllers do not directly interact with the host cluster.
   - **(Optional) Virtual Scheduler:** If enabled, it handles scheduling decisions for Pods *within* the virtual cluster's abstract node view. If disabled (default), the host scheduler schedules the actual synced Pods.
   - **Virtual Datastore:** Stores the state (API objects) of the virtual cluster. Defaults to SQLite, but can be etcd, or external SQL databases.
   - **Syncer:** The critical component that bridges the virtual and host clusters.
4. **Syncer Operations:**
   - The Syncer watches for certain types of resources in the virtual cluster (example, Pods, Services, ConfigMaps, Secrets, and PVCs).
   - When such a resource is created/updated in the virtual cluster, the Syncer creates/updates a corresponding "*physical*" resource in the host cluster's namespace.
   - **Translation:** During this sync, the Syncer performs the following translations:
     - **Name Rewriting:** Physical resource names are often mangled (for example, `virtual-pod-name-x-virtual-namespace-x-vCluster-name`) to avoid collisions in the host namespace.
     - **Namespace:** All synced physical resources are placed into the vCluster's single host namespace.
     - **Labels/Annotations:** Specific labels/annotations are added for vCluster to manage the synced objects.

  - The Syncer also watches the status of these physical resources in the host cluster, and syncs relevant status information back to the corresponding virtual resources.
  - **High-Level vs. Low-Level Resources:**
    - High-level resources such as Deployments, StatefulSets, and CRDs created in the vCluster typically only exist in the **`VirtualDatastore,`** and are managed by the **`VirtualControllerManager`**.
    - The **`VirtualControllerManager`** (for example, deployment controller within vCluster) creates **`VirtualPodSpecs`**.
    - The Syncer then picks up these **`VirtualPodSpecs`**, and syncs them as actual Pod objects to the host cluster.

5. **Host Cluster Operations (Running Workloads):**
   - The physical Pods created by the Syncer in the host namespace are scheduled by the HostScheduler, and run by the HostKubelet on the host cluster's nodes.
   - These physical Pods use the host cluster's CNI for networking and CSI for storage (via synced PVCs being fulfilled by the host).
6. **Service Exposure:**
   - Services defined in the vCluster are synced to the host namespace by the Syncer.
   - These host services can then be exposed using standard Kubernetes mechanisms on the host cluster (for example, via the host's Ingress controller if Ingress objects are also synced, or LoadBalancers).
   - VCluster also typically runs its own CoreDNS for service discovery within the virtual cluster, with the Syncer, ensuring DNS mappings resolve correctly to the host cluster IPs where the actual Pods are running.
7. **Storage:**
   - PersistentVolumeClaims (PVCs) created in the vCluster are synced to the host cluster's namespace.
   - The host cluster's CSI driver and StorageClasses then fulfill these synced PVCs, provisioning actual storage.
   - The physical Pod running on the host mounts the volume provisioned by the host cluster.

Provisioning Isolated vCluster Instances

VCluster instances can be created using the vCluster CLI, which simplifies the deployment process, or by directly using Helm for more granular control. For any customized or production-oriented setup, a vCluster.yaml file (a standard Helm values file) is essential to define specific configurations that impact isolation, security, and resource management.

The vCluster provisioning mechanism is designed with flexibility in mind. Simple CLI commands cater to rapid development and testing needs, allowing developers to quickly spin up isolated environments. For more complex, production-like scenarios, or integration into existing Infrastructure-as-Code (IaC) and GitOps workflows, direct Helm usage or providing a detailed vCluster.yaml file offers the necessary sophisticated control. This dual approach ensures that vCluster is adaptable across diverse operational models and user skill levels, thereby enhancing its applicability.

Leveraging the vCluster CLI

The vCluster CLI provides the most direct method for creating a new virtual cluster.

```
vcluster create my-vCluster --namespace team-x 12.
```

This command creates a vCluster named my-vCluster within the team-x namespace on the host cluster. The --namespace flag is fundamental as it dictates where the vCluster's control plane (a StatefulSet) and all its synchronized resources will reside on the host, directly contributing to vCluster's principle of single namespace encapsulation.

The `--distro` flag allows selection of the Kubernetes distribution for the vCluster's control plane. Options include k3s (default, recommended for its small footprint), k0s (another lightweight alternative), or k8s (vanilla Kubernetes, which deploys a separate etcd, API server, and controller manager, incurring more overhead). The choice of distribution impacts the resource consumption and internal characteristics of the vCluster but does not need to match the host cluster's distribution.

For any customization beyond defaults, the `--values` (or `-f`) flag is used to provide a Helm values file, commonly named vCluster.yaml. This file allows for detailed configuration of all aspects of the vCluster.

Other useful flags include:

- `--connect=false`: Prevents the CLI from automatically attempting to connect to the vCluster after creation.
- `--expose`: Creates a LoadBalancer service in the host cluster to expose the vCluster's API server externally. While convenient, this can be costly in cloud environments.

Advanced Deployment with Helm and vCluster.yaml

Under the hood, all vCluster deployments utilize Helm charts; the vCluster create CLI command is essentially a user-friendly wrapper around Helm operations.1 For fine-grained control and integration into GitOps workflows, direct Helm usage or detailed vCluster.yaml configuration is standard practice.

A **`vCluster.yaml`** file allows users to specify values for the vCluster Helm chart, overriding defaults and tailoring the deployment.

```
create my-vcluster --namespace team-x --values vcluster.yaml
```

Accessing Your vCluster via Kubeconfig

Once a vCluster is provisioned, users interact with it using kubectl, just like any other Kubernetes cluster. The vCluster connects command facilitates by modifying the local kubeconfig file to point to the vCluster's API server. Executing **`connect my-vcluster -n my-namespace`** typically performs the following actions:

- Establishes API Server Accessibility
- Updates Kubeconfig
- Sets Authentication

Alternatively, the kubeconfig for a vCluster can often be retrieved directly from a Secret named **`vc-<vcluster-name>`** located in the host namespace where the vCluster is deployed.

Verifying Your vCluster Deployment

After initiating vCluster creation, it is important to verify its successful deployment and operational status.

- **CLI Wait:** The vcluster create command typically waits for the vCluster to become ready, unless the **`--skip-wait`** flag is used.
- **List vClusters:** The vcluster list command can be used to see running vClusters managed by the CLI or platform.
- **Host Namespace Check:** Examine the pods in the host namespace where the vCluster was deployed.

  ```
  kubectl get pods -n <vcluster-host-namespace>
  ```

  This should show the vCluster's control plane pod (for example, **`my-vcluster-0`**, if it is a StatefulSet) in a Running state, and typically a CoreDNS pod, if not using the embedded CoreDNS feature.

- **Internal vCluster Check:** Connect to the vCluster using **`vcluster connect...`** and then execute standard kubectl commands against it.
- **Log Inspection**: If issues arise, inspecting the logs of the vCluster components is crucial. These logs are accessed via kubectl logs in the host namespace.

Secure Decommissioning: Deleting vClusters

When a vCluster is no longer needed, it should be deleted to free up resources on the host cluster.

- The vCluster CLI command **`vcluster delete <VCLUSTER_NAME> --namespace <NAMESPACE>`** is used for this purpose.
- Several flags can control the deletion behavior such as:
    - **`--keep-pvc`**: If set, the **`PersistentVolumeClaim`** associated with the vCluster's control plane (if any) will not be deleted.
    - **`--auto-delete-namespace or --delete-namespace`**: If enabled, the host namespace containing the vCluster will also be deleted (use with caution, especially if the namespace was not created exclusively by/for vCluster).
    - **`--delete-context`**: Controls whether the corresponding kubeconfig context is removed. By default, when the vCluster's main resource (e.g., the StatefulSet in the host namespace) is deleted, Kubernetes' garbage collection, guided by owner references set by vCluster on synced resources, should automatically clean up associated objects such as Pods and Services in the host namespace.

Optimizing Resources: Pausing (Sleep Mode) and Resuming vClusters

VCluster offers a "**`Sleep Mode`**" feature, which is highly beneficial for cost optimization, particularly for development, testing, or CI/CD vClusters that are not continuously active.

- **To pause**: `vcluster pause <VCLUSTER_NAME>` (or `vcluster platform sleep vcluster <VCLUSTER_NAME>` for platform-managed instances).
- **To resume**: `vcluster resume <VCLUSTER_NAME>` (or `vcluster platform wakeup vcluster <VCLUSTER_NAME>`).

Comparing Performance and Resource Utilization

KubeVirt excels in providing robust and performant execution of virtual machines by deeply integrating mature virtualization technologies such as KVM and QEMU into the Kubernetes framework. This allows workloads running within KubeVirt VMs to achieve performance levels that can approach that of bare-metal execution, particularly for I/O-bound or CPU-intensive tasks.

A key advantage of KubeVirt is its provision of fine-grained control over VM resources, and a suite of optimization techniques, specifically designed for virtualized workloads. Features such as

- memory overcommit
- configurable CPU allocation
- NUMA topology awareness
- IOThread tuning

offer administrators and users powerful levers to balance VM density with performance requirements. Furthermore, KubeVirt's seamless integration with standard Kubernetes primitives such as Pods, Services, and **`PersistentVolumeClaims`** allows for unified management of VMs alongside containers, while critically retaining the true isolation and environmental characteristics of a virtual machine.

KubeVirt is the preferred solution in several scenarios such as:

- Migrating Existing VM-Based Applications
- Specific Operating System or Kernel Requirements
- Strong Hardware-Level Isolation
- Direct Hardware Access Needs
- Complex, Monolithic "*Tenant*" Workloads

VCluster carves out a distinct and valuable niche by offering a compelling solution for creating multiple, isolated Kubernetes control planes with minimal resource overhead. This makes it highly suitable for development teams needing sandboxed environments, CI/CD pipelines requiring ephemeral Kubernetes clusters for testing, and SaaS providers looking to offer "*Kubernetes-as-a-service*" like experiences to their customers, without the cost and complexity of provisioning full physical clusters per tenant.

The strength of vCluster lies in its API-level isolation and efficient resource sharing at the data plane (that is, worker nodes and underlying infrastructure). It allows many sets of containerized applications to run across different virtual clusters, all sharing the same physical host cluster resources. From a KubeVirt user's perspective, vCluster addresses a fundamentally different problem: It is not about running virtual machines, but about partitioning an existing Kubernetes cluster at the control plane level to create multiple logical Kubernetes environments.

Ultimately, KubeVirt and vCluster are not direct competitors vying for the exact same use case. Instead, they represent complementary technologies within the broader Kubernetes ecosystem. KubeVirt is the go-to solution when the workload itself is a virtual machine, or requires the characteristics of one. vCluster, on the other hand, is a solution when the primary need is for multiple, isolated Kubernetes environments to run already containerized workloads. Understanding this fundamental distinction is crucial for architects and engineers when choosing the right tool for their specific objectives. KubeVirt provides a robust pathway for virtual machines to become first-class, manageable citizens within Kubernetes, complete with performance and resource management capabilities tailored to their nature. vCluster provides an innovative way for Kubernetes itself to be "*virtualized*" to serve multi-tenancy and environment isolation needs for container-native applications.

Hybrid Workloads vs. Multi-Tenant Environments

In the Kubernetes context, "*hybrid workloads*" refer to scenarios where virtual machines and containerized applications must coexist, be managed, and interact within a unified orchestration framework. This is not merely about running VMs in one system and containers in another; it signifies a deeper integration where both workload types are treated as first-class citizens by Kubernetes.

Several factors drive the adoption of hybrid workload models such as:

1. Legacy Application Modernization
2. Specialized Workload Requirements
3. Phased Modernization Strategies
4. Development and Testing

KubeVirt is engineered to natively manage virtual machines within Kubernetes, making it a cornerstone technology for hybrid workload scenarios. Its core approach involves extending the Kubernetes API through Custom Resource Definitions (CRDs), primarily VirtualMachine (VM) and VirtualMachineInstance (VMI). These CRDs allow Kubernetes to understand, orchestrate, and manage the entire lifecycle of VMs, using the same familiar API, tools (like kubectl and the KubeVirt-specific virtctl), and declarative configurations used for containers. KubeVirt intelligently delegates core orchestration functions such as scheduling, networking, and storage to Kubernetes, while it focuses on providing the specialized virtualization functionality.

Advantages in Hybrid Contexts

- Unified Management Plane
- Leveraging Kubernetes Ecosystem
- Consistent CI/CD Pipelines
- Resource Optimization

VCluster's primary function is to create virtual Kubernetes clusters that operate on top of an existing, physical host Kubernetes cluster. Its fundamental design goal is to provide strong isolation, and enable multi-tenancy by equipping each tenant (or virtual cluster instance) with its own independent control plane components.

VCluster itself does not directly manage the execution of VMs or containers in the same way KubeVirt manages VMs. Instead, it focuses on managing virtual Kubernetes clusters. Its role in hybrid workload scenarios is therefore indirect. A virtual cluster provisioned by vCluster can, however, become an environment capable of supporting hybrid workloads if it is integrated with a KubeVirt installation running on the host cluster. In such an integrated setup, tenants who are users of the vCluster can deploy and manage VMs, using KubeVirt CRDs. These KubeVirt resources, defined within the vCluster, are then synchronized by vCluster's syncer component to the host cluster, where the actual KubeVirt operators process them and run the VMs. vCluster emulates a fully functional Kubernetes cluster, which implies it could theoretically host any workload that Kubernetes can, provided the necessary extensions (like KubeVirt) are made available to it from the host.

Integrating KubeVirt with vCluster

While KubeVirt and vCluster address different primary challenges—VM orchestration and Kubernetes virtualization, respectively—their capabilities can be combined to create sophisticated solutions, particularly for multi-tenant environments that require VM provisioning.

VCluster, particularly in its Pro or Enterprise editions, offers an integration that allows a virtual cluster to leverage an existing KubeVirt installation running on the host Kubernetes cluster. This integration is typically enabled and configured through the vCluster.yaml manifest used to deploy or update a vCluster instance.

The synergy between KubeVirt and vCluster enables several compelling use cases, particularly in scenarios demanding both strong multi-tenancy and VM provisioning capabilities:

- Multi-Tenant Platforms Offering Self-Service VMs
- Enhanced Isolation for Development and Testing with VMs

- Securely Exposing VM Management to Less Trusted Tenants
- Building Internal "VM-*Enabled Platform-as-a-Service (PaaS)*"

Benefits and Limitations of the Combined Approach

Combining KubeVirt with vCluster offers distinct advantages, but also comes with certain limitations and considerations:

Benefits:

- Strong Tenant Isolation for VM Workloads
- Tenant Autonomy for VM Provisioning
- Simplified Management for Host Administrators (Potentially)
- Resource Efficiency

Limitations:

- VCluster Pro/Enterprise Feature
- Limited KubeVirt Resource Syncing
- Increased Complexity
- Potential Performance Overhead
- Dependency on Host KubeVirt Installation

Feature/Aspect	**KubeVirt**	**VCluster (Perspective on Hybrid Workloads)**
Primary Role	Direct orchestration of VMs alongside containers within a Kubernetes cluster.	Indirect; provides isolated Kubernetes environments (vClusters) that *can* host KubeVirt-managed VMs via integration with host KubeVirt.
VM Management	Native, core feature. Manages VM lifecycle, storage, networking directly via CRDs.	Via integration with host KubeVirt; not a core vCluster function. Relies on syncing KubeVirt resources.
Unified Kubernetes Management	Extends Kubernetes API to natively understand and manage VMs as first-class resources.	Provides a complete virtual Kubernetes control plane; workloads (VMs or containers) *within* the vCluster are K8s-managed.

Isolation for Hybrid Components	Relies on standard Kubernetes namespaces, RBAC, and NetworkPolicies for isolating VMs and containers.	Isolates entire Kubernetes environments (control planes). Hybrid components within a vCluster are then subject to that vCluster's rules.
Key Strengths	Seamless VM integration into Kubernetes, leverages full K8s ecosystem for VMs, ideal for legacy application migration and stateful VM services.	Strong environmental isolation for tenants who can then manage their own hybrid mix, flexibility in K8s versions/CRDs within vCluster.
Best Fit Scenario	Organizations needing to run and manage VMs as integral parts of a single Kubernetes cluster, leveraging unified operations.	Multi-tenant platforms where tenants require fully isolated Kubernetes environments and may optionally choose to run VMs using an integrated KubeVirt.

Table 11.3: *KubeVirt vs. vCluster for Hybrid Workloads*

In the following *Table* 11.4, we compare the two technologies based on multi-tenant environments:

Feature/Aspect	**KubeVirt (Leveraging Kubernetes Primitives)**	**VCluster**
Isolation Model	Kubernetes Namespaces, RBAC, Network Policies, and Resource Quotas applied on the host cluster.	Virtualized Kubernetes Control Plane per tenant (dedicated API server, controller manager, and data store).
Control Plane Sharing	Tenants share the host Kubernetes control plane.	Each tenant has a dedicated virtual control plane, isolated from the host and other tenants' control planes.
Tenant Autonomy (CRD Mgmt, K8s Versions)	Limited; typically no independent CRD management or K8s versioning per tenant.	High; tenants can manage their own CRDs, and potentially run different Kubernetes API versions within their vCluster.
Resource Management	Host cluster ResourceQuotas applied to tenant namespaces.	Host cluster `ResourceQuotas` on the vCluster's host namespace, plus internal resource management/quotas possible within the vCluster.
Security Boundary	Kubernetes API-level and network-level isolation based on host cluster policies.	Stronger API boundary due to separate API servers. Data plane isolation still relies on host cluster policies (NetworkPolicy, etc.).

Complexity to Implement Tenancy	Relies on well-configured Kubernetes multi-tenancy features on the host; can be complex to set up correctly.	Adds vCluster components (control plane pod, syncer) but can simplify the tenant experience for achieving cluster-like access.
Key Strengths	Consistent with Kubernetes container tenancy models, simpler if already using robust K8s tenancy practices.	Superior control plane isolation, high tenant autonomy, avoids CRD conflicts between tenants, reduces API load on host.
Best Fit Scenario	Trusted tenants within an organization, need for consistent policy enforcement with containers, simpler VM tenancy requirements.	Untrusted tenants, SaaS offerings, tenants requiring full (virtual) cluster admin rights, or independence in CRD/API version management.

Table 11.4: *KubeVirt vs. vCluster for Multi-Tenant Environments*

Decision Framework

This section will guide you through the process of deciding between KubeVirt and vCluster, considering various use cases and technical requirements. It outlines specific scenarios where each technology proves to be the optimal choice, and provides a comprehensive comparison table to facilitate informed decision-making.

Choosing KubeVirt

KubeVirt is the definitive choice when the requirements align with its core capability: running and managing full virtual machines within a Kubernetes environment. Several scenarios clearly indicate KubeVirt as the appropriate solution.

Scenarios Demanding Full Virtual Machine Capabilities: The most straightforward reason to choose KubeVirt is when the workload itself necessitates a full virtual machine environment. This includes:

- Unmodified Legacy Applications
- Specific Operating System Requirements
- Applications with Deep OS Dependencies
- Direct Hardware Access Needs (Virtualized)

Prioritizing Kernel-Level Isolation and Hardware Access: When security policies, compliance mandates, or the nature of the workload demands strong, kernel-level isolation between different applications or tenants, KubeVirt's hypervisor-based approach is superior. This is particularly relevant when:

- Running Untrusted Code

- Meeting Strict Compliance Requirements
- Preventing Kernel Exploits from Spreading

Consolidating the Existing VM Infrastructure onto Kubernetes

- Unify Orchestration
- Leverage Kubernetes Ecosystem
- Modernize Incrementally

Choosing vCluster

VCluster is the preferred solution, when the primary goal is to provide isolated, fully functional Kubernetes environments with agility and cost-efficiency, rather than running individual virtual machines. Its architecture is tailored for scenarios where Kubernetes-native multi-tenancy, and rapid environment provisioning are the key.

Scenarios Requiring Strong Kubernetes Multi-Tenancy

- Namespace Limitations are Insufficient.
- Full Administrative Control within Tenant Environment is Needed.
- Serving Multiple Customers on Shared Infrastructure.

Optimizing Cost, Speed, and Resource Efficiency for K8 Environments

- Minimizing Infrastructure Costs.
- Rapid Provisioning and Decommissioning.
- Higher Density of K8s Environments.

Empowering Developer Self-Service and CI/CD Pipelines

- Developer Sandboxes
- Ephemeral CI/CD Environments
- Experimentation and Learning

Key Requirement / Scenario	Primary Choice	Rationale / Key Considerations
Running unmodified legacy Windows/Linux applications.	KubeVirt	Requires a full OS environment that KubeVirt provides.
Needing strong kernel-level isolation for untrusted or sensitive workloads.	KubeVirt	Hypervisor-based isolation offers deeper security boundaries than shared-kernel models.
Providing multiple development teams with isolated Kubernetes sandboxes.	VCluster	Lightweight, rapid provisioning, strong API isolation, and cost-effective for multiple K8s environments.

Rapidly provisioning ephemeral environments for CI/CD testing of K8s apps.	VCluster	Fast spin-up/tear-down times are ideal for CI/CD pipelines.
Minimizing infrastructure costs for providing multiple K8s environments.	VCluster	Shares host cluster resources, significantly reducing overhead compared to multiple full clusters.
Requiring full admin control over CRDs and operators within isolated K8s environments.	VCluster	Tenants can manage cluster-scoped resources independently within their vCluster.
Consolidating an existing VM farm (for example, VMware, KVM) onto Kubernetes.	KubeVirt	Allows migration of existing VMs to Kubernetes for unified management.
Needing to test applications against different Kubernetes API versions or distributions.	VCluster	Can spin up vClusters with different K8s versions/ distributions without impacting the host.
Offering delegated VM provisioning to tenants who already have vCluster access.	KubeVirt + vCluster (Enterprise Integration)	VCluster acts as a multi-tenant frontend to KubeVirt; KubeVirt runs the VMs. Subject to integration limitations.
Running applications that require specific kernel modules or direct hardware access.	KubeVirt	VMs offer greater control over the kernel and better (though still virtualized) access to underlying hardware features than standard containers.
Managing diverse workloads (VMs and isolated K8s environments) on one platform.	KubeVirt and vCluster (Coexisting)	Host cluster runs KubeVirt for VMs and also hosts vClusters for isolated K8s environments, serving different needs on shared infrastructure.

Table 11.5: *Decision-Making Guide- When to Choose KubeVirt or vCluster*

Conclusion

In conclusion, both KubeVirt and vCluster offer powerful solutions within the Kubernetes ecosystem, addressing distinct needs. KubeVirt excels at integrating and managing virtual machines as first-class Kubernetes citizens, ideal for hybrid workloads, and consolidating the existing VM infrastructure.

Conversely, vCluster provides lightweight, isolated Kubernetes control planes, perfect for multi-tenancy, rapid environment provisioning, and developer self-service.

While serving different primary purposes, their capabilities can be combined to create sophisticated platforms that offer both VM provisioning and strong tenant isolation, allowing organizations to leverage the full power of Kubernetes for diverse computing requirements. The choice between them, or their combined use, hinges on specific use cases, isolation requirements, and operational goals.

The next chapter will delve into advanced KubeVirt VM lifecycle management, focusing on cloning and golden images. It will also cover creating VM templates, efficient image imports and DataVolume creation with CDI, as well as customizing VM deployments for consistency and security.

CHAPTER 12
Cloning, Golden VM Images, and the CDI Project

Introduction

This chapter covers advanced Virtual Machine (VM) lifecycle management in KubeVirt, using cloning and golden images with the Containerized Data Importer (CDI). Learn to create templates from the existing VMs for fast provisioning and consistent configurations. The key topics include, using CDI for efficient VM image import and management, streamlining DataVolume creation, customizing VM clones, and using golden images for standardized, secure VM deployments.

Hence, by the end of this chapter, you will understand how to optimize VM provisioning, maintain and update golden image repositories, and automate deployments with KubeVirt and CDI, enabling scalable and consistent VM management across hybrid environments.

Structure

In this chapter, we will cover the following topics:

- Benefits and Use Cases
- Creating and Managing Golden Images
- Containerized Data Importer (CDI) and its Role in Image Management
- Customizing VM Clones for Unique Workload Requirements

Benefits and Use Cases

Virtual Machine (VM) cloning is a foundational operation in virtualization, enabling the creation of identical copies of VMs. In the KubeVirt ecosystem, this capability is not merely an add-on but is deeply integrated with Kubernetes principles, offering a powerful, API-driven approach to managing virtualized workloads alongside containers. This section defines VM cloning within KubeVirt, introduces the key components that facilitate this process, and outlines the high-level mechanisms involved.

At its core, VM cloning is the process of creating an exact, independent, and fully functional replica of an existing VM. This duplicate encompasses the source VM's entire state, including its configuration, operating system, installed applications, and all the data residing on its virtual disks. Once created, the clone operates as a completely separate VM instance, with its own identity and lifecycle, distinct from the original.

The KubeVirt approach to VM cloning distinguishes itself significantly from traditional virtualization platforms. In conventional systems, cloning is often a hypervisor-specific, imperative operation managed through a centralized console or proprietary APIs. KubeVirt, however, reimagines virtualization within the Kubernetes paradigm. It extends the Kubernetes API with Custom Resource Definitions (CRDs) and dedicated controllers, enabling VM management, including cloning, through Kubernetes-native constructs, and its declarative API model. This means that cloning operations are defined, initiated, and monitored as Kubernetes resources, aligning VM lifecycle management with the well-established practices of container orchestration. KubeVirt's fundamental design allows organizations to run and manage traditional VM workloads and containerized applications side-by-side within a single Kubernetes cluster, providing a unified operational platform.

Advantages of KubeVirt VM Cloning

The integration of VM cloning into the Kubernetes-native KubeVirt framework offers a multitude of strategic advantages that enhance agility, efficiency, and reliability for managing virtualized workloads. These benefits stem directly from the combination of traditional virtualization capabilities with the power and flexibility of Kubernetes orchestration, and the specialized data handling of the Containerized Data Importer (CDI).

Accelerating VM Provisioning and Deployment

One of the most immediate and impactful benefits of KubeVirt VM cloning is the significant acceleration of VM provisioning and deployment processes. Instead of undergoing lengthy manual operating system installations, software configurations, and application deployments for each new VM, cloning allows for the rapid creation of new instances from an existing, fully configured VM or, more commonly, from a pre-configured "*golden image*" or `VirtualMachineSnapshot`. This can reduce provisioning times from hours to minutes, especially when CDI can leverage storage-efficient cloning methods such as CSI volume cloning or snapshot-based smart cloning.

Ensuring Consistency and Standardization Across Environments

Cloning produces identical copies of a source VM or snapshot, thereby ensuring a high degree of consistency and standardization across different deployment environments–such as development, testing, staging, and production. By deploying VMs from a common, vetted golden image, organizations can minimize configuration drift, and eliminate the notorious "*it works on my machine*" problem that often plagues software development lifecycles.

Enabling Efficient Scalability of Virtualized Workloads

KubeVirt VM cloning provides a practical mechanism for scaling out VM-based applications, particularly stateful ones that may not be easily managed by standard Kubernetes ReplicaSets designed for stateless workloads. This is useful for adding capacity to web farms, application server clusters, or database replicas. While KubeVirt's VirtualMachineInstanceReplicaSet (VMIRS) is suitable for scaling stateless ephemeral VMs, cloning offers a path to scale VMs that might have a unique initial state derived from a master instance, or require a full, independent copy of their disk.

Bolstering Disaster Recovery Capabilities

VM cloning, especially when combined with **`VirtualMachineSnapshots`**, plays a vital role in Disaster Recovery (DR) and business continuity planning. Production VMs can be regularly snapshotted, and these snapshots (or direct clones of VM disks) can be replicated to a secondary Kubernetes cluster, or an offsite storage location. In the event of a primary site failure, the cloned VMs, or VMs restored from these replicated snapshots, can be quickly brought online at the DR site.

Creating and Managing Golden Images

The concept of a "*golden image*" is foundational to efficient and scalable Virtual Machine (VM) management. Before delving into its specific implementation within the KubeVirt ecosystem, it is necessary to establish a clear understanding of what a golden image is, and the universal benefits it offers. This understanding will provide the context for appreciating KubeVirt's approach to VM templating and provisioning.

A golden image, also referred to as a master image, base image, or clone image, represents a meticulously prepared template of a VM, server, or even a hard disk drive configuration. It serves as a pre-configured, fully functional "snapshot" of a computer system or software setup, embodying the "*golden standard*" that an organization aims to replicate across multiple instances. The core idea is to capture a system in its ideal state–its "*perfect form*"–so that it can be used as a blueprint for deploying new, identical systems.

Typically, a golden image contains a pre-installed operating system, a suite of essential applications, necessary drivers, and specific software configurations tailored to meet organizational or workload requirements. The process of creating a golden image involves installing and configuring the OS and applications on a reference machine or VM, applying updates and patches, and setting up specific options and preferences. Once perfected, this configuration is saved as a template or image file.

The "*Golden Disk Image*" in the KubeVirt Ecosystem

In the KubeVirt context, a "*Golden Disk Image*" is precisely defined as an immutable disk image that is stored within a Kubernetes PersistentVolumeClaim (PVC). This PVC-backed image can then be cloned by a VirtualMachine to serve as its root operating system image. This approach is functionally analogous to how Amazon Machine Images (AMIs) are used in AWS.

The Containerized Data Importer (CDI), a companion project to KubeVirt, plays a crucial role in this process. CDI facilitates the import of external VM images (from various sources such as URLs or container registries) and stores them within the cluster's storage, typically manifesting as a PVC. This stored and prepared image effectively becomes the Golden Disk Image that KubeVirt can reference for provisioning new VMs. For instance, Red Hat, a significant contributor to KubeVirt and OpenShift Virtualization, publishes its official golden images as "*container disks.*" These are virtual machine images packaged within container images, and hosted in secure registries. CDI is then used to poll these registries, and import the container disks into the Kubernetes cluster, storing them as PVCs or VolumeSnapshots that can be used as golden images. The immutability of these golden disk images is a key characteristic, ensuring that every VM cloned from them starts from an identical and uncorrupted state.

The Central Role of PersistentVolumeClaims

`PersistentVolumeClaims` (PVCs) are fundamental to KubeVirt's storage architecture, serving as the Kubernetes-native abstraction for how storage is provisioned and consumed by virtual machines. The concept of golden images in KubeVirt is intrinsically tied to PVCs. The prepared, bootable disk image that constitutes the golden image is stored within a PVC. The CDI orchestrates the population of these PVCs with image data imported from various external or internal sources.

CDI-Based Cloning

The CDI provides robust functionality for cloning an existing **`PersistentVolumeClaim`** (the golden image PVC) to a new target PVC that will serve as the root disk for a new virtual machine. This operation can be initiated in a couple of ways:

- Using **`DataVolume`** with **`source.pvc`**
- Using PVC Annotation **`k8s.io/CloneRequest`**: `"<src-namespace>/<src-pvc-name>"`

CDI is designed to perform this cloning operation efficiently. It will attempt to leverage any underlying storage backend capabilities for fast, storage-level clones, if available. If the storage system does not offer native cloning features that CDI can use, it will fall back to a network-based copy, where the data is read from the source PVC, and written to the target PVC by CDI-managed pods.

CDI's StorageProfile Custom Resource allows administrators to define or discover preferred cloning strategies for different Kubernetes StorageClasses.

Leveraging the `VirtualMachineClone` API with VM Snapshots

KubeVirt provides another mechanism for creating copies of virtual machines through its **`VirtualMachineClone`** Custom Resource Definition which is part of the clone.kubevirt.io API group.

A significant use case for the **`VirtualMachineClone`** API is the creation of "*golden VM images*" by first taking a **`VirtualMachineSnapshot`** of a fully prepared and configured reference VM, and then using the **`VirtualMachineClone`** resource to instantiate new VMs from this snapshot. The typical workflow is:

1. Create a base VirtualMachine.
2. Power it on, and prepare the "*golden environment*" inside the guest OS (install applications, configure users, settings, and so on).
3. Take a VirtualMachineSnapshot of this prepared VM.
4. Optionally, delete the original base VM, if it is no longer needed.

5. To provision new VMs, create **`VirtualMachineClone`** objects where the spec. source field points to the previously created VirtualMachineSnapshot.

This method offers a way to template not just the disk image, but potentially the entire VM configuration (CPU, memory, devices, and so on) as captured at the moment of the snapshot. The choice between CDI-based PVC cloning, and using the VirtualMachineClone API often depends on the desired granularity of templating. CDI cloning is ideal, when the primary goal is to replicate a standard OS disk, with VM-specific hardware configurations (CPU, memory, and devices) being defined separately in the VirtualMachine manifest that consumes the cloned disk.

Referencing Golden Images in VirtualMachine Definitions

We shall discuss the following different ways available for us to reference Golden Images with Data Volume Templates:

- **Using `DataVolumeTemplates` with `sourceRef` to a DataSource**: A **`dataVolumeTemplate`** defines a **`DataVolume`** that will be dynamically created and processed by CDI, when the VirtualMachine is started. By setting the sourceRef field in this embedded DataVolume to point to a DataSource.
- **Direct Reference to Versioned Golden Image PVCs in `DataVolumeTemplates`**: For scenarios requiring strict control over the image version used by a VM, or for pinning a VM to a specific, validated version of a golden image, a DataVolumeTemplate can be configured to clone directly from a known golden image PVC. This is done by specifying **`spec.source.pvc`** within the DataVolume definition embedded in the **`dataVolumeTemplate`**, providing the name and namespace of the exact golden image PVC to clone.

```
apiVersion: kubevirt.io/v1
kind: VirtualMachine
metadata:
  name: my-pinned-vm
spec:
  runStrategy: Always
  dataVolumeTemplates:
    - metadata:
        name: rootdisk-dv
      spec:
        source:
          pvc:
            namespace: golden-image-ns
            # Direct reference to a versioned PVC
            name: my-os-image-v1.2.3-stable
        pvc:
```

```
          accessModes:
            - ReadWriteOnce
          resources:
            requests:
              storage: 30Gi
  template:
    spec:
      domain:
        #... VM domain spec...
      volumes:
        - name: rootdisk
          dataVolume:
            name: rootdisk-dv
```

Best Practices for Golden Image Lifecycle Management

Let us discuss some of the core best practices that we should keep in mind, when creating the base Golden Images for our workloads:

- **Purpose-Specific Images:** Instead of a one-size-fits-all approach, create multiple, lean golden images tailored for specific roles, applications, or environments.
- **Minimalism:** Each golden image should include only the essential software, libraries, and configurations required for its designated purpose.
- **End-to-End Automation:** The entire process–from base OS installation, package management, customization, security hardening, generalization (**`virt-sysprep`**), testing, and finally, importing into CDI or uploading to a container registry–should be automated.
- **CI/CD Tools:** Leverage general-purpose CI/CD tools such as Jenkins, GitLab CI, or GitHub Actions, or specialized image building tools such as HashiCorp Packer or OS-specific builders or Red Hat Image Builder.
- **Tekton for Kubernetes-Native CI/CD:** For environments deeply integrated with Kubernetes, Tekton Pipelines provide a Kubernetes-native framework for defining and running CI/CD pipelines.
- **Rigorous Security:** Embed security configurations, hardening measures and compliance checks directly into the automated image build process.
- **Continuous Patching:** Golden images are not static. They must be regularly updated with the latest security patches, operating system updates, and application version upgrades.

Updating Live Virtual Machines from New Golden Image Versions

KubeVirt provides foundational mechanisms, known as VM rollout strategies, that define how changes made to a **`VirtualMachine`** (VM) object's specification are propagated to its corresponding running **`VirtualMachineInstance`** (VMI). These strategies are configured globally in the KubeVirt Custom Resource.

- **LiveUpdate:** When this strategy is enabled, KubeVirt attempts to apply changes to a running VMI as soon as possible, if the change supports live application. An example is CPU hotplug, where changing the number of CPU sockets in the VM spec might trigger an immediate update to the running VMI.
- **Stage:** This is the default strategy. With Stage, any changes made to the VM object's spec are staged, and will only take effect the next time the VM is restarted (that is, the VMI is stopped and started again).

CDI and its Role in Image Management

The CDI's primary goal is to provide a declarative, automated mechanism for importing, cloning, and uploading VM disk images onto PVCs. This simplifies storage management for KubeVirt VMs by abstracting the complexities of data transfer and image preparation. The key objectives include:

- **Declarative Data Population:** Enabling users to define the desired state of a PVC (that is, populated with a specific image) through Kubernetes custom resources.
- **Multiple Data Sources:** Supporting image import from various locations, including HTTP/S URLs, S3-compatible object storage, container registries, and direct uploads from a client machine. It also supports cloning the existing PVCs.
- **Image Format Handling:** Automatically processing common VM disk image formats (for example, **`qcow2`**, **`raw`**) and compression types (for example, **`gz`**, **`xz`**), including conversion to formats optimal for KubeVirt.
- **Integration with Kubernetes Storage:** Working seamlessly with standard Kubernetes storage primitives such as PVCs, PersistentVolumes (PVs), and StorageClasses.
- **Golden Image Management:** Facilitating the creation and use of "*golden VM images*"–standardized templates for VM provisioning.

Core Components

CDI's functionality is delivered through several key components that run as pods, within the Kubernetes cluster, typically in a dedicated namespace.

- **`cdi-operator`:** This component is responsible for installing, managing, and upgrading the CDI components within the cluster. It watches the CDI custom resource which triggers the deployment and configuration of other CDI components.
- **`cdi-controller` (Deployment Controller):** This is the primary long-lived controller that monitors DataVolume custom resources and PVC annotations. Upon detecting a new DataVolume, or a PVC with specific CDI annotations (for example, for import or clone), the cdi-controller initiates the appropriate data population process. It is responsible for creating and managing the lifecycle of worker pods (importer or cloner pods) that perform the actual data transfer and processing. It also updates the status of DataVolume CRs and PVC annotations to reflect the progress and outcome of operations.
- **`cdi-apiserver`:** This component serves as an API endpoint for specific CDI operations, most notably for handling UploadTokenRequest CRs related to direct image uploads. When a user initiates an image upload using virtctl image-upload, virtctl communicates with the cdi-apiserver to obtain a secure, short-lived token. This token is then used to authenticate the upload stream to the cdi-uploadproxy. The cdi-apiserver thus plays a crucial role in the security and orchestration of the image upload workflow. It also handles requests for VM export tokens.
- **`cdi-importer` (Importer Pods):** These are short-lived worker pods created by the cdi-controller to handle the import of data from external sources such as HTTP/S, S3, or container registries into a PVC. An importer pod typically mounts the target PVC, and streams data from the specified source into it. It also performs the necessary data transformations such as decompression and image format conversion (example, qcow2 to raw) using tools like qemu-img. The naming convention for these pods is often **`importer-<datavolume-name>-<random-suffix>`**.
- **`cdi-cloner` (Cloner Pods):** Similar to importer pods, these are temporary worker pods responsible for cloning data from a source PVC to a target PVC. For host-assisted cloning (when storage-native cloning is not available), a source cloner pod and a target cloner pod are typically created. These pods establish a connection (often TLS-secured) to transfer data between the volumes.
- **`cdi-uploadproxy`:** This service acts as a secure gateway for direct image uploads initiated by virtctl image-upload. It receives the authenticated data stream from the client, and forwards it to the appropriate upload-server-pod

(which might be an importer pod configured for upload) that writes the data to the target PVC. The cdi-uploadproxy service needs to be exposed externally (for example, via NodePort, LoadBalancer, or Ingress) for client uploads to function.

- **`upload-server-pod`:** This is a pod (often an importer pod in a specific mode) that runs an HTTP server to receive the uploaded data from the cdi-uploadproxy, and write it to the target PVC.

Interaction Flow for DataVolume Processing

In this section, we go in detail discussing how the control and interaction flow happens in case of processing a DataVolume CRD.

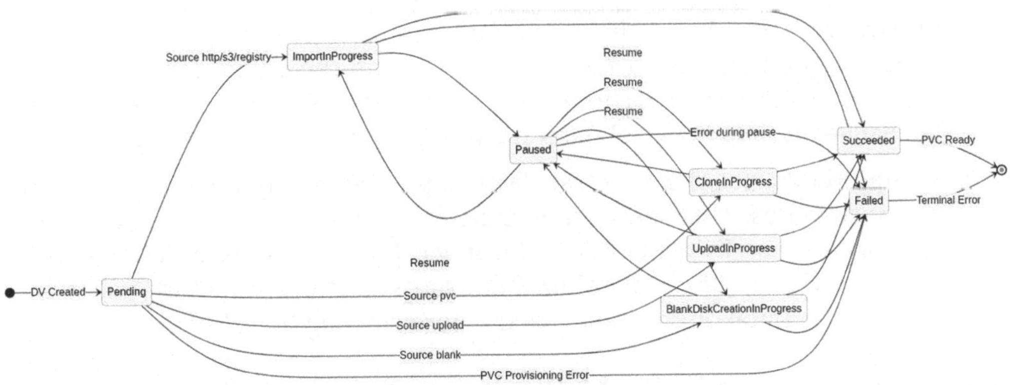

***Figure 12.1:** Data Volume Processing Interaction Flow*

The processing of a DataVolume involves a coordinated effort between these components:

- **DataVolume Creation:** A user creates a DataVolume manifest specifying the data source (for example, HTTP URL, S3 bucket, source PVC for cloning, or an upload request) and the target PVC characteristics.
- **Controller Detection:** The **`cdi-controller`** observes the creation of the new DataVolume CR.
- **PVC Provisioning:** The **`cdi-controller`** creates a corresponding PVC, based on the DataVolume specification. If dynamic provisioning is used, the underlying storage provisioner creates a PV.
- **Worker Pod Orchestration:**
    - **For Imports (HTTP, S3, and Registry):** The cdi-controller launches a cdi-importer pod. This pod is configured with the source details from the DataVolume (example, URL, secret reference for credentials). The importer pod mounts the target PVC, downloads/extracts the data, performs any

necessary conversions (for example, qcow2 to raw and decompression), and writes it to the PVC.

- **For Cloning:** If storage-native cloning (smart clone/CSI clone) is available and configured, CDI attempts to use it. Otherwise, for host-assisted cloning, the cdi-controller typically creates a source cloner pod, and a target cloner pod. These pods coordinate to copy the data from the source PVC to the target PVC.
- **For Uploads:** When a DataVolume with an upload: `{}` source is created, the cdi-controller prepares the system for an upload. The virtctl image-upload command then requests an upload token from the **`cdi-apiserver`**. Once the token is granted, virtctl streams the image to the **`cdi-uploadproxy`** which forwards it to an upload-server-pod that writes to the PVC.

- **Status Updates:** Throughout the process, the worker pods and the cdi-controller update annotations on the PVC, and the status of the DataVolume CR to reflect the progress (for example, **`ImportInProgress`**, **`CloneInProgress`**, **`UploadReady`**) and the final outcome (for example, Succeeded, Failed).
- **Completion:** Once the data transfer and processing are complete, the worker pod terminates. The DataVolume status changes to Succeeded, and the PVC is ready for use by a KubeVirt VM. If the DataVolume was defined within a VirtualMachine CR's dataVolumeTemplates section, KubeVirt will typically wait for the DataVolume to succeed before starting the VM.

Key CDI Functionalities for Image Management

CDI provides a versatile set of functionalities for managing VM images, catering to different sources and use cases. These are primarily orchestrated through the DataVolume custom resource.

Importing VM Images from Various Sources

CDI supports importing VM images from several external and internal locations.

1. **Importing from HTTPs/URLs**

```
apiVersion: cdi.kubevirt.io/v1beta1
kind: DataVolume
metadata:
  name: fedora-dv-http
spec:
  source:
    http:
      url: "https://download.fedoraproject.org/pub/fedora/linux/
```

```
releases/39/Cloud/x86_64/images/Fedora-Cloud-Base-39-1.5.x86_64.
raw.xz"
      # secretRef: "my-http-secret" # Optional: for basic
authentication
      # certConfigMap: "my-custom-ca-bundle" # Optional: for
custom CA certs
  pvc:
    accessModes:
      - ReadWriteOnce
    resources:
      requests:
        storage: 10Gi
    # storageClassName: "your-storage-class" # Optional
```

2. **Importing from S3-Compatible Storage**

```
apiVersion: cdi.kubevirt.io/v1beta1
kind: DataVolume
metadata:
  name: image-dv-s3
  namespace: default
spec:
  source:
    s3:
      # The URL should be the full path to the object, including
the S3 endpoint, bucket, and object key.
      # Example for AWS S3: "s3://s3.amazonaws.com/my-bucket/
images/my-image.qcow2"
      # Example for MinIO (if not using TLS): "http://minio-
service.minio-ns.svc:9000/my-bucket/images/my-image.qcow2"
      # Example for MinIO (using TLS): "https://minio-service.
minio-ns.svc:9000/my-bucket/images/my-image.qcow2"
      url: "s3://<your-s3-endpoint-and-bucket>/<path/to/image.
qcow2>"
      secretRef: "my-s3-secret" # References the Secret defined
      # certConfigMap: "s3-ca-bundle" # Optional: for custom CA
certificate for the S3 endpoint
      # region: "us-east-1" # Optional: specify the S3 region if
necessary
  pvc:
    accessModes:
      - ReadWriteOnce
    resources:
      requests:
        storage: 20Gi
    # storageClassName: "your-s3-optimized-storage-class" #
Optional
```

3. **Importing from Container Registries**

```
apiVersion: cdi.kubevirt.io/v1beta1
kind: DataVolume
metadata:
  name: containerdisk-dv
spec:
  source:
    registry:
      # The URL should specify the full image path, including the
tag or digest.
      # The 'docker://' prefix is common, but check CDI
documentation for exact format.
      url: "docker://quay.io/kubevirt/fedora-cloud-container
-disk-demo:latest"
      # secretRef: "my-private-registry-secret" # Optional: for
private registries
      # certConfigMap: "my-registry-custom-ca" # Optional: for
registries with custom/self-signed CAs
      # pullMethod: "pod" # Default. Alternative is "node" (less
common).
  pvc:
    accessModes:
      - ReadWriteOnce
    resources:
      requests:
        storage: 10Gi
    # storageClassName: "your-storage-class" # Optional
```

Cloning the Existing `PersistentVolumeClaims`

```
apiVersion: cdi.kubevirt.io/v1beta1
kind: DataVolume
metadata:
  name: cloned-fedora-dv
  namespace: target-namespace # Namespace where the new cloned
PVC will be created
spec:
  source:
    pvc:
      namespace: "source-namespace"   # Namespace of the source
PVC
      name: "golden-fedora-pvc"     # Name of the source PVC to
clone
  pvc:
    accessModes:
      - ReadWriteOnce
```

```
    resources:
      requests:
        storage: 10Gi # Must be the same size or larger than the
source PVC
    # storageClassName: "your-storage-class" # For smart/CSI
cloning, usually must match source PVC's StorageClass
    # volumeMode: Filesystem # Or Block, usually must match
source PVC's volumeMode for smart/CSI cloning
```

Understanding contentType

Let us discuss the `contentType` field in a bit more detail, and the options available for its value. The **`contentType`** field in a KubeVirt CDI DataVolume specifies the format of the data being imported. It tells the CDI how to handle the source data to make it usable as a virtual machine disk.

KubeVirt (Default Content Type)

- This indicates that the source data is intended to be a bootable or attachable virtual disk image for a KubeVirt VM.
- CDI performs several key operations for this content type:
  - **Decompression:** If the source image is compressed (for example, **`.raw.gz`**, **`.qcow2.xz`**), CDI automatically decompresses it.
  - **Format Conversion:** If the decompressed image is in qcow2 format, CDI converts it to raw format. This conversion to raw is a standard practice within CDI to ensure a consistent and often more performant disk format for KubeVirt.
  - **Resizing:** The resulting raw image is automatically resized to utilize the full capacity of the target PVC. The guest OS within the VM will then need to be configured to recognize and use this potentially larger disk space.

archive

- This indicates that the source data is a tar archive (for example, a **`.tar`** file).
- CDI will extract the contents of the tar archive into the root directory of the target PVC.
- This contentType is useful for populating a PVC with a filesystem structure that can then be mounted by a regular Kubernetes pod, or by a KubeVirt VM using KubeVirt's filesystem volume type (for example, **`virtiofs`**).
- Initially, compression for archives (for example, **`.tar.gz`**) was not directly supported for extraction by CDI itself, meaning the source would need to be an uncompressed tarball.

Creation, Maintenance, and Consumption Patterns

CDI fundamentally transforms the management of golden VM images from what might traditionally be a manual, external process (for example, maintaining templates in a vSphere Content Library) into a Kubernetes-native, declarative, and automatable workflow. The combination of CDI's import and cloning capabilities effectively allows the creation of an in-cluster "**`Content Library`**" for KubeVirt, often realized as a dedicated namespace holding these master PVCs. The lifecycle of golden images using CDI typically follows these patterns:

Creation

- **Initial Import:** An administrator defines a DataVolume to import a chosen base OS image (example, a generic cloud image or an ISO) into a PVC. This PVC is often created in a dedicated and restricted namespace (for example, golden-images, vm-templates) to protect it from unintended modifications.
- **(Optional) Customization:** To create a more specialized golden image, a KubeVirt VM can be launched using the initially imported base PVC. Inside this VM, administrators can perform customizations: install additional software, apply security configurations, configure services, and so on, using tools such as virt-customize, cloud-init, or manual setup. Once customized, the disk of this VM needs to be captured as a new golden image. This might involve shutting down the VM, and then cloning its PVC to create a new, "**`customized`**" golden image PVC.
- **ContainerDisk Approach:** An increasingly popular method is to package the prepared VM disk image (raw or qcow2) into a container image (a "**`ContainerDisk`**") and push it to a container registry. This allows versioning and distribution using standard container tooling. CDI then imports this ContainerDisk via its registry source to create the golden PVC. This method aligns VM image management closely with container image workflows.

Maintenance and Updating

- When a golden image needs to be updated (for example, to apply OS patches, update embedded software, or fix security vulnerabilities), a new version of the image is created.
- This typically involves repeating the creation process: importing an updated base image or building a new ContainerDisk with the changes, resulting in a new golden PVC (example, **`fedora-39-golden-v2`** if **`fedora-39-golden-v1`** was the previous version).

- The old golden image PVC can be retained for a period to allow for rollback, or to support VMs that still require the older version. Eventually, outdated golden images can be decommissioned and their PVCs deleted.
- When using DataVolumes to create the golden image PVCs themselves, the annotation **`cdi.kubevirt.io/storage.deleteAfterCompletion: "false"`** is often used. This prevents the DataVolume object that created the golden PVC from being automatically deleted upon successful import. This is beneficial if the DataVolume definition is managed via GitOps, as it stops the system from continuously attempting to recreate the (already existing and populated) golden PVC.
- **Consumption:**
    - End-users or automation systems create new KubeVirt VMs by referencing the desired golden image.
    - This is typically done by defining a DataVolume in the user's working namespace that specifies the golden image PVC (from the golden-images namespace) as its source.pvc. CDI then clones the golden PVC into a new PVC for the VM.
    - Alternatively, if KubeVirt VirtualMachine objects are used, their spec. dataVolumeTemplates section can define a DataVolume that clones a golden image. This automates the disk provisioning as part of the VM creation process. The lifecycle of such a DataVolume (and its cloned PVC) is then tied to the VirtualMachine object.
    - If CDI Volume Populators are used, a VolumeCloneSource CR can be defined in the golden-images namespace pointing to the golden PVC. User PVCs in other namespaces can then reference this VolumeCloneSource via their dataSourceRef to get a clone.

Customizing VM Clones for Unique Workload Requirements

In KubeVirt, this capability to clone Virtual Machines is a cornerstone of efficient virtualization management, enabling rapid provisioning, disaster recovery, and the creation of standardized environments as well as is significantly enhanced by the **`VirtualMachineClone`**, Custom Resource Definition (CRD) and the Containerized Data Importer (CDI) project. These tools not only facilitate the creation of VM replicas, but also provide extensive mechanisms to customize these clones to meet diverse and specific workload requirements. This section delves into the various strategies for tailoring VM clones, from basic metadata adjustments to deep modifications of hardware, storage, network configurations, and operating system-level settings.

Let us see some of these unique workload requirements that can arise in various scenarios, and how we can tackle them in the context of KubeVirt.

Ensuring Uniqueness: MAC Addresses and SMBIOS

For a cloned VM to function correctly on a network, and be uniquely identifiable at a pseudo-hardware level, its MAC addresses and SMBIOS serial numbers must be distinct.

- **`newMacAddresses`:** This field is a map where keys are interface names (defined in the source VM's template, for example, "**`default`**", "**`eth1`**") and values are the desired MAC addresses for the clone. By default, KubeVirt strips all MAC addresses from the cloned VM's interfaces. This allows external mechanisms like kube-mac-pool (if deployed) to automatically assign fresh, valid MAC addresses. However, newMacAddresses provides explicit control for scenarios requiring deterministic MAC assignment such as integration with external DHCP/IPAM systems that rely on specific MACs, or software licensing tied to MAC addresses.
- **`newSMBiosSerial`:** This field allows setting a specific SMBIOS serial number for the cloned VM. If not specified, KubeVirt assigns an auto-generated serial number based on the target VM's name. A custom SMBIOS serial can be important for asset tracking, licensing, or maintaining consistent system identity across different environments.

These mechanisms for setting unique identifiers are foundational. Without unique MAC addresses, network collisions and communication failures are inevitable. While KubeVirt's default behavior of stripping MACs is generally safe, the explicit controls offered by newMacAddresses and newSMBiosSerial are invaluable for precise identity management, ensuring that each clone, regardless of its source, can be uniquely and correctly identified at the virtual hardware layer.

Modifying Virtual Hardware Configuration

Beyond CPU and memory, other aspects of the virtual hardware platform can be customized to meet specific requirements such as guest OS compatibility or enabling particular hardware features.

- **Machine Type:** The QEMU machine type (for example, **`q35`**, **`pc-i440fx-2.10`**) can be changed via a JSON patch to **`spec.template.spec.domain.machine.type`**. KubeVirt defaults to QEMU's newest q35 type, but older operating systems or specific use cases might require an alternative.

- **Firmware Settings:** Firmware characteristics, including the SMBIOS uuid and serial (though newSMBiosSerial in VirtualMachineClone is often preferred for the latter), and the bootloader (to switch between BIOS and UEFI via **`efi: {}`**), can be modified under **`spec.template.spec.domain.firmware`**. Enabling UEFI boot, for example, might be necessary for modern operating systems or features like Secure Boot. Secure Boot itself requires the SMM CPU feature to be enabled.
- **Virtualization Features:** Various virtualization features exposed by the hypervisor such as acpi, apic, and hyperv enlightenments (for example, relaxed, vapic, and spinlocks), can be enabled, disabled, or tweaked under **`spec.template.spec.domain.features`**. These can be crucial for guest OS stability, performance, or compatibility, especially for non-Linux guests.

Altering these fundamental virtual hardware aspects via JSON patches during cloning provides significant flexibility. It allows a standard golden image to be adapted for diverse guest OS needs or specific hardware dependencies, without the need to prepare and maintain separate base images for each distinct hardware profile. For instance, a legacy OS might necessitate an older machine type, while a modern OS could leverage UEFI, and its associated security features.

Connecting to NetworkAttachment Definitions (NADs)

NetworkAttachmentDefinitions (NADs), with apiVersion: **`k8s.cni.cncf.io/v1`**, are Kubernetes CRDs used by Multus to define available secondary networks. These NADs can configure various CNI plugins (for example, bridge, host-device, SR-IOV, and MACVTAP) to provide diverse network capabilities.

```
spec:
 template:
   spec:
     domain:
       devices:
         interfaces:
           name: prod-network
           model: virtio
           # For a bridge-based NAD, or remove if NAD type han-
dles it (e.g. SR-IOV)
           # The type here (bridge, masquerade, and so on) should
align with how the NAD is expected to be used by the VM.
           bridge: {}
     networks:
       name: prod-network  # Must match the interface name above
       multus:
```

```
          # Name of the NetworkAttachmentDefinition in the VM's
namespace
          networkName: production-vlan-nad
```

Interface Types (bridge, masquerade, slirp, SR-IOV)

KubeVirt supports several interface types, each with different characteristics:

- **masquerade:** The default for the primary pod interface if not otherwise specified. VM traffic is NATed using the pod's IP address. This is simple to set up, but hides the VM's actual IP from the external network.
- **bridge:** Connects the VM's interface to a Linux bridge on the node. For the primary interface, this connects to the pod network bridge. For secondary interfaces (via Multus NADs), this can connect the VM to other host bridges, effectively placing it on the same L2 segment as the bridge.
- **slirp:** Provides user-mode networking via slirp: {}. It does not require special privileges on the host and allows outbound connections, but generally has lower performance than bridge or masquerade modes.
- **SR-IOV:** Enables direct assignment of a Virtual Function (VF) from an SR-IOV capable Physical NIC on the host to the VM. This offers very high performance and low latency by bypassing much of the host's networking stack. It requires SR-IOV hardware, corresponding device plugins (for example, SR-IOV network device plugin), and an SR-IOV NAD. The interface is defined with:

  ```
  sriov:
    resourceName: "vendor.com/sriov_vf_pool_A"
  ```

where resourceName matches the resource advertised by the device plugin.

Static IP and MAC Address Considerations

Ensuring predictable network identity for cloned VMs often involves setting static MAC addresses and, where possible, static IP addresses. Directly assigning static IP addresses to VMs through the VirtualMachine CRD is not a general KubeVirt feature for the default pod network; IPAM is typically managed by other layers:

- **CNI Plugin:** Some CNI plugins (such as Kube-OVN) support static IP and MAC assignment via annotations on the Pod or VM object. To use this for a clone, the necessary annotations would need to be applied to the target VirtualMachine object, likely via JSON patches to its metadata.annotations or spec.template.metadata.annotations.
- **Cloud-init/Sysprep:** Static IP configuration can be injected into the guest OS during its first boot, using cloud-init (for Linux) or Sysprep (for Windows). The

cloud-init or Sysprep data source within the VM template would need to be modified via JSON patch to include the desired network configuration.

- **DHCP Reservation:** If an external or CNI-provided DHCP server is in use, it can be configured to assign a specific IP address to the VM based on its (statically assigned) MAC address.

While MAC address assignment is relatively straightforward with VirtualMachineClone, achieving static IP configuration for clones often requires a coordinated approach. This typically involves using JSON patches to either inject CNI-specific annotations, or to modify the guest OS initialization data (**cloud-init/Sysprep**), underscoring the flexibility required from the cloning mechanism to integrate with various IPAM strategies.

```
apiVersion: clone.kubevirt.io/v1beta1
kind: VirtualMachineClone
metadata:
  name: clone-static-mac-and-cni-ip
spec:
  source:
       kind: VirtualMachine
       apiGroup: kubevirt.io
       name: dynamic-network-vm
  target:
       kind: VirtualMachine
       apiGroup: kubevirt.io
       name: fixed-identity-appliance
       patches:
       # Example: Add Kube-OVN annotation for static IP on the
       # 'default' interface (eth0 in pod)
       # This annotation is hypothetical; actual annotation may
vary
       - op: add
       # '~1' is JSON Pointer for '/'
       path: /spec/template/metadata/annotations/kubeovn.io~1ip_
address
       value: "default:192.168.1.100" # Format depends on CNI
```

Using Cloud-init for Linux VMs (user data, SSH keys, and network)

Cloud-init is the de facto standard for early boot customization of Linux virtual machines in cloud environments. KubeVirt integrates cloud-init by allowing **userData** (containing cloud-config YAML or shell scripts) and networkData (for guest network configuration) to be passed to the VM via special volumes, typically of type cloudInitNoCloud or cloudInitConfigDrive. This data can be provided inline within the **VirtualMachine** manifest, or more commonly for reusability and security, referenced from Kubernetes Secrets or ConfigMaps. When cloning a VM, its cloud-init configuration can be tailored for the new instance, using JSON patches.

```
apiVersion: kubevirt.io/v1
kind: VirtualMachine
metadata:
 name: vm-with-cloudinit-example
spec:
 running: false # Set to true to start the VM automatically
 template:
   metadata:
     labels:
       kubevirt.io/domain: vm-with-cloudinit-example
   spec:
     domain:
       cpu:
         cores: 1
       resources:
         requests:
           memory: 1Gi
       devices:
         disks:
           - name: containerdisk # An example OS disk
             disk:
               bus: virtio
           - name: cloudinitdisk # The cloud-init disk
             disk:
               bus: virtio
         interfaces: # Default pod network interface
           - name: default
             masquerade: {}
     networks: # Default pod network
       - name: default
         pod: {}
     volumes:
       - name: containerdisk # Define the OS disk source
         containerDisk:
             # Example image
           image: kubevirt/cirros-container-disk-demo:latest
       - name: cloudinitdisk # Define the cloud-init volume
         cloudInitNoCloud:
           userData: | # You can put your cloud-config data here
             #cloud-config
             hostname: my-custom-vm
             users:
               - name: myuser
                 ssh_authorized_keys:
```

```
                  - ssh-rsa <your public key here user@example.
com>
                # grant full sudo access without a password
                sudo: ALL=(ALL) NOPASSWD:ALL
          runcmd:
            - [touch, /tmp/cloud-init-was-here.txt]
```

Conclusion

Thus, this chapter delved into advanced VM lifecycle management in KubeVirt, emphasizing the power of cloning and golden images facilitated by the Containerized Data Importer (CDI). We explored how these capabilities accelerate VM provisioning, ensure consistency, and enhance disaster recovery. The key topics covered included the creation and management of golden images (especially "**Golden Disk Images**" backed by PVCs), CDI's role in importing and cloning images, and detailed methods for customizing VM clones to meet unique workload requirements, including network configuration and OS-level settings via cloud-init. Ultimately, understanding these mechanisms is crucial for optimizing and automating VM deployments, within KubeVirt's Kubernetes-native framework.

The next chapter will cover managing Virtual Machines (VMs) with KubeVirt across various environments, including multiple cloud providers and on-premises infrastructure. It will detail VM migration strategies, utilization of cloud-specific features, ensuring interoperability between VMs in hybrid and multi-cloud settings, along with storage and networking management.

CHAPTER 13
KubeVirt in Hybrid and Multi-Cloud Environments

Introduction

The adoption of hybrid and multi-cloud architectures has become a defining strategy for organizations seeking flexibility, resilience, and performance across their digital infrastructure. As workloads diversify and evolve, enterprises increasingly require infrastructure models that transcend single-cloud limitations, while enabling seamless integration of private data centers and public cloud resources. In the context of KubeVirt and OpenShift Virtualization, hybrid and multi-cloud designs provide a foundational bedrock for extending Virtual Machine (VM) workloads beyond traditional boundaries, ensuring scalability, fault tolerance, and efficient resource utilization.

Structure

In this chapter, we will cover the following topics:

- Understanding Hybrid and Multi-Cloud Architecture
- Workload Portability: Migrating VMs across Clouds with KubeVirt
- Networking Considerations for Hybrid and Multi-Cloud Environments
- Multi-Cloud Workload Scaling and Disaster Recovery Strategies
- Security Challenges and Best Practices in Hybrid/Multi-Cloud Setups
- Real-World Use Cases for KubeVirt in Hybrid and Multi-Cloud Scenarios

Understanding Hybrid and Multi-Cloud Architectures

Hybrid cloud refers to an IT architecture that connects private cloud (or on-premises infrastructure) with public cloud environments, allowing data and applications to move between them. In contrast, a multi-cloud strategy involves using two or more public cloud platforms from different providers, often for specific service advantages, redundancy, or cost optimization.

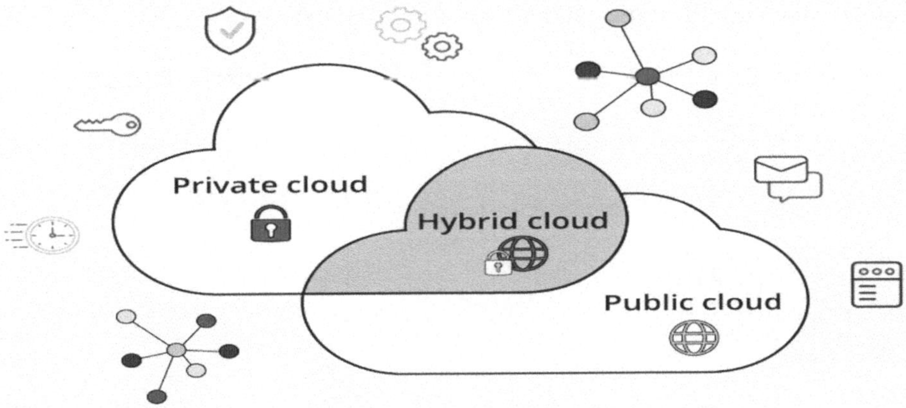

Figure 13.1: *Hybrid Cloud*

While hybrid cloud is focused on bridging on-premises with cloud platforms (for example, combining OpenShift running on bare metal with AWS EC2 instances), multi-cloud spans multiple cloud service providers (for example, running workloads across AWS, Azure, and GCP).

Key Characteristics:

- **Portability:** Applications and services can move across environments.
- **Interoperability:** Services can communicate and interoperate securely and efficiently.
- **Federation:** A governance layer ensures unified policy, identity, and access control across platforms.

Real-World Use Case: A financial institution maintains sensitive customer data within an on-premises OpenShift environment for regulatory compliance. At the same time, it leverages public cloud compute instances to process high-volume analytics workloads during peak hours. This blend exemplifies hybrid clouds in practice.

Business Drivers behind Hybrid and Multi-Cloud Adoption

Modern organizations pursue **hybrid** and **multi-cloud strategies** to achieve:

- Avoidance of vendor lock-in.
- Improved disaster recovery and High Availability (HA).
- Geographic distribution for latency-sensitive applications.
- Cost efficiency through workload optimization.
- Compliance with regional data sovereignty laws.

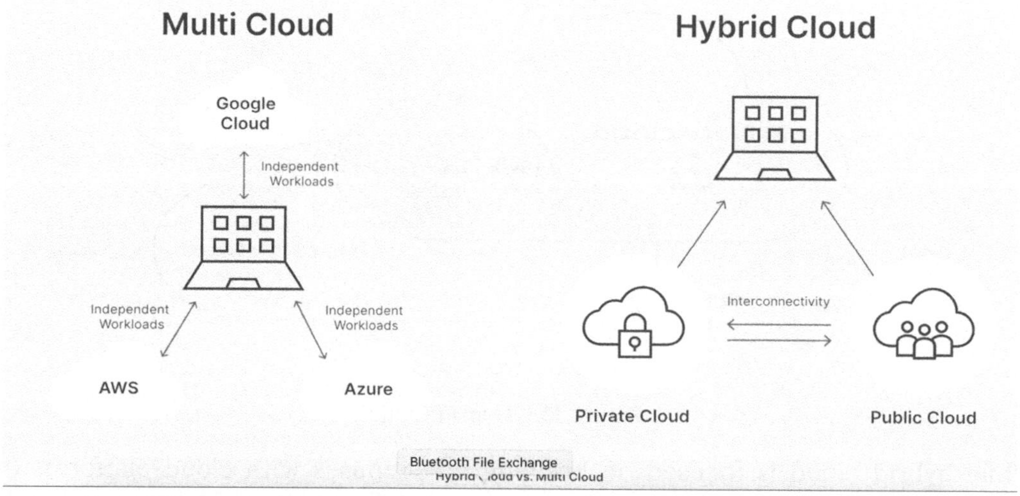

Figure 13.2: *Multicloud and Hybrid Cloud*

These drivers align directly with infrastructure platforms such as OpenShift and KubeVirt which support consistent deployment patterns and workload orchestration across varied infrastructure.

Example: An e-commerce enterprise utilizes AWS for web-tier services due to global reach, but retains its transaction-processing VM workloads on OpenShift with KubeVirt in its private data center. This approach balances cost, security, and availability.

Architectural Patterns for Hybrid and Multi-Cloud Deployments

Successful hybrid and multi-cloud deployments require architectural planning.

KubeVirt on OpenShift provides a flexible virtualization layer that coexists with containerized applications. The following patterns illustrate common designs:

- **Cloud Bursting:** Burst VM workloads from on-premises OpenShift environments to public cloud, when demand exceeds capacity.
- **Data Gravity and Processing Proximity:** Keep data local (for example, in on-prem object storage) while processing workloads in the public cloud to reduce latency.
- **Disaster Recovery:** Deploy passive or active VM replicas across cloud environments for failover using KubeVirt migration strategies.
- **Federated Control Planes:** Use Red Hat Advanced Cluster Management (RHACM) to manage multiple OpenShift clusters across clouds.

Network and Storage Considerations

Networking and storage are foundational elements in hybrid and multi-cloud systems. To ensure consistency and interoperability, architects must consider the following:

Networking:

- **East-West traffic flow** between on-prem and cloud must be encrypted and optimized.
- **SDN integration** between OpenShift and external networks should use overlay networks or direct VPN tunnels.
- **Load balancing** strategies must support multi-region and cross-cloud traffic.

Storage:

- Use **CSI-compatible storage providers** across environments (for example, Ceph, and Portworx).
- Ensure that **data replication** strategies across clouds are in place.
- Consider **ReadWriteMany (RWM)** volumes for shared VM workloads in hybrid clusters.

Example: A hybrid setup may use OpenShift Data Foundation (ODF) with Ceph to provide persistent volumes across both on-prem and AWS-hosted OpenShift clusters, enabling seamless migration and availability for KubeVirt VMs.

KubeVirt's Role in Hybrid and Multi-Cloud Ecosystems

KubeVirt extends Kubernetes by enabling it to orchestrate VMs alongside containers, offering a unified control plane. In hybrid and multi-cloud environments, this unification is essential for:

- **Consistency:** Developers interact with VMs and containers via the same APIs and tools.
- **Mobility:** VM images and definitions can be replicated across OpenShift clusters, using GitOps practices.
- **Interoperability:** KubeVirt integrates with OpenShift Pipelines, Service Mesh, and GitOps to streamline cross-cloud deployments.

Integration Example: A telecommunications provider deploys network functions as VMs, using KubeVirt and containers using standard Kubernetes APIs. These functions are distributed across on-prem and Azure-based OpenShift clusters. With GitOps and RHACM, deployments and policy controls are consistent and auditable.

Challenges and Best Practices

Despite its benefits, hybrid and multi-cloud introduces complexity in areas such as security, governance, and observability. The following are the best practices:

Security:

- Implement **Zero Trust architectures** across cloud boundaries.
- Use **Centralized Identity Providers** **`(IdPs)`** with **`OpenID Connect (OIDC)`** for federated authentication.
- Need to ensure **end-to-end encryption of VM and pod traffic**.

Governance:

- Need to define **namespace-level policies** for workload placement.
- Need to use **OPA Gatekeeper or Kyverno** for policy enforcement.

Observability:

- Centralize **logs and metrics with tools like Prometheus, Grafana, and Loki**.
- Correlate **VM and container metrics** to identify bottlenecks or anomalies.

Operations:

- Employ **Infrastructure as Code (IaC) with Terraform or Ansible** for reproducibility.
- Automate deployment pipelines using **Tekton and ArgoCD**.

Workload Portability: Migrating VMs across Clouds with KubeVirt

In hybrid and multi-cloud environments, workload portability is no longer a luxury—it is a necessity. Enterprises are increasingly seeking mechanisms that allow seamless migration of Virtual Machines (VMs) across cloud boundaries, without vendor lock-in or complex platform rewrites. KubeVirt, when integrated with OpenShift Virtualization, provides a robust abstraction layer that enables this kind of cross-cloud mobility, while leveraging Kubernetes-native constructs. This section examines how KubeVirt facilitates workload portability, explores the architecture required to enable migration across heterogeneous environments, and offers real-world patterns and considerations for designing and executing such migrations.

Understanding Workload Portability in the Context of Virtualization

Workload portability refers to the capability to move application workloads across disparate infrastructure environments with minimal configuration or modification. In the context of VMs, this includes not only the movement of the VM image itself, but also associated configurations such as network policies, storage mappings, and security contexts. Achieving portability involves addressing several layers:

- **Compute Abstraction:** Consistent CPU and memory definitions across environments.
- **Network Compatibility:** Aligning overlay or underlay network configurations across clusters.
- **Storage Compatibility:** Ensuring volume types and persistent storage backends are either standardized or translatable.
- **State Preservation:** Guaranteeing that the VM state (cold or live) is preserved during the transition.

KubeVirt enhances this portability by leveraging Kubernetes CRDs (Custom Resource Definitions) to represent VMs in a declarative format, thus making VM definitions infrastructure-agnostic.

Architectural Foundations for Multi-Cloud VM Migration

A successful VM migration strategy across clouds with KubeVirt hinges on certain architectural decisions:

- **Federated or Interconnected Clusters:** Clusters deployed on different clouds (for example, AWS, Azure, GCP, and on-prem) must be capable of communicating through a secure tunnel (for example, VPN, interconnect, and so on). Red Hat Advanced Cluster Management (RHACM), for instance, can manage multiple OpenShift clusters spread across clouds, offering a centralized control plane for orchestrating VM migrations.
- **Storage Abstraction Layer:** Using container-native storage solutions such as OpenShift Data Foundation (ODF) ensures that persistent volumes are not tied to a specific cloud provider's block storage. ODF supports replication and snapshot mechanisms critical for VM migrations. In cases where ODF is not feasible, CSI plugins must be configured consistently across environments.
- **Image Registry and VirtualDisk Management:** VM images must be accessible in both source and destination environments. Hosting them in a centralized or replicated container registry (for example, Quay and Harbor) ensures accessibility. KubeVirt utilizes **`DataVolume`** resources managed by CDI (Containerized Data Importer) for importing, cloning, and transferring disk images.

Step-by-Step Process for Cross-Cloud VM Migration

Migrating VMs between clouds, using KubeVirt involves the following stages:

Step 1: Export the VM Definition

Use **`kubectl get vm <vm-name> -o yaml`** to extract the VM manifest. Ensure that dependent resources (for example, volumes, secrets, and configMaps) are also exported.

Example:

```
kubectl get vm ubuntu-vm -o yaml > ubuntu-vm.yaml
kubectl get pvc ubuntu-vm-disk -o yaml > pvc.yaml
```

Step 2: Transfer VM Disk Image

If the disk is stored in a PVC backed by ODF or a CSI-compatible storage class, snapshot and export the image, using the **`VolumeSnapshot`** API or **`virtctl image-upload`**.

Example:

```
virtctl image-upload dv ubuntu-vm-disk \
  --size=10Gi \
  --image-path=./ubuntu-disk.qcow2 \
  --storage-class=ocs-storagecluster-ceph-rbd
```

Alternatively, the disk can be uploaded to an intermediate object storage bucket (for example, S3) and then imported in the destination cluster using CDI.

Step 3: Replicate the Manifest and Resources

Deploy the exported YAMLs to the destination OpenShift cluster:

```
oc apply -f pvc.yaml
oc apply -f ubuntu-vm.yaml
```

Ensure that storage classes, network attachment definitions (if using Multus), and service accounts are identical or compatible in the target environment.

Step 4: Validate and Start the VM

Once the resources are deployed, one needs to verify the VM status:

```
kubectl get vmi
virtctl start ubuntu-vm
```

Monitor the VM boot logs and application readiness to confirm successful migration.

Real-World Example: Migrating from On-Prem OpenShift to AWS ROSA

An enterprise maintains an on-prem OpenShift cluster for development workloads, and a managed OpenShift (ROSA) cluster on AWS for production. As part of a DR strategy, select VMs need to be periodically backed up, and restorable on ROSA:

- **Image Management:** The enterprise hosts VM disk images in an S3-compatible object store, accessible from both environments.
- **Networking:** Both clusters are connected via AWS Direct Connect, and a shared internal DNS.
- **Storage:** ODF runs on-prem, while EBS-backed CSI volumes are used in ROSA. The migration pipeline uses disk snapshots transferred via S3.
- **Automation:** A Tekton pipeline orchestrates the export, transfer, and import process, ensuring minimal downtime.

This model allows the organization to maintain workload continuity, even in the face of infrastructure failure or planned maintenance.

https://www.redhat.com/en/blog/modernizing-with-openshift-on-aws-using-rosa

Considerations and Best Practices

- **Stateful vs. Stateless Workloads:** While stateless workloads can be migrated using container images and Helm charts, VMs often encapsulate state and OS-level dependencies. Plan for cold migrations, unless live migration support is available across environments.

- **Resource Compatibility:** Need to ensure that CPU models and memory configurations are compatible. Some cloud environments may impose constraints (for example, CPU passthrough restrictions).
- **Security Contexts and SELinux:** Preserve VM security configurations such as SELinux contexts and service account bindings. These must be re-established on the destination cluster.
- **Namespace and RBAC Consistency:** Maintain consistent namespace mappings and role bindings across clusters to avoid access control issues post-migration.
- **Observability and Logging:** Use tools like Prometheus and Grafana to monitor the migration. Log collection should be unified (for example, via Loki or Fluentd) to capture any post-migration issues.

Future Outlook: Live Migration and Edge Computing

While KubeVirt supports live migration within a single cluster, live migration across cloud clusters is still an evolving area. As network latencies and storage replication techniques improve, we can expect future releases to introduce enhanced support for cross-cluster live migration.

Edge computing presents another interesting application. Devices in edge locations may periodically synchronize VMs with central cloud environments, using KubeVirt. This model provides resilience in disconnected or semi-connected scenarios.

Networking Considerations for Hybrid and Multi-Cloud Environments

In modern cloud-native architectures, especially those leveraging KubeVirt to manage both containerized and virtualized workloads, networking plays a critical role in ensuring performance, scalability, and security. Hybrid and multi-cloud environments introduce additional layers of complexity due to the heterogeneity of infrastructure, disparate network topologies, and the need for consistent communication across multiple platforms. This section provides an in-depth examination of networking considerations crucial for successfully deploying and operating KubeVirt workloads in hybrid and multi-cloud scenarios.

Introduction to Hybrid and Multi-Cloud Networking

Hybrid cloud combines on-premises infrastructure with one or more public cloud providers, whereas multi-cloud refers to the use of multiple public cloud platforms simultaneously. In both models, networking must facilitate low-latency, secure, and reliable communication across heterogeneous environments.

With KubeVirt, the situation becomes more nuanced. Virtual Machines (VMs) introduced into Kubernetes clusters require integration with Kubernetes-native networking constructs, while maintaining the isolation and functionality of traditional virtualization environments.

Network Design Principles

Designing a network strategy for KubeVirt in hybrid and multi-cloud environments should consider the following principles:

- **Interoperability:** Networks across different environments must be interoperable to support seamless VM and container communication.
- **Consistency:** Uniform policy enforcement such as ingress/egress rules, DNS resolution, and IP addressing schemes.
- **Scalability:** The ability to scale networking resources in proportion to workload demands.
- **Security:** Encrypted communication, network segmentation, and zero-trust networking models.
- **Resiliency:** Failover mechanisms, redundant paths, and intelligent routing protocols to ensure service continuity.

KubeVirt Networking Architecture

KubeVirt VMs rely on the Kubernetes Container Network Interface (CNI) for network connectivity. The default bridge-based binding enables VMs to share the pod network interface, but KubeVirt also supports more advanced configurations such as Multus CNI for attaching VMs to multiple networks.

Pod Network vs. Additional Network Interfaces

- **Pod Network:** Ideal for integrating VMs with Kubernetes services.
- **Multus and Secondary Networks:** Necessary when VMs require L2 adjacency or connection to legacy systems.

Example: In a financial services application where backend VMs need direct access to a mainframe over VLANs, secondary interfaces configured via Multus can bridge the VM directly to the legacy network.

Inter-Cluster Networking

In multi-cluster or multi-cloud environments, workloads often span across regions or providers. Establishing inter-cluster connectivity is fundamental.

- **VPN and Direct Connect**
    - **Site-to-Site VPNs:** Useful for quick setup, but can introduce latency.
    - **Cloud Interconnects (for example, AWS Direct Connect and Azure ExpressRoute):** Provide high throughput and low latency, but require more upfront planning.
- **Service Mesh Integration:** Service meshes like Istio can abstract service discovery, secure communication, and observability across hybrid environments. However, integrating VMs into service meshes requires sidecar injection, and proper IP routing.

  Example: In a global retail enterprise, KubeVirt VMs hosting payment processing services can be integrated into Istio to ensure secure, encrypted traffic between clusters in AWS and GCP.

DNS and Service Discovery

Service discovery is pivotal in distributed systems. Kubernetes-native service discovery mechanisms are DNS-based. However, across clouds and on-prem environments, DNS configuration must account for split-horizon DNS, and domain forwarding.

- **CoreDNS Customization:** To resolve external services.
- **External DNS Tools:** Integrate with Route53, Cloud DNS, or private DNS zones.

Load Balancing and Traffic Management

In hybrid and multi-cloud setups, load balancing strategies should be adapted to handle traffic routing between VMs and containers across networks.

- Ingress Controllers
- **Cloud-Native Ingress:** Cloud provider-specific.
- **HAProxy/Nginx/Contour:** Suitable for on-prem and hybrid clusters.

Global Load Balancers

- **GSLB (Global Server Load Balancers):** Route traffic based on latency, geo-location, or availability.

Example: A SaaS provider uses GSLB to distribute requests to KubeVirt VMs running in an on-prem data center and cloud-native microservices in Azure Kubernetes Service (AKS).

Security and Policy Management

Networking security in a distributed, multi-cloud setup is non-trivial. Kubernetes Network Policies can enforce rules at the pod level, but may not be sufficient for VM traffic.

Layered Security

- **Network Policies:** Pod-to-pod and pod-to-VM restrictions.
- **Service Mesh MTLS:** Encrypts traffic at the application layer.
- **Cloud Firewall Rules:** Apply at the infrastructure level.

Example: An e-commerce application utilizes Calico for Kubernetes network policies, Istio for MTLS, and AWS Security Groups for ingress traffic filtering to KubeVirt VMs.

Observability and Troubleshooting

Effective troubleshooting requires complete observability across the entire network stack.

Monitoring Tools

- **Prometheus and Grafana:** Monitor traffic metrics, latency, and availability.
- **Kiali:** Visualize service mesh communication.
- **Wireshark/tcpdump:** For low-level packet inspection.

Common Issues

- **MTU Mismatches:** Especially between VPN-connected networks.
- **IP Conflicts:** Duplicate IP addressing across environments.
- **DNS Resolution Failures:** Misconfigured or incomplete domain forwarding.

Multi-Cloud Workload Scaling and Disaster Recovery Strategies

As organizations expand their IT footprints across hybrid and multi-cloud environments, achieving scalable, resilient, and fault-tolerant infrastructure becomes paramount. KubeVirt, when integrated with OpenShift and managed using a GitOps-driven model, empowers architects to deploy, scale, and recover workloads across cloud boundaries with confidence. This section delves into the practical strategies for workload scaling and Disaster Recovery (DR) in multi-cloud scenarios, with particular emphasis on virtualized workloads managed through KubeVirt.

Understanding Multi-Cloud Scalability and Its Challenges

Multi-cloud workload scaling refers to the ability to dynamically expand or contract workloads across multiple Cloud Service Providers (CSPs) such as AWS, Azure, GCP, and on-premises environments. The core challenges include:

- **Latency and bandwidth variability** across regions and providers.
- **Inconsistent resource types** and VM instance characteristics.
- **Lack of uniform APIs** and orchestration layers, without an abstraction like OpenShift.
- **Data gravity**—especially when stateful VMs need to replicate or relocate data.

With KubeVirt acting as a bridge between container-native workloads and traditional virtual machines, organizations can encapsulate VM-based applications within Kubernetes-native constructs, and scale them using the same primitives as stateless workloads.

Scaling Virtual Workloads across Multi-Cloud OpenShift Clusters

To achieve seamless scalability of KubeVirt workloads, organizations typically employ a combination of horizontal and vertical scaling strategies. OpenShift provides native constructs such as `MachineSets` and `ClusterAutoscaler`, while KubeVirt supports VM scaling via `VirtualMachineInstanceReplicaSet` and CPU/memory adjustments.

Horizontal Scaling across Clusters

Scaling across clusters involves distributing virtual machine workloads between clusters located in different cloud providers or regions. This approach is essential when dealing with:

- Regional failovers.
- Proximity to users or data centers.
- Cloud cost arbitrage.

Example: A financial services firm runs its risk-analysis engine on OpenShift/KubeVirt across GCP (`us-west1`) and Azure (`eastus`). Using GitOps workflows via ArgoCD or OpenShift GitOps, it deploys a `VirtualMachine` YAML configuration across both clusters. An external DNS and load-balancing layer (for example, F5 BIG-IP or AWS Global Accelerator) routes traffic to the appropriate region based on latency or availability.

To enable this, a service mesh (such as Istio or OpenShift Service Mesh) can be extended across clusters with federation or multicluster mesh gateways. This ensures secure and observable communication between services and VMs, even across cloud boundaries.

Vertical Scaling within Nodes

In scenarios where workloads are constrained within a single region or cloud, vertical scaling of the VMs—for example, adding more CPU cores or memory to an existing VMI—can be achieved using live migration combined with custom resource updates. KubeVirt supports CPU/memory hotplugging in specific configurations.

Note: *Careful tuning of* `KubeVirtLiveMigrationConfiguration` *and resource quotas is required to ensure seamless vertical scaling in production environments.*

Disaster Recovery (DR) for Virtual Machines in Multi-Cloud Setups

Disaster recovery strategies vary, based on Recovery Time Objective (RTO) and Recovery Point Objective (RPO) requirements. In a multi-cloud world, this entails architecting systems that can fail over virtual machines across CSPs with minimal disruption and data loss.

Cold DR with GitOps and Immutable VM Definitions

In many use cases, a **cold DR strategy** is acceptable, where VMs are defined declaratively using GitOps practices, but are only instantiated upon failover.

Workflow:

1. VM manifests (YAML) are stored in Git repositories.
2. Cluster A (primary) runs the production VM.
3. Cluster B (standby, in a different cloud) remains in sync via GitOps, but does not instantiate the VM until a failover trigger.
4. Upon failure detection in Cluster A (using Prometheus or external heartbeat monitors), a GitOps pipeline (ArgoCD or FluxCD) triggers the deployment in Cluster B.

Pros: Low cost, simple architecture.

Cons: Slower RTO, requires external data synchronization mechanism.

Warm DR Using Persistent Volumes and Periodic Sync

A **warm DR** approach involves periodically syncing persistent volumes, and keeping VM images up to date in the secondary cluster. This is particularly useful for applications that are semi-critical, and need shorter recovery times.

- **Volume replication tools:** OpenShift Data Foundation (ODF) with RBD mirroring, Velero with Restic, or external volume replication (for example, AWS EBS snapshots + S3 replication).
- **VM sync mechanism:** Need to Scheduled `virtctl export,` and reapply operations or KubeVirt snapshotting.

Example: A healthcare provider replicates patient record systems rightly from their primary OpenShift cluster in Azure to a secondary cluster in AWS. They use Velero to back up both Kubernetes objects and attached volumes, and the recovery time is under 20 minutes for critical VMs.

Hot DR with Continuous Replication

In mission-critical environments (for example, high-frequency trading or industrial automation), **hot DR** is essential. This means running redundant VMs in parallel across multiple clusters or clouds with real-time synchronization.

Mechanisms:

- **Live VM replication:** Achievable via advanced storage replication (for example, Ceph RBD mirroring) combined with VM templates in standby mode.
- **IP failover:** Floating IP management across cloud providers, using BGP (for example, MetalLB) or third-party routing services.

Considerations:

- Clock synchronization across VMs and clusters.
- Consistency of distributed stateful services (for example, databases).
- Monitoring the health of VM instances via Prometheus alerting rules.

Practical Architecture for Multi-Cloud Scaling and DR

Let us explore a reference architecture that brings these concepts together:

Architecture Components

- **OpenShift Clusters**: Deployed in AWS and GCP using ROSA and GKE, respectively.
- **KubeVirt:** Deployed with identical configurations across both clusters.
- **GitOps Tool:** ArgoCD with applications deployed via Helm charts and Kustomize.
- **Storage:** OpenShift Data Foundation with asynchronous mirroring enabled between clouds.
- **Service Mesh:** Istio multicluster configuration for east-west traffic.
- **Monitoring and Alerts:** Prometheus + `Alertmanager` integrated with PagerDuty or Slack.
- **DNS and Load Balancing:** ExternalDNS + cloud-native load balancers with health checks.

Failover and Recovery Flow

- **Primary Site Failure:** GCP experiences a regional outage.
- **Health Check Triggers DR:** Alert from `Alertmanager` fires an incident response.
- **GitOps Promotion:** ArgoCD promotes standby VMs in AWS to active state.
- **Volume Attachment:** Replica volumes are mounted and verified.
- **DNS Update:** ExternalDNS re-points to the healthy site's ingress endpoints.
- **Post-Mortem Analysis:** Metrics collected for root cause analysis.

Best Practices and Recommendations

- **Standardize VM Definitions:** Use CRD-based VM templates with `metadata.labels` to tag applications for DR policies.
- **Enable Observability:** Integrate Prometheus and Grafana dashboards, specifically for KubeVirt metrics such as `kubevirt_vmi_phase` and `kubevirt_migrations`.
- **Test Regularly:** Simulate DR scenarios using tools like Chaos Mesh to inject faults, and validate readiness.
- **Ensure Cloud Quotas:** Pre-allocate cloud resources (IP, storage classes, and so on) in secondary sites to prevent DR failures due to quota limits.

- **Document and Automate:** Every step of scaling and DR should be codified and version-controlled for auditable automation.

Security Challenges and Best Practices in Hybrid/Multi-Cloud Setups

As enterprises adopt hybrid and multi-cloud strategies to achieve operational resilience, cost optimization, and performance efficiency, security emerges as a foundational concern that influences every layer of infrastructure and application management. KubeVirt, when used within OpenShift in these distributed environments, must operate within a rigorously secured framework to ensure consistent policy enforcement, and minimize exposure to threats. This section explores the critical security challenges inherent in hybrid/multi-cloud deployments, and outlines the best practices aligned with KubeVirt-based virtualization.

Security Challenges in Hybrid and Multi-Cloud Architectures

Hybrid and multi-cloud environments face fragmented security controls and inconsistent identity management across platforms, increasing the risk of misconfigurations and breaches. The lack of unified visibility and governance makes it harder to detect threats and enforce policies consistently.

- **Inconsistent Security Policies across Environments:** In a hybrid/multi-cloud environment, organizations often deal with disparate cloud providers—each with its own set of security configurations, policy definitions, and access controls. This leads to challenges in achieving uniform enforcement of policies related to network segmentation, Identity and Access Management (IAM), encryption standards, and runtime protection.

  Example: Consider a financial services company deploying virtual machines via KubeVirt on OpenShift clusters in AWS, Azure, and an on-premises datacenter. If IAM policies are not consistently enforced, a misconfigured role in Azure could grant elevated privileges to a user that would otherwise be restricted in AWS, resulting in a potential privilege escalation.

- **Expanded Attack Surface:** Distributed workloads across multiple platforms inherently increase the attack surface. Each cloud environment introduces unique APIs, interfaces, and service endpoints, making it more difficult to maintain consistent monitoring, and threat detection mechanisms.

  Example: A misconfigured API Gateway in a secondary cloud provider might expose VMs running sensitive workloads to unauthorized external access, even if the primary cloud environment is properly secured.

- **Lack of Unified Identity Management:** Fragmented identity and access control across multiple cloud vendors can result in inconsistent user authentication and authorization mechanisms. This challenge becomes more pronounced when integrating KubeVirt workloads with identity federation services or SSO (Single Sign-On) systems.
- **Data Residency and Compliance Risks:** Different jurisdictions have varied data protection laws. When VMs are instantiated across regions, regulatory requirements such as GDPR, HIPAA, or PCI-DSS can be violated inadvertently due to improper workload placement.

  Example: A healthcare provider using KubeVirt to launch patient-data-intensive workloads across OpenShift clusters in both the U.S. and EU might breach GDPR policies, if those workloads move patient data outside of the EU region, without appropriate safeguards.
- **Complexity in Monitoring and Incident Response:** Monitoring tools and SIEM (Security Information and Event Management) solutions may not provide complete visibility across heterogeneous environments. Limited observability makes it difficult to detect threats such as lateral movement between cloud providers or anomalies in inter-cluster VM traffic.

Security Best Practices for KubeVirt in Hybrid/Multi-Cloud

Implement Centralized Identity and Access Management: Leverage federated identity systems (for example, Azure AD, AWS IAM Identity Center, and Keycloak) that integrate with OpenShift and KubeVirt to ensure a consistent authentication mechanism across environments.

- We can use OpenShift OAuth and RBAC to enforce least privilege access.
- Need to integrate with LDAP or SAML for legacy on-prem systems.
- Leverage cloud-native tools such as AWS SSO or Google Cloud Identity for federated identity.

Enforce Consistent Network Security Policies: Network segmentation, encryption, and policy enforcement should be uniformly applied regardless of cloud provider. Leverage tools such as OpenShift Service Mesh (Istio) and CNI plugins (for example, Calico) to enforce egress and ingress controls.

- Define and manage network policies through GitOps to ensure version-controlled, auditable deployments.
- Implement east-west traffic inspection with Envoy proxies in service mesh layers.

Secure VM Images and Workloads: Adopt a secure image pipeline for KubeVirt VMs:

- Sign and scan VM base images using tools like Clair, Trivy, or Red Hat Quay.
- Maintain golden images for standardized deployments.
- Isolate sensitive VMs using SELinux/AppArmor profiles within OpenShift.

Example: For a government agency deploying classified workloads, hardened VM images built using STIG benchmarks and scanned, before deployment prevent vulnerabilities from propagating in production environments.

Use End-to-End Encryption: Ensure all data in transit and at rest is encrypted using provider-specific and platform-agnostic encryption mechanisms.

- Utilize OpenShift secrets management backed by external key management services (for example, AWS KMS, HashiCorp Vault).
- Enforce mTLS for all service-to-service communication.

Centralized Logging and Monitoring: Unify observability tools across cloud platforms using cloud-native and open-source monitoring stacks:

- Use Prometheus and Grafana for metrics aggregation.
- Integrate Fluent Bit or Loki for centralized log collection.
- Forward security events to a central SIEM platform like Splunk or ELK.

Example: In a retail multi-cloud environment, centralized logging helps detect anomalies across customer-facing VM-based services by correlating logs from multiple OpenShift clusters.

Automate Security Posture Management via GitOps: By integrating GitOps workflows into OpenShift and KubeVirt management, teams can define security configurations as code, and audit them continuously.

- Use ArgoCD or FluxCD to manage security policy deployments.
- Incorporate automated policy validation using OPA Gatekeeper or Kyverno.

Apply Zero Trust Principles: Zero Trust Architecture (ZTA) enforces continuous verification of identity, context, and device posture.

- Use micro-segmentation to restrict lateral movement.
- Continuously authenticate user and machine identities.
- Monitor and validate runtime behavior of workloads.

Real-World Use Cases for KubeVirt in Hybrid and Multi-Cloud Scenarios

KubeVirt offers a powerful virtualization extension to Kubernetes, enabling the seamless coexistence of virtual machines and containers within the same orchestration layer. As organizations transition from monolithic architectures to cloud-native paradigms, many face the challenge of integrating legacy systems with modern containerized applications. KubeVirt, deployed on Red Hat OpenShift, presents an elegant solution for these hybrid demands, particularly in environments where multi-cloud strategies are a necessity.

This section provides an in-depth analysis of real-world use cases where KubeVirt is leveraged in hybrid and multi-cloud scenarios. Each use case illustrates the practical benefits of combining VM-based workloads with container-native services, using OpenShift Virtualization.

Modernizing Legacy Applications While Ensuring Continuity

Use Case: A financial services provider operating a mix of mainframe-based batch processing applications and containerized microservices requires a phased modernization approach.

Scenario: The provider deploys OpenShift clusters across both on-premises and public cloud environments (AWS and Azure). Legacy workloads, such as COBOL-based services encapsulated in VMs, are virtualized using KubeVirt. Meanwhile, customer-facing APIs and analytics pipelines are containerized.

Technical Benefits:

- **Workload Co-location:** Both VM and container workloads are orchestrated on the same OpenShift cluster, simplifying management.
- **Consistent CI/CD Pipelines:** Pipelines built on Tekton or Jenkins can deploy updates to VMs and containers simultaneously.
- **Policy Uniformity:** RBAC, network policies, and storage classes are uniformly enforced across VM and container workloads.

Outcome: This hybrid deployment model allows the provider to continue using critical legacy software, while investing in cloud-native transformation, ultimately reducing the technical debt.

Disaster Recovery and High Availability across Cloud Boundaries

Use Case: A government agency responsible for critical infrastructure needs a resilient Disaster Recovery (DR) strategy for legacy systems that cannot yet be containerized.

Scenario: Primary workloads run on an OpenShift cluster in a private datacenter with KubeVirt-managed VMs hosting legacy applications. A secondary OpenShift cluster on Google Cloud serves as the failover site.

Technical Approach:

- **VM Snapshotting and Backup:** Integration with tools such as Velero or Restic enables automated backup of VM disk images and configurations.
- **Cross-Cluster Migration:** KubeVirt's DataVolume and CDI components facilitate replicating VM images across clusters.
- **Geo-Redundant DNS and Load Balancers:** Traffic is routed via multi-region load balancers and cloud-native DNS solutions such as AWS Route 53 or GCP Cloud DNS.

Outcome: In case of a datacenter failure, VMs can be re-instantiated in the cloud environment with minimal downtime. The consistent OpenShift layer ensures compatibility and operational continuity.

Edge Computing and Telco Network Function Virtualization (NFV)

Use Case: A telecommunications company deploying 5G infrastructure requires edge nodes capable of running both containerized and VM-based network functions.

Scenario: OpenShift clusters with KubeVirt are deployed at the network edge (for example, base station sites or local data hubs). Containerized services like telemetry collectors and network monitoring tools run alongside VM-based Virtual Network Functions (VNFs) that require kernel-level access or specific driver support.

Technical Considerations:

- **Hardware Affinity:** Node selectors and CPU pinning are used to assign VMs to nodes with appropriate hardware accelerators (for example, SR-IOV NICs).
- **Low Latency Requirements:** KubeVirt's support for real-time workloads, and CPU isolation ensures minimal jitter and packet loss.

- **Multi-Tenant Isolation:** vCluster and OpenShift's multi-tenancy model are employed for tenant segmentation at the edge.

Outcome: KubeVirt enables Telco to consolidate network functions and telemetry services within a unified platform, optimizing resource usage, while reducing operational complexity.

Cross-Cloud Bursting for Seasonal Demand

Use Case: An e-commerce enterprise experiences seasonal spikes in web traffic, and requires elastic compute capacity, without migrating core VM-based applications.

Scenario: The enterprise operates its baseline workloads on an on-prem OpenShift cluster. During peak seasons (for example, Black Friday), it bursts into OpenShift clusters hosted on AWS or Azure.

Key Strategies:

- **Workload Cloning:** VMs are cloned using KubeVirt's VM export features, and stored in object storage (for example, S3-compatible endpoints).
- **Auto-Scaling Hooks:** Kubernetes HPA is extended with custom metrics to trigger VM instantiations, based on traffic patterns.
- **Storage Replication:** Data is replicated via block-level mirroring or cloud-native storage gateways to ensure consistency.

Outcome: This model achieves scalable elasticity, enabling the enterprise to maintain performance under heavy load, without re-architecting legacy applications.

Dev/Test Environments for Heterogeneous Application Stacks

Use Case: A multinational software company develops and tests software across various operating systems, including legacy Windows Server and modern Linux distributions.

Scenario: Development teams leverage OpenShift Virtualization to provision ephemeral VMs for application testing. The environments are spun up in both private data centers and public clouds.

Technical Workflow:

- **Self-Service VM Provisioning:** Developers request VM templates using OpenShift Developer Console or CLI integrations.
- **GitOps Integration:** VM manifests and templates are stored in Git repositories, and Argo CD is used to manage their lifecycle.

- **Ephemeral and Persistent Modes:** Depending on test scenarios, VMs are instantiated with either ephemeral disks or persistent PVC-backed volumes.

Outcome: This approach offers agility for testing across heterogeneous environments, while enforcing governance through GitOps workflows and OpenShift policies.

Security-Sensitive Workloads in Regulated Environments

Use Case: A healthcare provider processes patient data under HIPAA regulations, and requires isolated compute environments with auditable access.

Scenario: Sensitive applications such as those handling medical imaging or EHR processing are deployed as VMs within OpenShift clusters in both on-prem and FedRAMP-compliant cloud environments.

Security Enhancements:

- **Dedicated VM Nodes:** Using taints and tolerations, VMs run on hardened nodes with FIPS-compliant OS images.
- **Role-Based Access:** OpenShift RBAC policies are extended with audit logging to monitor all access to VMs.
- **Network Isolation:** VMs are placed in isolated network segments using OpenShift SDN or OVN-Kubernetes.

Outcome: KubeVirt ensures compliance with stringent security mandates, while offering a unified platform for deploying and managing workloads.

Conclusion

KubeVirt has emerged as a strategic enabler for organizations navigating the complexities of hybrid and multi-cloud environments. By extending Kubernetes with native virtualization capabilities, it allows enterprises to unify their management of virtual machines and containers under a consistent, declarative, and automated platform like OpenShift. Throughout this chapter, we explored how KubeVirt facilitates workload portability, multi-cloud scaling, robust disaster recovery, and secure deployment practices—each supported by real-world use cases that underscore its versatility.

As cloud-native adoption accelerates and legacy systems continue to play a role in enterprise IT, KubeVirt offers a critical bridge. It empowers architects to modernize at their own pace, protect prior investments, and innovate across a federated cloud landscape. When integrated thoughtfully, KubeVirt not only simplifies multi-cloud operations, but also sets the foundation for future-ready infrastructure that is agile, resilient, and secure.

The next chapter explores GPU-accelerated workloads in KubeVirt, detailing GPU passthrough, device plugin integration, and the best practices for deploying high-performance virtualized machine learning and video processing tasks.

CHAPTER 14

Advanced Topics in KubeVirt

Introduction

This chapter delves into advanced KubeVirt use cases, focusing on running GPU-accelerated workloads within virtual machines. We will explore integrating KubeVirt with device plugins, and exposing GPUs to VMs for tasks like machine learning and video processing, as well as GPU passthrough. The chapter also covers potential challenges and performance considerations, when running GPU workloads in virtualized environments.

Challenges and best practices for deploying GPU workloads in virtualized environments are also covered, including considerations for resource management, compatibility, and performance tuning. By the end of this chapter, you will have a deep understanding of leveraging GPUs with KubeVirt in OpenShift, empowering them to run advanced workloads efficiently.

Structure

In this chapter, we are going to cover the following topics:

- GPU Workloads
- Kubernetes Device Plugins for GPU Support
- GPU Passthrough for KubeVirt VMs
- Best Practices for Performance Tuning of GPU Workloads
- Managing GPU Resources and Monitoring Usage
- Challenges and Troubleshooting GPU Workloads in KubeVirt

GPU Workloads

A Graphics Processing Unit (GPU) is a specialized electronic circuit designed to rapidly manipulate and alter memory to accelerate the creation of images in a frame buffer intended for output to a display device. Their highly parallel structure makes them more efficient than general-purpose Central Processing Units (CPUs) for algorithms where processing of large blocks of data is done in parallel. While CPUs are optimized for sequential processing with complex control logic, GPUs feature a massive array of simpler cores, enabling massive parallel execution. For instance, modern accelerators can feature up to 1,472 independent processing tiles, each containing thousands of threads operating in parallel, compared to high-performance CPUs which might contain 8-64 cores. This architectural distinction is fundamental to their efficacy in accelerating specific types of computational tasks.

GPU-accelerated workloads span a variety of domains, primarily Machine Learning (ML), scientific computing, and High-Performance Computing (HPC).

In Machine Learning, GPUs are indispensable for the following use cases that we are going to discuss here:

- **Training Deep Learning Models:** The parallel nature of GPUs dramatically improves the training speed of complex neural networks, including Convolutional Neural Networks (CNNs) for image processing and Transformer models for Natural Language Processing (NLP). Deep learning computations often spend 65-80% of their execution time in matrix multiplication operations which map efficiently to the Single-Instruction Multiple-Data (SIMD) paradigm employed by GPUs
- **Inference Acceleration:** Deploying trained ML models for real-time predictions also benefits significantly from GPU acceleration, achieving low latency for demanding applications.
- **Data Preprocessing:** GPUs can accelerate the preprocessing of large datasets, especially for high-dimensional data like images and videos.
- **Scientific Computing and HPC:** GPUs are leveraged for tasks such as Molecular dynamics, computational fluid dynamics, and N-body simulations in physics and chemistry. Genomic sequence alignment, financial modeling, and weather forecasting.

GPU virtualization technology allows a single physical GPU to be divided into virtual instances shareable by multiple users or VMs simultaneously across a network. This approach offers several advantages:

- **Efficient Resource Utilization:** Physical GPUs are expensive, and often underutilized in dedicated setups. Virtualization allows multiple VMs to share GPU resources, significantly increasing utilization, and reducing the idle time.
- **Cost Reduction:** Sharing GPUs reduces the need for multiple physical units, leading to lower hardware, power, and cooling costs.

- **Remote Access and Flexibility:** Users can access powerful GPU capabilities remotely, irrespective of their local hardware. This is particularly beneficial for distributed teams and cloud environments.
- **Streamlined Management:** Centralized management of GPU resources simplifies allocation, monitoring, and maintenance.

Types of GPU Virtualization

This section outlines different types of GPU virtualization, including pass-through, mediated pass-through, and API-level remoting, along with their respective uses and performance characteristics.

- **Pass-through (Direct Device Assignment):** An entire physical GPU is dedicated to a single VM. This offers near-native performance, and is suitable for high-end gaming, intensive machine-learning workloads, and scientific simulations.
- **Mediated Pass-through (for example, NVIDIA vGPU, and Intel GVT-g):** A GPU is shared among multiple VMs with the help of a vendor driver that mediates access. Hardware features are often used to provide isolated contexts to VMs. This offers medium to high performance, and is used in Virtual Desktop Infrastructure (VDI), AI/ML training, and 3D rendering.
- **API-level Remoting:** Graphics or compute API calls from an application are intercepted and forwarded to a remote GPU for processing. Performance is typically medium, suitable for remote desktops and cloud gaming.

Kubernetes Device Plugins for GPU Support

Kubernetes, by default, manages CPU and memory resources. To enable awareness and scheduling of specialized hardware resources like GPUs, it utilizes the device plugin framework. Device plugins are vendor-specific components that run on nodes, discover these specialized hardware resources, register them with the Kubelet, and manage their lifecycle. This framework allows pods to request and consume these resources in a manner analogous to CPU and memory.

Device plugins abstract the hardware specifics from the Kubernetes scheduler, enabling it to make placement decisions for pods, based on the availability of these custom resources. This abstraction is crucial for heterogeneous clusters containing different types of specialized hardware. Vendor-specific operators such as the NVIDIA GPU Operator, further simplify this process by automating the deployment and lifecycle management of not only the device plugin, but also associated drivers, container runtimes, and monitoring tools, significantly reducing the operational burden.

NVIDIA GPU Support

Setting up NVIDIA GPU support in Kubernetes involves several prerequisites and components, typically managed by the NVIDIA GPU Operator.

Prerequisites

- Compatible NVIDIA GPUs installed on worker nodes.
- Appropriate NVIDIA drivers installed on the host
- nvidia-container-toolkit installed on each GPU node.
- nvidia-container-runtime configured as the default runtime for the container engine (for example, Docker, containerd, and CRI-O).

Installation: The recommended method is using the NVIDIA GPU Operator which can be installed via Helm. The operator automates the deployment of drivers, the device plugin, container toolkit, DCGM for monitoring, and other necessary components.

```
helm repo adds nvidia https://nvidia.github.io/gpu-operator
helm repo update
helm install --wait --generate-name \
      -n gpu-operator --create-namespace \
      nvidia/gpu-operator
```

Alternatively, the NVIDIA device plugin can be deployed as a static DaemonSet, though this is less common for production environments.

Key Components Deployed by the Operator:

- **NVIDIA drivers:** Ensures that the correct drivers are running on the host.
- **NVIDIA device plugin:** Implements the Kubernetes device plugin API to expose nvidia.com/gpu resources.
- **NVIDIA Container Toolkit:** Enables containers to utilize NVIDIA GPUs.
- **GPU Feature Discovery (GFD):** Labels nodes with detailed GPU characteristics (for example, model, memory, and MIG capability), allowing for more precise scheduling.
- **DCGM (Data Center GPU Manager) Exporter:** For monitoring GPU metrics.

AMD GPU Support

AMD GPUs can also be exposed as schedulable resources in Kubernetes, using the AMD GPU Device Plugin.

Prerequisites

- ROCm-capable AMD GPU hardware on worker nodes.

- ROCm stack or AMD GPU drivers installed on these worker nodes.

Installation: The plugin is typically deployed as a Kubernetes DaemonSet to run on all nodes with AMD GPUs. A pre-built Docker image is available, and deployment can be done using a YAML manifest. A helm chart is also available for deployment.

```
kubectl create -f https://raw.githubusercontent.com/ROCm/k8s-device-plugin/master/k8s-ds-amdgpu-dp.yaml
```

Components and Functionality

- Implements the Kubernetes Device Plugin API for AMD GPUs.
- Exposes AMD GPUs as amd.com/gpu resources in Kubernetes.
- An optional Node Labeler can be deployed to automatically label nodes with detailed GPU properties (device ID, VRAM, compute units), aiding in scheduling.

```
kubectl create -f https://raw.githubusercontent.com/ROCm/k8s-device-plugin/master/k8s-ds-amdgpu-labeller.yaml
```

Once installed, the pods can request AMD GPUs via their resource limits:

```
apiVersion: v1
kind: Pod
metadata:
  name: amd-gpu-pod
spec:
  containers:
    - name: amd-gpu-container
      image: rocmining/rocm-hip-sample
      resources:
        limits:
          amd.com/gpu: 1
```

Device plugins are typically written in Go. They implement the DevicePluginServer gRPC interface defined by Kubernetes which includes methods like ListAndWatch (to report available devices and their health) and Allocate (called by Kubelet, when a container needs the device). Developers creating custom device plugins, or contributing to the existing ones would work extensively with these Go interfaces and Kubernetes client libraries.

GPU Passthrough for KubeVirt VMs

GPU passthrough, also known as direct device assignment, allows a physical GPU to be directly accessed by a KubeVirt Virtual Machine Instance (VMI). This method provides near-native performance as the VM's guest operating system interacts directly with the GPU hardware, bypassing most of the hypervisor overhead for GPU operations.

This is particularly beneficial for demanding workloads such as high-performance computing, AI/ML model training, and professional graphics applications. Configuring GPU passthrough in KubeVirt involves a multi-layered setup process, spanning from host hardware and BIOS settings to Kubernetes and KubeVirt configurations. Each layer must be correctly configured for successful passthrough.

Host Preparation

Proper host preparation is foundational for GPU passthrough. Following are the steps involved:

Enable IOMMU (Input/Output Memory Management Unit)

The IOMMU (Intel VT-d for Intel CPUs or AMD-Vi/AMD IOMMU for AMD CPUs) must be enabled in the host system's BIOS/UEFI. This hardware feature allows direct memory access (DMA) remapping, and isolates devices for secure assignment to VMs.

Setting Kernel Parameters

The host kernel must be booted with appropriate parameters to activate IOMMU.

- `For Intel: intel_iommu=on`
- `For AMD: amd_iommu=on`

These parameters are typically added to the **`GRUB_CMDLINE_LINUX`** in **`/etc/default/grub`**, followed by regenerating the grub configuration, and rebooting the host.

Load `vfio-pci` Driver and Bind GPU

The vfio-pci kernel module is responsible for providing direct device access to userspace applications like QEMU/KVM which KubeVirt uses. This module must be loaded.

```
sudo modprobe vfio-pci
```

The target GPU must be unbound from its default host driver (for example, **`nvidia`**, **`nouveau`**, **`amdgpu`**) and bound to the **`vfio-pci`** driver. This can be done manually using **`sysfs`** commands.

```
# Replace 0000:XX:YY.Z with the GPU's PCI address (e.g.,
0000:01:00.0)
echo "0000:XX:YY.Z" > /sys/bus/pci/drivers/nvidia/unbind # Or
other default driver
echo "vfio-pci" > /sys/bus/pci/devices/0000:XX:YY.Z/driver_override
echo "0000:XX:YY.Z" > /sys/bus/pci/drivers/vfio-pci/bind
```

The NVIDIA GPU Operator can automate this binding process, when nodes are correctly labeled with **nvidia.com/gpu.workload.config=vm-passthrough**. This label instructs the operator to prepare the node for GPU passthrough to VMs which includes managing driver states.

Configuring KubeVirt Custom Resource (CR) for permittedHostDevices

KubeVirt requires administrators to explicitly allowlist PCI devices that can be passed through to VMs. This is a security measure and a way to manage device availability. This configuration is done by editing the KubeVirt CR, usually named KubeVirt and located in the KubeVirt namespace (or **openshift-cnv** for OpenShift environments).

The **spec.configuration.permittedHostDevices.pciHostDevices** array is used to define these permissions.

```
apiVersion: kubevirt.io/v1
kind: KubeVirt
metadata:
  name: kubevirt
  namespace: kubevirt
spec:
  configuration:
    developerConfiguration:
      featureGates:
        - GPU # Ensure GPU feature gate is enabled
        # May also be relevant depending on KubeVirt version
        # - HostDevices
      permittedHostDevices:
        pciHostDevices:
          # Example: NVIDIA Tesla P4 (VendorID:DeviceID)
          - pciVendorSelector: "10DE:1BB3"
            # Must match device plugin advertisement
            resourceName: "nvidia.com/GP104GL_TESLA_P4"
            # Crucial when using vendor device plugins
            externalResourceProvider: true
            # Example: AMD Radeon Pro VII
          - pciVendorSelector: "1002:731F"
            resourceName: "amd.com/gpu"
            externalResourceProvider: true
```

A few critical notes about the configuration have been described in the preceding command.

pciVendorSelector: A string combining the PCI Vendor ID and Product ID (for example, "10DE:1BB3"). This can be found using **lspci -nn** on the host.

resourceName: This is a critical field. It defines the name under which KubeVirt recognizes this type of GPU. This name **must** match the resource name advertised by the Kubernetes device plugin (for example, **nvidia.com/GA102GL_A10**, **amd.com/gpu**).

This name appears in the output of kubectl describe node **<node-name>** under Allocatable resources.

VirtualMachineInstance (VMI) Specification for GPU Passthrough

Once the host and KubeVirt CR are configured, VMs can request GPUs. VMIs request GPU resources through the gpus array, or the more generic hostDevices array within spec.domain.devices.

```
apiVersion: kubevirt.io/v1
kind: VirtualMachineInstance
metadata:
  name: vmi-gpu-passthrough-nvidia
spec:
  domain:
    resources:
      requests:
        memory: "8Gi"
      limits:
        memory: "8Gi"
      cpu:
        cores: 4
      devices:
        gpus:
          - name: "gpu1"
            # Matches resourceName in KubeVirt CR
            deviceName: "nvidia.com/GP104GL_TESLA_P4"
...
...
```

Best Practices for Performance Tuning of GPU Workloads

Optimizing the performance of GPU workloads within KubeVirt VMs requires a holistic approach, considering not only the GPU configuration itself but also the surrounding Kubernetes and host environment. Effective tuning ensures that these resource-intensive applications achieve their maximum potential.

In clusters with diverse GPU types (for example, NVIDIA A100, Tesla T4, and AMD Instinct), it is crucial to ensure that VMs are scheduled onto nodes equipped with the appropriate GPU model for their specific needs. **Node Feature Discovery (NFD)**, often integrated with or utilized by GPU operators (like NVIDIA's GFD), to automatically detect and apply detailed hardware labels to nodes.

Leveraging NUMA Alignment and CPU Pinning

For optimal performance, especially in multi-socket server systems, NUMA (Non-Uniform Memory Access) awareness is the key.

- **NUMA Alignment:** Ensure that the VMI and its assigned GPU(s) reside on the same NUMA node. Accessing memory or devices across NUMA nodes introduces latency. KubeVirt offers features to influence NUMA placement.
- **CPU Pinning/DedicatedCPUs:** For latency-sensitive or compute-intensive GPU workloads, enabling dedicatedCpuPlacement in the VMI spec pins vCPUs to specific physical CPU cores. This reduces context switching and improves cache coherency. Combining this with NUMA alignment (ensuring pinned CPUs are on the same NUMA node as the GPU) can yield significant performance benefits.
- **Topology-Aware Scheduling:** Kubernetes schedulers can be configured for topology awareness, helping to co-locate interdependent workloads (for example, a VM and its data processing pods) on the same physical host or within the same network topology to minimize the communication latency.

Utilizing Fractional GPU Resources

For workloads that do not require the full capacity of a GPU, leveraging sharing technologies such as NVIDIA MIG (Multi-Instance GPU) or time-slicing can significantly improve the overall GPU utilization and cost-effectiveness. These technologies allow a single physical GPU to be partitioned or shared among multiple VMs or pods. We will talk about GPU Slicing and other techniques in a later section of this chapter in more detail.

Storage Performance

GPU applications, particularly in AI/ML, often process vast amounts of data. Ensure that VMs have access to high-performance storage solutions such as local NVMe SSDs or network file systems (for example, NFS, Lustre, and so on) optimized for high throughput and low latency. The choice of storage backend for KubeVirt (for example, Ceph RBD, local storage, and hostDisk) can impact I/O performance.

HugePages for VMs

Configuring KubeVirt VMs to use hugepages (for example, 2MB or 1GB page sizes instead of the default 4KB) can enhance performance for memory-intensive applications. Hugepages reduce the number of Translation Lookaside Buffer (TLB) entries needed, minimizing TLB misses, and improving memory access speeds. KubeVirt supports configuring hugepages for VMs.

Managing GPU Resources and Monitoring Usage

Effective management and monitoring of GPU resources are crucial for maintaining performance, ensuring availability, and optimizing costs in a KubeVirt environment. This involves leveraging Kubernetes' own resource management features, alongside specialized GPU monitoring tools.

KubeVirt VMs, being managed as Kubernetes pods, benefit from standard Kubernetes resource management mechanisms:

- **Namespaces:** Isolate GPU workloads, and manage resources on a per-project or per-team basis.
- **`ResourceQuotas`:** Apply **`ResourceQuota`** objects at the namespace level to limit the total number of GPUs (for example, **`count/nvidia.com.gpu: "10"`**) that can be consumed by all the VMs and pods within that namespace. This ensures fair sharing, and prevents any single project from monopolizing scarce GPU resources.
- **LimitRanges:** Define default resource requests and limits for containers (and thus VMIs) within a namespace, although GPU limits are typically explicitly set in the VMI spec.

Monitoring GPU Metrics with Prometheus and Grafana

A robust monitoring stack is necessary for visibility into GPU utilization, performance, and health. The combination of NVIDIA Data Center GPU Manager (DCGM), Prometheus, and Grafana is a widely adopted solution.

NVIDIA Data Center GPU Manager (DCGM)

DCGM is a comprehensive suite of tools for managing and monitoring NVIDIA GPUs in data center environments. It provides detailed telemetry and health diagnostics. This low-overhead tool offers a range of functions: Active health monitoring, diagnostics, and system validation, alongside policies, power and clock management, along with group configuration, and accounting.

Of particular interest are GPU utilization metrics (for monitoring Tensor Cores, FP64 units, and so on), memory metrics, and interconnect traffic metrics. DCGM offers bindings for various languages such as C and Python, and these are included in the installer packages. For integration with the container ecosystem where Go is popular as a programming language, there are Go bindings based on the DCGM APIs.

DCGM Exporter

The dcgm-exporter is a key component that collects a wide array of GPU metrics from DCGM, and exposes them in a format that Prometheus can scrape. The NVIDIA GPU Operator typically deploys the dcgm-exporter as part of its stack. The key metrics exposed include:

- GPU Utilization (compute, memory controller, encoder, and decoder)
- Framebuffer Memory Usage (used, free, and total)
- GPU Temperature
- Power Consumption
- Clock Speeds (SM, memory)
- PCIe Throughput
- ECC Errors (Correctable and Uncorrectable)

Prometheus Setup

Prometheus needs to be configured to discover and scrape metrics from the `dcgm-exporter` endpoints. A common approach is to add a scrape job to the Prometheus configuration, targeting the service exposed by dcgm-exporter (for example, `dcgm-exporter-service.gpu-operator.svc.cluster.local:9400`).

In environments like Azure Kubernetes Service (AKS) with **Azure Managed Prometheus**, this can involve creating a PodMonitor Custom Resource Definition (CRD) that selects the dcgm-exporter pods, and specifies the metrics endpoint.

Grafana Dashboards

Grafana is used to visualize the metrics collected by Prometheus. NVIDIA provides official Grafana dashboards for DCGM, which can be imported into Grafana, using their dashboard ID from the Grafana dashboard repository **- eg ID 12239: NVIDIA DCGM Exporter Dashboard**

Key GPU Metrics for Monitoring

The following table provides a concise comparison of Multi-Instance GPU (MIG) and Time-Slicing, highlighting their key features, operational mechanisms, and suitability for different KubeVirt VM scenarios. This summary aims to guide the selection of the most appropriate GPU sharing strategy based on specific workload requirements for isolation, performance predictability, and supported hardware.

Metric Name (DCGM)	Description	Why it's Important
DCGM_FI_DEV_GPU_UTIL	Percent of time over the last sample period during which one or more kernels was executing on the GPU.	Indicates how busy the GPU's compute units are. Consistently low utilization might suggest underused resources.
DCGM_FI_DEV_MEM_COPY_UTIL	Percent of time over the last sample period during which the GPU's memory controller was busy.	High memory controller utilization can indicate memory bandwidth bottlenecks.
DCGM_FI_DEV_FB_USED	Amount of framebuffer memory used (in MiB).	Monitors GPU memory consumption; helps prevent out-of-memory errors and identify memory-hungry workloads.
DCGM_FI_DEV_FB_FREE	Amount of framebuffer memory free (in MiB).	Complements DCGM_FI_DEV_FB_USED for a full picture of memory availability.
DCGM_FI_DEV_POWER_USAGE	Power consumption of the GPU in Watts.	Useful for power management, thermal monitoring, and understanding workload energy efficiency.
DCGM_FI_DEV_GPU_TEMP	GPU temperature in degrees Celsius.	Critical for GPU health; high temperatures can lead to performance throttling or hardware damage.
DCGM_FI_DEV_SM_CLOCK	SM (Streaming Multiprocessor) clock frequency in MHz.	Indicates the operational speed of compute units; can be affected by power or thermal limits.
DCGM_FI_DEV_MEM_CLOCK	Memory clock frequency in MHz.	Indicates the operational speed of GPU memory; impacts memory bandwidth.

DCGM_FI_DEV_PCIE_REPLAY_COUNTER	Count of PCIe replays.	Increased replays can indicate issues with PCIe link quality or signal integrity, impacting performance.
DCGM_FI_DEV_ECC_SBE_VOL_TOTAL	Total single-bit ECC errors (volatile).	Indicates memory corruption that was corrected; high rates might signal impending hardware issues.
DCGM_FI_DEV_ECC_DBE_VOL_TOTAL	Total double-bit ECC errors (volatile).	Uncorrectable errors that can lead to data corruption or application crashes; critical for GPU health.

Table 14.1: *DCGM Metrics Name and Their Description*

The NVIDIA GPU Operator ecosystem greatly simplifies the integration of monitoring by often including the DCGM Exporter by default, and providing standardized dashboards. However, administrators must still ensure proper configuration for Prometheus scraping (for example, PodMonitor CRDs in AKS or appropriate scrape configurations in Prometheus itself) to make these metrics available for visualization and alerting.

Challenges and Troubleshooting GPU Workloads in KubeVirt

Deploying and managing GPU workloads in KubeVirt, while powerful, can present several challenges. Effective troubleshooting requires a systematic approach, understanding the various layers involved, from hardware to the application running inside the VM.

vfio-pci Binding Problems

For GPU passthrough, the GPU on the host must be unbound from its default driver (for example, nvidia, nouveau, and so on) and bound to the vfio-pci driver. Failures in this process prevent KubeVirt from assigning the device.

Troubleshooting:

- On the host, use **`lspci -nnk`** to check which driver is currently bound to the GPU. If not **`vfio-pci`**, manually **`unbind/bind`** or verify the GPU Operator's configuration (for example, **`nvidia.com/gpu.workload.config=vm-passthrough`** label).
- Ensure kernel modules like **`vfio-pci`**, **`vfio`**, **`vfio_iommu_type1`** are loaded (**`lsmod`**).
- Check for IOMMU grouping issues; sometimes other devices in the same IOMMU group can interfere.

IOMMU Misconfigurations

The IOMMU (Intel VT-d or AMD-Vi) must be enabled in the host's BIOS/UEFI, and correctly configured in the kernel (for example, `intel_iommu=on` or `amd_iommu=on kernel parameters`).

Troubleshooting: Verify BIOS/UEFI settings. Check kernel boot parameters (`cat /proc/cmdline`). Examine `dmesg` output on the host for IOMMU-related errors or warnings.

Incorrect KubeVirt CR `permittedHostDevices` Configuration

The KubeVirt Custom Resource must correctly list the GPUs that are permitted for passthrough, with accurate PCI vendor/device IDs and resource names.

Troubleshooting:

- Double-check PCI IDs, using `lspci -nn` on the host.
- Ensure the resourceName in the KubeVirt CR matches exactly what the device plugin advertises (visible in `kubectl describe node <node-name>`).
- Crucially, set `externalResourceProvider: true`, when using vendor device plugins (like NVIDIA's).

GPU Slicing, GPU Time Sharing, and Multi-Instance GPU (MIG)

While GPU passthrough offers dedicated performance, it can lead to underutilization, if workloads do not consistently require a full GPU. GPU sharing technologies aim to improve utilization by allowing multiple VMs or containers to concurrently use a single physical GPU. The primary methods, especially in the context of NVIDIA GPUs, are Time-Slicing and Multi-Instance GPU (MIG). NVIDIA vGPU is another important technology for sharing via mediated devices.

The choice between these strategies involves a trade-off between resource density, performance predictability, isolation, and cost. Understanding these options is crucial for optimizing GPU resources in a KubeVirt environment.

GPU Slicing/Time-Sharing (Primarily NVIDIA context)

Concept: Time-sharing is a software-based technique where multiple workloads (VMs or containers) share a single physical GPU by having their execution contexts rapidly switched on the GPU's processing units. Each workload effectively gets a "*slice*" of the GPU's time.

Mechanism: The NVIDIA device plugin, when configured for time-slicing, advertises multiple "*replicas*" of a physical GPU as distinct Kubernetes resources. For example, a single physical GPU might be presented as 4 schedulable `nvidia.com/gpu` resources. The GPU driver then manages the scheduling of tasks from these different replicas onto the physical GPU in a round-robin or similar fashion.

Use Cases:

- Workloads that are bursty, or have significant idle periods (for example, development, testing environments, and so on).
- Lightweight inference tasks that do not saturate a full GPU.
- Maximizing user density and GPU utilization for tasks where peak performance or strong isolation is not paramount.
- Enabling GPU sharing on older generations of NVIDIA GPUs that do not support MIG.

Drawbacks:

- **No Hardware Isolation:** Critically, time-slicing does not provide memory or fault isolation between the shared workloads. A misbehaving workload (for example, causing a driver crash or consuming excessive memory) can impact all other workloads sharing that GPU.
- **Performance Variability:** Latency and throughput can be unpredictable, and will degrade as more workloads contend for the GPU's time. Performance is not guaranteed.
- **Not suitable for performance-critical applications** requiring consistent low latency or high throughput, nor for security-sensitive applications demanding strong isolation.

Multi-Instance GPU (MIG) (NVIDIA Specific)

Concept: MIG is a hardware-level partitioning feature available on NVIDIA Ampere architecture GPUs (for example, A100, A30, and H100) and newer. It allows a single physical GPU to be divided into multiple, smaller, fully isolated GPU instances. An A100 GPU, for example, can be partitioned into up to **seven** such instances.

Mechanism: Each MIG instance has its own dedicated set of hardware resources: Streaming Multiprocessors (SMs), memory, L2 cache, and memory bandwidth controllers. This provides strong isolation and predictable performance for each instance, making them appear as independent, and smaller GPUs to the operating system or hypervisor.

This provides several useful advantages such as:

- **Strong Hardware Isolation:** Provides fault, memory, and performance isolation between MIG instances. Also, ensures Quality of Service (QoS) for memory bandwidth.
- **Predictable Performance:** Each instance delivers consistent performance, based on its allocated resources.
- **Enhanced Security:** Suitable for multi-tenant scenarios due to hardware-enforced boundaries.

While there are also some downsides:

- Limited to newer NVIDIA GPU architectures (Ampere and later).
- **Static Partitioning:** MIG profiles (the size and number of instanccs) arc configured at the node level, often using nvidia-smi commands. While the configuration can be changed, it is not as dynamic as software-based time-slicing, and may require a GPU reset or specific operator actions. The partitions are fixed until reconfigured.
- A predefined set of instance sizes ("MIG *profiles*") are available for each GPU model.

NVIDIA vGPU (Mediated Devices) in KubeVirt

Concept: NVIDIA vGPU technology enables a physical GPU to be shared among multiple VMs by creating virtual GPU (vGPU) instances. Each VM receives a dedicated, non-overcommitted portion of the GPU's framebuffer, and access to its compute capabilities, all managed by the NVIDIA vGPU software drivers on the hypervisor (host), and within the guest VM.

Mechanism: vGPU leverages the Linux kernel's mediated device (mdev) framework. The NVIDIA vGPU Manager, a driver component running on the host, is responsible for creating and managing various vGPU profiles (for example, NVIDIA A10-8Q, and Tesla P4-2Q) which define the amount of framebuffer and types of capabilities allocated to each vGPU instance.

Use Cases:

- Virtual Desktop Infrastructure (VDI) for graphics-intensive applications.
- Professional graphics workstations running in VMs.
- AI/ML workloads that can benefit from shared but guaranteed slices of GPU resources.

NVIDIA vGPU deployments typically require licensing. Guest VMs running vGPU drivers need to connect to an NVIDIA license server to activate their vGPU capabilities.

Feature	Multi-Instance GPU (MIG)	Time-Slicing
Partition Type	Hardware (Spatial)	Software (Temporal)
Max Partitions/ Replicas	Up to 7 instances per GPU (for example, A100)	Configurable (example, 4, 8, or more replicas per GPU)
Isolation Level		
- Fault	Strong (Hardware)	None
- Memory	Strong (Hardware, dedicated memory per instance) [29]	None (Shared framebuffer)
- Performance	Predictable per instance	Variable, depends on contention
Quality of Service (QoS)	Hardware-guaranteed (example, memory bandwidth)	None (Best-effort sharing)
Reconfiguration Effort	Static; changes may require GPU reset/specific ops	Dynamic (via ConfigMap, but plugin restart may be needed)
GPU Architecture Support	NVIDIA Ampere and newer (A100, H100, and so on.)	Most CUDA-compatible NVIDIA GPUs
KubeVirt Usage Method	Passthrough of a MIG instance (for example, `nvidia.com/mig-1g.5gb`)	Passthrough of a time-sliced replica (example, `nvidia.com/gpu`)

Table 14.2: *Comparing Multi-Instance GPU (MIG) vs. Time-Slicing for KubeVirt VMs*

Conclusion

The integration of GPU acceleration into KubeVirt VMs opens up a vast array of possibilities for running demanding applications within a Kubernetes-managed infrastructure. This chapter has explored the advanced facets of this integration, from understanding diverse GPU workloads, and the critical role of Kubernetes device plugins, to the detailed configuration of GPU passthrough. Best practices for performance tuning highlight that optimal GPU utilization is a multifaceted endeavor, encompassing careful resource management, appropriate driver selection, and leveraging Kubernetes' scheduling capabilities.

The ability to monitor GPU resources effectively, using tools like Prometheus and Grafana, often facilitated by vendor operators such as the NVIDIA GPU Operator, is paramount for maintaining system health and optimizing costs. While powerful, GPU workloads in KubeVirt are not without their challenges; a systematic approach to troubleshooting, covering layers from hardware to guest OS, is essential for resolving issues related to drivers, device binding, and resource allocation.

Furthermore, advanced GPU sharing technologies such as NVIDIA's Time-Slicing, Multi-Instance GPU (MIG), and vGPU provide flexible mechanisms to enhance resource utilization, catering to different performance and isolation requirements. Choosing the appropriate sharing strategy—or opting for dedicated passthrough—requires a careful assessment of workload characteristics and business needs.

Throughout these advanced topics, the Go programming language, via KubeVirt/client-go, offers a robust programmatic interface for managing KubeVirt VMs, including those with complex GPU configurations. As GPU virtualization technologies continue to evolve, KubeVirt, in concert with the broader Kubernetes ecosystem, is poised to provide an increasingly sophisticated platform for unifying containerized and VM-based GPU-accelerated workloads.

The next and final chapter concludes the book by exploring the best practices for implementing KubeVirt in OpenShift Virtualization environments, and discussing the emerging trends shaping the future of virtualization and cloud-native technologies. The chapter is designed to help optimize the deployments, ensure long-term success, and stay ahead of technological advancements.

CHAPTER 15
Best Practices and Future Trends

Introduction

This final chapter concludes the book by exploring the best practices for implementing KubeVirt in OpenShift Virtualization environments, and discussing the emerging trends shaping the future of virtualization and cloud-native technologies. This chapter is designed to help optimize the deployments, ensure long-term success, and stay ahead of technological advancements.

This chapter dives into future trends of virtualization and Kubernetes. Topics include the evolution of hybrid and multi-cloud solutions, the growing adoption of edge computing, and advancements in networking and storage technologies for virtualized environments. The potential for AI-driven automation and observability in managing virtual workloads is also discussed, providing a glimpse into the next wave of innovation.

For years, these two worlds—virtual machines and containers—operated in parallel, are managed by distinct platforms, toolchains, and teams. KubeVirt stands at the confluence of these two streams, representing not merely a tool to run virtual machines (VMs) on Kubernetes, but the catalyst for a fundamental convergence. By treating VMs as first-class citizens within the Kubernetes ecosystem, KubeVirt dissolves the boundary between traditional and modern application architectures, creating a single, unified control plane for all workloads.

This chapter explores the profound implications of this convergence and charts, a course through the best practices and future trends that will define the next epoch of virtualization.

By the end of this chapter, you will have a roadmap for leveraging KubeVirt effectively, while staying prepared for future opportunities and challenges in virtualization.

Structure

In this chapter, we will cover the following topics:

- Trends in Hybrid and Multi-Cloud Virtualization
- The Role of Edge Computing and Virtualization
- AI and Automation in Virtual Workload Management

Trends in Hybrid and Multi-Cloud Virtualization

The move toward hybrid and multi cloud architectures is no longer a niche strategy, but a mainstream reality for modern enterprises. This shift is driven by a desire for flexibility, resilience, and the avoidance of dependency on a single cloud provider. However, it also introduces significant operational complexity, particularly when managing a mix of traditional virtualized applications and new containerized services. KubeVirt emerges in this context as a pivotal technology, offering a unified approach that addresses the core challenges of this new landscape. This section explores the macro-trends driving KubeVirt's adoption, the strategic pathways it opens for modernization, and the critical best practices for building production-grade infrastructure that spans multiple environments.

The Unified Control Plane: A New Operational Paradigm

At its core, KubeVirt's most transformative contribution is the creation of a single, unified control plane to orchestrate both virtual machines and containers. This is not achieved by bolting a separate virtualization manager onto Kubernetes; instead, KubeVirt natively extends the Kubernetes API itself. Through the use of Custom Resource Definitions (CRDs), it introduces new resource types like

VirtualMachine (VM) and VirtualMachineInstance (VMI) that Kubernetes can understand and manage just like it manages Pods or Deployments. A KubeVirt VM is, architecturally, a regular Kubernetes Pod that contains a KVM-based virtual machine process, allowing it to be scheduled, networked, and managed, using the same primitives as any other containerized workload.

The significance of this unification extends far beyond technical elegance; it represents a strategic response to major industry pressures. The primary drivers for this shift are as much economic and strategic, as they are technical. In the recent years, the virtualization market has seen significant consolidation, leading to concerns about soaring costs and vendor lock-in, particularly with established platforms like VMware. Many organizations are actively seeking alternatives to de-risk their infrastructure, and regain control over their budgets.

This unified approach yields profound operational efficiencies. It dismantles the organizational and technical silos that have long separated virtualization administrators from container platform teams. Instead of maintaining two disparate infrastructure stacks–each with its own hardware, management tools, monitoring systems, and required skill sets–organizations can consolidate onto a single platform. This allows a single operations team to use a consistent set of cloud-native tools such as kubectl, Helm charts, and GitOps workflows, to manage the entire application portfolio, regardless of whether a component runs in a VM or a container. This reduction in operational complexity and management overhead is a key benefit driving adoption.

Frame KubeVirt adoption as a strategic initiative to de-risk infrastructure from vendor lock-in and reduce licensing costs. The technical goal of a unified control plane should be presented as the enabler of these critical business outcomes.

Strategic Modernization

One of the most significant barriers to enterprise modernization has been the challenge of dealing with legacy applications. Many of these systems, while critical to the business, were not designed for the cloud-native world, and cannot be easily containerized due to complex dependencies, tight coupling with specific operating systems, or prohibitive refactoring costs. KubeVirt provides a crucial bridge, offering a pragmatic and iterative path to modernization that avoids the "*all-or-nothing*" approach of traditional rip-and-replace projects.

KubeVirt enables several distinct modernization strategies, allowing organizations to choose the path that best fits their application portfolio and business objectives:

- **Lift and Shift:** The most straightforward approach is to move existing VMs as-is onto a KubeVirt-enabled Kubernetes cluster. While this does not change the application architecture, it provides immediate operational benefits by consolidating all workloads under a single management plane.
- **Refactor and Containerize:** KubeVirt excels at facilitating a gradual decomposition of monolithic applications. A legacy monolith can continue to run in a VM on Kubernetes, while new features or components are developed as containerized microservices on the same cluster. Because both the VM and the containers share the same Kubernetes networking and storage fabric, they can communicate seamlessly.
- **Hybrid Coexistence:** For many organizations, some workloads will remain in VMs for the foreseeable future. This may include applications that require a

full Windows OS, Commercial Off-The-Shelf (COTS) software distributed as virtual appliances, or workloads with specialized hardware dependencies.

The capability to enable pragmatism is arguably KubeVirt's most powerful feature. It transforms application modernization from a daunting, high-risk endeavor into a manageable, iterative process. By allowing the old and the new to coexist and interoperate, KubeVirt empowers teams to deliver business value continuously, while progressively evolving their architecture.

Best Practices for Production-Grade Networking

While KubeVirt masterfully unifies the control plane, it intentionally delegates the complex task of networking to the underlying Kubernetes cluster. This design choice allows KubeVirt to leverage the vast and innovative Kubernetes networking ecosystem, but it also means that the capabilities of a KubeVirt deployment are fundamentally defined by the chosen Container Network Interface (CNI) plugin. For simple, single-cluster deployments, default Kubernetes networking may suffice. However, for production-grade hybrid and multi-cloud environments, advanced networking solutions are not just a recommendation; they are a requirement to address challenges related to live migration, security, multi-tenancy, and performance. The following are the key networking patterns, and the solutions that enable them:

- **Network-Transparent Live Migration:** A critical feature for enterprise virtualization is the ability to migrate a running VM from one host to another without downtime. While KubeVirt supports live migration, the default networking setup can present challenges such as the VM's IP address changing upon migration, or significant network interruption.

  To solve this, specialized CNI projects such as Kube-OVN have developed sophisticated mechanisms like traffic replication, and advanced port binding techniques to ensure that the VM's IP address is preserved, and network downtime is reduced to sub-second levels.

- **Unified Security and Observability with eBPF:** To achieve a true zero-trust security model that spans both VMs and containers, a CNI that can apply consistent policy, and provide deep visibility into all traffic is essential.

  Cilium, which leverages the power of eBPF in the Linux kernel, is a leading solution in this space. It can enforce rich, identity-based Layer 3-7 network policies, and provide detailed observability for all traffic, regardless of whether it originates from a container or a KubeVirt VM.

- **High-Performance and Specialized Networking:** For workloads with demanding performance requirements, such as financial trading applications or real-time data processing, KubeVirt offers several paths for network acceleration. It supports SR-IOV (Single Root I/O Virtualization), which allows a VM to bypass the host's network stack, and directly access a physical network interface card (NIC), providing near-native performance.

For environments requiring both high performance and the flexibility of Software-Defined Networking (SDN), integration with OVS-DPDK (Open vSwitch with Data Plane Development Kit) provides user-space network acceleration.

- **Complex Network Topologies with Multus:** A common requirement, when migrating applications from traditional virtualization, is the ability to connect a VM to multiple distinct networks simultaneously. The Multus CNI meta-plugin is the standard solution for this in the Kubernetes ecosystem. It allows a pod–and by extension, a KubeVirt VM–to attach to multiple network interfaces, each connected to a different underlying CNI, enabling the creation of complex and segmented network topologies.

High-Performance, Resilient Storage in Hybrid/Multi-Cloud

In parallel with networking, KubeVirt delegates all storage operations to the underlying Kubernetes storage infrastructure via the Container Storage Interface (CSI). This provides not only immense flexibility, but also places the responsibility of providing performant, resilient, and feature-rich storage squarely on the chosen CSI driver and storage backend. Stateful VMs, particularly those running databases or other mission-critical applications, have stringent storage requirements that must be met to ensure data persistence, high availability, and disaster recovery in a hybrid or multi-cloud setting.

The following are the key storage requirements for production KubeVirt deployments, and the solutions that address them:

- **ReadWriteMany Access:** The most crucial storage requirement for enabling VM live migration is the ability for a Persistent Volume (PV) to be mounted and accessed by multiple nodes simultaneously. This is known as the ReadWriteMany (RWX) access mode. While many file-based storage systems (like NFS) support RWX, achieving this for high-performance block storage is more complex. **Ceph RBD** (with the appropriate configuration), and **Longhorn** are specifically designed to provide RWX access for block volumes, making them suitable for stateful KubeVirt workloads that require live migration.
- **High Availability (HA) and Disaster Recovery (DR):** For multi-site and multi-cloud architectures, ensuring data availability during a site failure is

paramount. This requires robust storage replication. A significant challenge arises in two-site HA scenarios where a 50% infrastructure loss can cause traditional quorum-based systems to fail, leading to a "*split-brain*" condition.

The Role of Edge Computing and Virtualization

The relentless expansion of data generation, and the demand for low-latency processing are pushing computation away from centralized clouds toward the physical edge–factories, retail stores, hospitals, and telecommunication outposts. This domain, known as edge computing, presents a unique set of challenges and opportunities. Unlike the resource-rich data center, the edge is characterized by constraints in hardware, power, and connectivity. It is in this demanding environment that KubeVirt's ability to unify diverse workloads on a single platform becomes not just a convenience, but a critical enabler. This section explores the architectural drivers for virtualization at the edge, the necessary components of a KubeVirt edge stack, and the best practices for overcoming the inherent challenges of resource management, high availability, and security in distributed deployments.

Integrating KubeVirt with Lightweight Kubernetes

A standard Kubernetes distribution can be too resource-intensive for a typical edge device. The Kubernetes control and worker plane components can consume multiple gigabytes of RAM and significant CPU cycles, leaving little room for the actual application workloads. This has led to the rise of lightweight Kubernetes distributions, which are specifically engineered for resource-constrained environments. These distributions achieve their small footprint by replacing heavy components (for example, using SQLite instead of etcd), packaging components into a single binary, and removing non-essential features, all while remaining fully API-compliant.

Choosing the right lightweight Kubernetes distribution is a critical first step in building a viable KubeVirt edge stack. The most prominent options include:

- **K3s:** Developed by Rancher (now part of SUSE), K3s has become a de facto standard for edge and IoT deployments. It is delivered as a single binary smaller than 100 MB, and can run a single-node cluster with as little as 512 MB of RAM. Its use of SQLite as the default datastore significantly reduces its memory footprint. It also has strong support for ARM architectures which are common at the edge.
- **MicroK8s:** Developed by Canonical, MicroK8s is distributed as a snap package which simplifies installation, and enables transactional, automatic updates.

It also has a small footprint and a rich ecosystem of add-ons that can be enabled with a single command. It strikes a balance between simplicity and functionality, making it suitable for both development and small production deployments.

- **Other distributions like K0s** offer similar benefits, while tools like **Minikube** and **Kind** are excellent for local development and testing of edge scenarios, often using emulation mode for KubeVirt, if hardware virtualization is not available.

Resource Management

Deploying KubeVirt at the edge introduces a unique confluence of challenges stemming from hardware constraints, the need for resilience, and an expanded threat surface. A production-grade edge architecture requires a holistic approach that addresses these challenges across the entire stack, from the hardware up to the application.

Virtual Machines (VMs) are inherently more resource-intensive than containers. On a constrained edge device, a single VM that is not properly configured can easily consume all available CPU and memory, starving the Kubernetes control plane, and other critical containerized services.

When defining a VirtualMachine or VirtualMachineInstance, it is crucial to specify resource requests, and limits for both CPU and memory. KubeVirt offers advanced features such as automatically setting resource limits based on namespace-level ResourceQuota objects, providing an administrative safeguard against runaway resource consumption.

High Availability (HA)

Traditional Kubernetes high availability relies on a three-node control plane to maintain etcd quorum. Many edge locations, however, may only have one or two physical nodes due to cost and space constraints. In a two-node cluster, the failure of a single node represents a 50% infrastructure loss, making it impossible for etcd to maintain a majority quorum, and leading to a "split-brain" scenario where the cluster ceases to function.

A two-node HA architecture that replaces direct etcd communication with kine, a shim that translates etcd API calls to a supported backend database (like SQLite or MySQL). This allows the control plane's state store to remain functional, even when one of the two nodes goes offline.

Security

Edge devices are often deployed in physically insecure locations, and operate on potentially untrusted networks. This dramatically increases the attack surface compared to a secured data center. Securing KubeVirt at the edge demands a defense-in-depth, zero-trust strategy that hardens every layer of the stack like:

- **Immutable Operating System:** The foundation of a secure edge device is an immutable OS like **Talos Linux** or **Flatcar Container Linux**. These systems run from a read-only filesystem, preventing configuration drift and unauthorized changes. They are often managed exclusively via an API, with no SSH or shell access, which significantly reduces the local attack surface.
- **KubeVirt Security Fundamentals:** KubeVirt's own security principles must be rigorously applied. This includes enforcing the principle of least privilege for all components, establishing clear boundaries between trusted components (virt-handler) and untrusted components (virt-launcher).
- **Hardware-Level Security:** For the highest level of security, leverage hardware-based features. This includes using a Trusted Platform Module (TPM) for measured boot and full-disk encryption, and employing confidential computing technologies like Intel® Trust Domain Extensions (TDX) to encrypt VM memory, protecting workloads even if the hypervisor or host kernel is compromised.

AI and Automation in Virtual Workload Management

This section explores the future of KubeVirt management, focusing on how the Go-based Operator Pattern provides the bedrock for automation, and how the emerging field of AIOps is set to transform virtual workload management from a reactive discipline into a predictive and autonomous one.

The Operator Pattern and Go Controllers

The engine of automation in the Kubernetes ecosystem is the Operator Pattern. An Operator is, in essence, a piece of software that encodes the operational knowledge of a human expert for a specific application. It extends the Kubernetes API with CRDs to represent the application's desired state, and runs one or more custom controllers that continuously work to make the actual state of the system match that desired state. This is achieved through a perpetual reconciliation loop: the controller watches for changes to its CRDs, compares the desired state with the current state of the cluster, and takes action to resolve any discrepancies.

KubeVirt is a prime example of the Operator Pattern in action. The entire project is architected as a set of operators and controllers, overwhelmingly written in the Go programming language (over 94% of the codebase), which is the native tongue of the cloud-native world.

These controllers are sophisticated Go applications that utilize the official Kubernetes client-go library to communicate with the Kubernetes API server. Go is the language of choice for building Kubernetes automation for a simple reason: The core Kubernetes project and its essential libraries–including client-go, controller-runtime, and the Operator SDK–are all written and maintained in Go. This provides developers with the most stable, feature-rich, and up-to-date foundation for creating custom controllers.

AIOps in Practice: Predictive Scaling and Anomaly Detection

As KubeVirt deployments grow in scale and complexity, managing them with static rules and reactive alerts becomes increasingly challenging. The sheer volume of telemetry data and the intricate dependencies between mixed workloads can overwhelm human operators. This is where **AIOps (AI for IT Operations)** enters the picture. AIOps leverages Machine Learning (ML) and big data analytics to automate IT operations and, crucially, to move from a reactive posture (responding to failures) to a proactive and predictive one (anticipating and preventing failures).

Standard Kubernetes autoscaling mechanisms such as the Horizontal Pod Autoscaler (HPA), are reactive. An AIOps-driven approach is far more intelligent like:

- **Data Collection:** It begins by collecting rich, historical time-series data from KubeVirt VMs and the underlying nodes. This data is typically scraped, and stored by a monitoring system like Prometheus.
- **Forecasting:** Using this historical data, ML models–often based on time-series forecasting algorithms and implemented in languages like Python–are trained to recognize recurring patterns and cycles in workload demand (for example, peak traffic every weekday at 9 AM, or end-of-month batch processing).
- **Proactive Action:** Based on these forecasts, the AIOps system can proactively scale VM resources (by adjusting CPU or memory allocations) or the number of VM replicas, before the anticipated demand spike occurs. This ensures that sufficient resources are always available to maintain performance SLAs, while also avoiding the cost of permanent over-provisioning.

The management of large-scale, hybrid KubeVirt deployments presents a perfect use case for AIOps. The complexity is simply beyond human scale. The trend is moving toward open frameworks, and the direct integration of these capabilities into

Kubernetes management platforms. The future of KubeVirt operations lies in this intelligent automation.

Automating Day-2 Operations

While the KubeVirt Operator automates the core lifecycle of a VM (creation, scheduling, and deletion), a wide range of "*Day-2*" operations—such as in-guest software configuration, patching, and application deployments—still require robust automation strategies. A mature KubeVirt environment relies on a combination of tools, each suited for a different aspect of the automation challenge.

- **Initial Bootstrapping with `Cloud-init`:** For the initial configuration of a VM at first boot, cloud-init is the industry standard. KubeVirt has first-class support for **`cloud-init`**, allowing users to inject startup scripts, user data (for application configuration), and SSH keys via Kubernetes ConfigMaps and Secrets. A key best practice is to use KubeVirt's accessCredential API to inject SSH keys separately from the main userData script. This cleanly separates access credentials from application configuration, improving security and maintainability.
- **Declarative Management with GitOps:** The ultimate goal for managing the state of the VMs themselves is a fully declarative GitOps workflow. Tools like ArgoCD or FluxCD should be used to manage the YAML manifests for VirtualMachine resources, within a Git repository. When a change is committed to Git—for example, updating a VM's memory allocation, or changing the container disk image—the GitOps controller automatically applies this change to the cluster. This ensures that the Git repository is the single source of truth for all virtualized infrastructure, providing a complete, auditable, and easily reproducible history of the environment's state.

Towards Self-Healing and Generative Infrastructure

The convergence of the declarative Operator Pattern with the predictive power of AIOps is setting the stage for the next evolution in infrastructure management: truly autonomous, and self-healing systems. This is not a distant vision, but an emerging reality built upon the programmable foundation that KubeVirt and Kubernetes provide.

A self-healing system goes beyond simple automated restarts. It involves intelligently detecting and preempting failures.

The next frontier in this evolution is the integration of Generative AI and Large Language Models (LLMs) to augment the capabilities of human operators. This moves beyond pure automation to create an interactive and intelligent assistance layer.

A prime example of this trend is the open-source project **K8sGPT**. This tool scans a Kubernetes cluster for issues, but instead of just printing raw error codes, it feeds the diagnostic data to an AI backend (such as OpenAI's models) to generate a root cause analysis, and a set of remediation suggestions in plain, human-readable English. This dramatically lowers the barrier to entry for troubleshooting the complex, and interconnected failures that can occur in a KubeVirt environment. The value of this approach is being recognized by platform vendors; for example, Kubermatic Kubernetes Platform is already integrating K8sGPT as a default tool in its web terminal to enhance cluster debugging.

This points to a future where the management of virtual workloads becomes less about writing complex scripts, and more about defining high-level intent as well as having a conversation with an intelligent system.

Conclusion

The journey through the best practices and future trends of KubeVirt reveals a technology that is far more than a simple hypervisor replacement. It is a catalyst for convergence, unifying the historically separate domains of virtual machines and containers under a single, powerful, and extensible control plane. This unification is not merely a technical convenience; it is a strategic enabler, offering enterprises a pragmatic path to modernize legacy applications, escape vendor lock-in, and reduce operational complexity across hybrid, multi-cloud, and edge environments.

Our analysis has shown that realizing the full potential of KubeVirt requires a holistic, ecosystem-aware approach. Success is thus not defined by the installation of KubeVirt alone, but by the thoughtful architecture of the entire cloud-native stack upon which it depends. Production-grade deployments demand sophisticated, Kubernetes-native solutions for networking and storage to enable critical enterprise features such as transparent live migration, robust multi-tenancy, and resilient high-availability.

Index

D

H

I

K

L

P

P

Q

R

S

V

W